OCT 0 7 '06	**DATE DUE**		
DEC 1 2 2006			
JAN 1 8 2007			
JAN 0 4 2007			

SHOOTING

WATER

SHOOTING
WATER

A MEMOIR OF SECOND CHANCES, FAMILY, AND FILMMAKING

DEVYANI
SALTZMAN

Newmarket Press • *New York*

First U.S. edition by Newmarket Press, April 2006

Published by arrangement with Key Porter Books Limited, Toronto, Canada

ISBN-13: 978-1-55704-711-3 Hardcover
ISBN-10: 1-55704-711-1 Hardcover

First Edition

10 9 8 7 6 5 4 3 2 1

Library of Congress Cataloging-in-Publication Data

Saltzman, Devyani, 1979-
  Shooting water : a memoir of second chances, family, and filmmaking / Devyani Saltzman.— 1st U.S. ed.
      p. cm.
  Includes index.
  ISBN 1-55704-711-1 (cloth : alk. paper)
  1. Saltzman, Devyani, 1979- 2. Motion picture actors and actresses—Canada—Biography. I. Title.
  PN2308.S25A3 2006
  791.4302'8092—dc22

                                        2005036810

QUANTITY PURCHASES
Companies, professional groups, clubs, and other organizations may qualify for special terms when ordering quantities of this title. For information or a catalog, write Special Sales Department, Newmarket Press, 18 East 48th Street, New York, NY 10017; call (212) 832-3575; fax (212) 832-3629; or e-mail info@newmarketpress.com.

www.newmarketpress.com

Manufactured in the United States of America.

To my mother, for introducing me to her love of books
To my father, for teaching me how to turn dreams into reality

Contents

INDIA 1999

15

OXFORD 2000

149

SRI LANKA 2004

163

AFTERWORD

269

EPILOGUE

271

ACKNOWLEDGEMENTS

275

INDEX

277

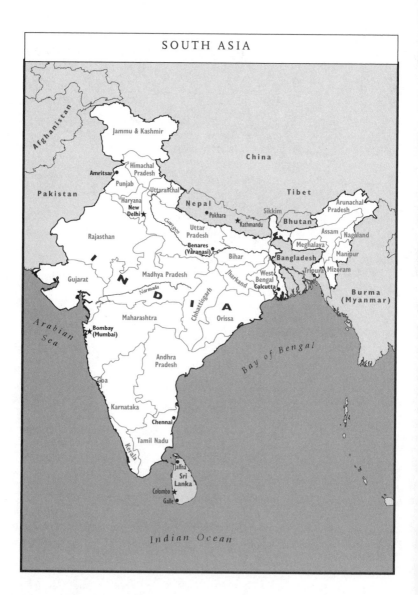

SOUTH ASIA

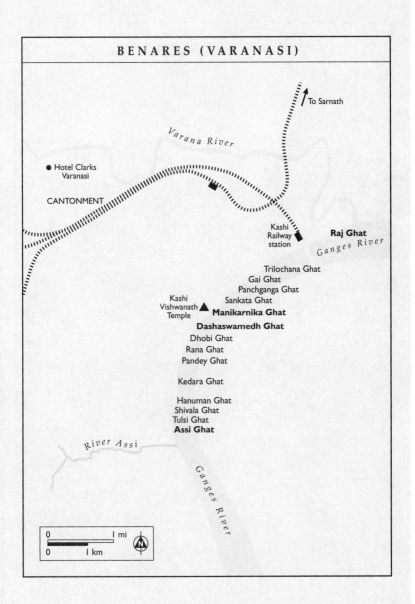

BENARES (VARANASI)

To Sarnath

Varana River

● Hotel Clarks
Varanasi

CANTONMENT

Kashi
Railway
station

Raj Ghat

Ganges River

Trilochana Ghat
Gai Ghat
Panchganga Ghat
Sankata Ghat

Kashi
Vishwanath ▲
Temple **Manikarnika Ghat**

Dashaswamedh Ghat

Dhobi Ghat
Rana Ghat
Pandey Ghat

Kedara Ghat

Hanuman Ghat
Shivala Ghat
Tulsi Ghat
Assi Ghat

River Assi

Ganges River

0   1 mi
0   1 km

Let grief be a fallen leaf
At the dawning of the day

PATRICK KAVANAGH, *RAGLAN ROAD*

We are all born with a weight. It holds us down like the grey morning rain, like a hook upon the wall on which we hang, and struggle to get off of. We spend our lives avoiding it, trying to face it, or off-loading it onto the people we love, only to see them stagger under what is not their own. Not a physical weight, like the six pounds, three and a half ounces I weighed when I was born, but something heavier and yet more elusive. Mine held me to the train berth I was lying on, and I felt my body grow heavy as it sank into the cold blue plastic.

India

1999

1

The train compartment smelled of incense and sour bodies. It was four in the morning as the Rajdhani Express sped eastward from New Delhi to Benares, the engine plowing through the darkened fields of Uttar Pradesh, the largest state in north India. Inside the second-class compartment it was completely quiet except for the low hum of the wheels against the rails. But I was awake. It was December 27, 1999, the verge of the new millennium. From my upper berth, tucked into the sheets and coarse wool blanket provided by the Eastern Railways, I could just make out the glow of the moon through the tinted glass of the train window. The fields were immersed in a thick grey fog, typical of December in north India. At the other end of my overnight train journey, my mother was sleeping peacefully in a small hotel room in Benares—a peace that would be short-lived, although neither of us knew it at the time.

In four weeks my mother, international award-winning film-maker Deepa Mehta, was going to begin shooting her fifth feature film, *Water*. She was born in India in 1950 and immigrated to Canada in 1973 after falling in love with my father, Paul Saltzman, a Canadian film producer and director. Together they started a small production company producing documentaries, television series and, eventually, feature films. She was thirty-eight when she directed her first movie.

I was their only child, a half-Hindu, half-Jewish daughter, born during a snowstorm in Canada. They raised me between Canada and India, where we visited my maternal grandparents every year in their house in New Delhi. Dressed in small Indian *lehengas* and *kurtas*, I was fed food by my *Nani*, my grandmother, with her soft hands. My first words were in Hindi. But when I was eleven years old, soon after my mother directed her first film, my parents divorced. It happened at the Cannes Film Festival in the south of France.

My mother's first film had been accepted into the Critics Week section of the festival. The whole family, including my maternal grandparents, went to Cannes to celebrate. The movie was about the unlikely relationship between two Canadian immigrants, an old Jewish man and his young Indian caregiver. It was received with praise and given a standing ovation, launching her career. But below the thin gauze of celebrity and success that was quickly beginning to envelop us, my parents' marriage of eighteen years was crumbling.

It ended on a warm spring evening after a screening, in the small apartment we had rented overlooking the Riviera. I was trying to do math homework, but sat frozen at the oval dining room table as their last fight raged. My grandparents sat on the couch, dumbfounded. And then my parents asked me to choose whom I was going to live with. The fringe of the red-and-white-striped awning on our little balcony moved gently back and forth in the breeze. I remember that, and the sound of my *Nani* crying as I walked down the narrow French staircase and out of our rented apartment, holding my dad's hand.

My choice haunted me every day afterward. My dad and I spent the rest of the afternoon sitting on a seawall overlooking the Mediterranean. He bought me an ice-cream cone, the first thing I asked for after he told me they would divorce, and we sat side by side, contemplating our futures in silence.

As an eleven-year-old with a child's instincts, it seemed only natural to choose him over my mother. I felt safe with him, while my mother's pain and anger sometimes scared me. The court decreed I could choose to live with whom I wished, and I spent the following eight years visiting my mother sporadically. Our time together was painful, and always haunted by my choice.

The train whistle blew, piercing the silence of the compartment. I sat up on the edge of the berth and dangled my legs over the side in darkness. The whistle faded and the compartment rocked back into comfortable silence, save for the quiet snores of the man on the opposite berth. I had just turned nineteen, and was taking a year off between high school and university. I was confused about the future and about myself. A deep uncertainty was holding me down. When my mother invited me to make a film with her in India for three months, I accepted, despite the painful memories between us.

I hadn't been to India for years, and the last time I had travelled there was with my father. We avoided New Delhi, where my grandparents lived, and when they tried to call me, my dad put down the receiver. In the pain after the divorce my father had wrapped me up in our own world in our home in Toronto, angrily pushing away any contact I may have had with my maternal grandparents. Since the divorce, my relationship with India had been slowly left to die, like a withered plant, untended and forgotten. Meanwhile, my mother's relationship with India grew, and she soon returned to the land of her birth through the medium of film, turning her attention to the position of women in Indian society.

In 1996 my mother wrote and directed her third feature film, *Fire*. It told the story of two middle-class Delhi sisters-in-law who find love in each other and turn away from their oppressive arranged marriages. The film was explosive in India, a country that has no word for "lesbian." It put my mother on the map as an international, and controversial, filmmaker. Movie theatres screening *Fire* in Bombay and Delhi were attacked by angry protesters who felt the film misrepresented Indian culture. They shouted that lesbianism didn't exist in India, burned the film poster, and broke down the theatre doors. She followed *Fire* with *Earth*, in 1998, based on the novel by Bapsi Sidhwa about the violent partition of India and Pakistan in 1947.

Water was the final film in what would come to be known as the Elements Trilogy. Set in the holy city of Benares in 1938, the film follows the lives of an almost invisible group of women in Indian society—Hindu widows. Women whose religion prescribed that they atone for their husbands' death by living as ascetics, wearing only white, the colour of mourning, shaving their heads to renounce vanity, and living in *ashrams*, or spiritual refuges. Hindu widows practised a different form of wifely devotion from the more widely known *sati*, in which a woman would throw herself on her husband's funeral pyre, burning herself to death. The *Manusmriti*, one of the sacred Hindu texts, explains that in life a woman is half her husband and therefore, in the event of his death, she is half-dead. The practice of ascetic widowhood still exists today.

My mother had given me the script to read in Toronto. I read all of her work before anyone else, despite the difficulties between us. The script was beautiful, set against the backdrop of India's struggle for independence from the British. It follows the lives of three Hindu widows living in an *ashram*: Shakuntala, a middle-aged woman hardened by her fate; Kalyani, a beautiful twenty-year-old, prostituted out to wealthy clients as one of the only means by which the *ashram* can earn an income; and Chuyia, a feisty child-widow of eight. Child marriage was a common practice in India and still exists in parts of the country. A young girl would be betrothed to an older man, sometimes twenty or even thirty years her senior, and join him in his household upon reaching puberty. Daughters were a financial burden to their families, and quickly off-loaded through marriage. On Chuyia's arrival at the *ashram*, Shakuntala and Kalyani are inspired to find freedom within the social constraints imposed upon them and to at last attain *moksha*—self-liberation.

The sky was still a deep blue as the train pulled into Benares Station. Passengers had begun to awaken and gather their luggage, descending from the sleeping berths to brush their teeth in the small metal basins between train carriages. The three months of filming would be the longest time my mother and I would have spent together in eight years.

I stepped onto the platform among a sea of sleeping travellers. The cold hit suddenly after the warmth of the compartment. I remembered that north Indian winters could be bitterly cold, enough to see one's breath in the dust-filled air. Men and women lay curled up on the narrow platform, waiting for their trains. The women wore saris, or *salwaar kameez*, while the men wore pants and shirts. Their babies were wrapped in blankets and shawls and placed carefully between their sleeping bodies. It was five in the morning, and the first signs of dawn were still an hour away. The film production car assigned to pick me up wouldn't arrive until six a.m.

The last of the Rajdhani's passengers exited the station, and I was left amid the dark mass of sleeping bodies. I felt uncomfortable in the darkness, edgy and alone. In an effort to blend in, I tried to hide my combat pants under my shawl. It was useless, since I was dragging an oversized Jack Wolfskin backpack with a Canadian flag sewn onto it. I found a place to sit on a cold concrete bench, and waited for the sun to rise.

The only light on the platform came from a small Indian *chai* stall a hundred metres away. I lifted my backpack and made my way past the sleeping families toward the glow of a single kerosene lamp. A small boy, with a red knit hat pulled low over his ears, was sitting on a stool behind a single gas burner, watching his stainless-steel kettle boil. Steam rose toward the station roof, fogging the narrow pane of glass that served as a barrier between customers and the flame. A pile of handmade clay cups were stacked loosely next to it. I asked for tea in broken Hindi. The words sounded awkward and unfamiliar as they left my mouth. He stared at me, waited a moment, and then reached for a cup. Picking up the kettle, he poured milky-sweet *masala chai*—a mixture of black tea, spices, and sugar—into the waiting container.

I sat down on the bench and cradled the warm clay between my hands. The station clock read five-thirty. I periodically glanced at it and searched the sky for streaks of light.

Water was written at the kitchen table in my mother's little Victorian house in Toronto. On the nights I would sleep over, I would wake up in the morning and come downstairs to find her sitting at the table with a cup of Earl Grey tea, a pack of Rothman cigarettes, and a spiral-bound Hilroy notebook. She had often been there since six in the morning, writing.

I wondered what it would be like to spend time with her again. If we could forget the pain in our time together, if something could change in the process of making a film. British director John Boorman said filmmaking was the act of converting "money into light." I hoped it would be more than that for us.

The first signs of life began to stir on the platform. Families were folding their blankets and the boy at the *chai* stall was now busy with customers. I looked at the sky. It was a pale blue. The station clock read five to six. Comforted by the sounds of morning, I walked toward the station exit as the day began to brighten.

A white Ambassador car was parked opposite the main gate of Benares Station. Ambassadors, manufactured in India, have the curves of a voluptuous woman and the suspension of a bullock cart. The fog had already begun to burn off in the heat, leaving the morning warm and slightly damp. Standing at the bottom of the station steps, among a throng of relatives, taxi drivers, and porters, was my mother. Her black hair fell below her shoulders, blending perfectly with her dark sweater. She wore small round sunglasses, and her face was darker than I remembered. Smiling, she motioned me toward the waiting car. The driver of the Ambassador tried to place my oversized backpack into the trunk, but it wouldn't fit. I helped him put it in the front seat. My mother waited patiently beside the open back door. When we hugged, I could smell her Diorissimmo perfume and was surprised by its comforting familiarity.

As I got into the back seat I realized there was someone else in the car. My mother introduced me to her assistant, Vikram. He was tall and lanky with warm, intelligent eyes. His black baseball cap was pushed back from his forehead, and he wore a single silver earring with a small blue bead suspended from it on his left ear. He was twenty-four and came from Bombay. The three of us sat squished in the back seat, with Vikram in the middle, as the Ambassador bounced along dusty rural roads toward Benares.

I looked out the streaked window at the pale yellow light falling on the flat expanse of mustard fields. Families were starting their day by pulling out *charpoys*, cots made of hemp and wood, so older relatives could sit and warm themselves in the winter sun. My mother sat silently, looking out the opposite window.

As I looked out over the fields I remembered the shape of the city, built like a crescent moon along a broad curve in the Ganges River. I had been in Benares for a brief visit a few years earlier and had fallen in love with it. One of my cousins in Delhi told me that she hated Benares. It was a dirty city with overcrowded streets, excessive traffic, and pollution. "You either hate it or love it, no in-betweens," she said. But I liked a city that demanded some form of commitment.

The Ganges, *Ganga-ma*, or Mother Ganges to Hindus, is the holiest river in India. And Benares is one of India's holiest cities, where many Hindus cremate their dead and immerse the ashes in the river. The Ganges flows through the high passes of the Himalayas to the tropical delta of the Bay of Bengal, carrying in its currents the sins of all those whose remains were placed in it.

The banks of the river are lined with *ghats*, hundreds of red sandstone steps running the length of the crescent moon and descending into the river. Each section of steps has its own name and corresponding maze of narrow *galis* (pronounced gullies), or laneways, that radiate back from the river into the centre of town. Maybe the word *gali* came from the Hindi word *gala*, or throat.

There was Assi *Ghat* on the south end of the city; Manikarnika *Ghat*, in the centre; and Raj *Ghat* at the north end near the train station. Each step is worn from centuries of pilgrims descending to the Ganges for morning prayers. While the devout purified themselves in the water, *dhobiwallahs*, washermen and women, stood knee-deep in the river, beating the city's laundry against the steps—the mundane and holy existing in perfect harmony. It is an ancient city with many incarnations, each with its own name. Benares is what the British called it. Recently it had been officially restored to its original Hindi form, Varanasi. But in its oldest incarnation it was known as Kashi—the City of Light.

The Ambassador started moving away from the rural roads, bypassing the *ghats* and knot of *galis* at the centre of town, toward Benares's cantonment. Dusty roads broadened into tree-lined boulevards, shaded from the sun by leafy *gulmohur* trees. The cantonment, or cantt, on the northwestern fringes of the city, three kilometres from the river, was the residential and administrative centre for the British during colonial rule until independence in 1947, a world away from the lives of the Raj's Indian subjects.

The cantt housed a handful of medium-size hotels, a number of private houses, and a small office that the production had rented for the duration of filming. The Ambassador pulled up to the Hotel Clarks Varanasi. A circular driveway curved up to the five-storey white building. Although it had just been built, whitewashed pillars and its location in the cantt gave it a faintly colonial air. The Ambassador came to a stop in front of large twin glass doors. I noticed that Vikram had hardly spoken during the drive to the hotel. He seemed thoughtful. David Hamilton, the producer of *Water* and my stepfather, stood waiting for us in the white-marble lobby.

David came into my life two years after the divorce, when I was thirteen. It was Christmas in Toronto, cold and grey. My mother was living in a development of pale pink townhouses just below Casa Loma, Canada's only castle. The grey carpets and walls of her house were accented with scant Indian furnishings, giving it an air of transience. The darkness pushed up against the windows and white flurries melted as soon as they collided with the glass. David arrived with a big square box wrapped tightly in clear plastic. He had bought a train set for me for Christmas. I refused to play with it.

David grew up on an Air Force base in the Yukon in northwest Canada. His mother, an Austrian immigrant, divided her time between working in a laundry and taking care of three children, while his father worked at the base. At the age of five David sold newspapers on street corners to supplement their meagre income. A scholarship to McGill University in Montreal allowed him to study engineering and eventually win a place at Harvard Business School. When I met him he was the CEO of a company based in Ottawa that provided high-tech services to corporations like Microsoft. Only after he met my mother did he begin applying his knowledge of finance toward film, transforming himself into a producer, like my father. David put together the financing for both *Fire* and *Earth*, piecing together money solely from independent investors.

The marble floor of the hotel lobby was freshly polished and the paint on the walls smelled new. David was wearing a white scarf wrapped once around his neck and a check-collared shirt on his small frame. His brown hair was cut neatly around his face. I put down my bag and reached forward to hug him. It had taken a few years to come to know and love him, but he was often the buffer between my mother and me, mediating any discord that erupted between us.

Over the next two weeks, an international cast and crew, including actresses Shabana Azmi and Nandita Das, who had played the lovers in *Fire*, would arrive in Benares to shoot *Water*. As I hugged David, I thought of my job. I was looking forward to working as the third assistant cameraperson in the cinematography department.

2

David and Vikram left for the production office, a five-minute walk from the hotel, while my mother and I made our way to her corner suite on the fourth floor. The hotel was quiet. We walked along a carpeted hallway toward a large plate-glass window. Outside I could see a narrow alley, and a brick wall lined with cakes of dung, fuel for a local resident. They were pressed flat against the red surface by someone's hand, the palm print still visible. To the right of the window were double wooden doors, room 421. It had been a month since we had last seen each other in Delhi, and now we were going to stay together in Benares. I was excited about being close to her, close to her creativity, but I was also nervous, and wanted my own room.

We walked into a small sitting area with a couch, two armchairs, and a TV. A low marble counter separated it from a king-size bed and a window overlooking the flat rooftops of nearby buildings.

Three small statues of Hindu gods were placed on the marble counter. Each one was three inches high, carved out of wood, and painted in bright saffrons, reds, and greens. Laxmi, the goddess of wealth; Ganesha, the god of success; and Brahma, the creator. Small personal touches in an otherwise impersonal room. My Indian family had never been active followers of Hinduism, although my mother did her degree in Hindu philosophy at Delhi University.

"Come, I have something you have to listen to."

She pulled me toward the pale yellow two-seater and turned on a black portable tape player on the coffee table. A beautiful male voice filled the room, haunting and sweet, singing in Hindi. Behind the voice was the rhythm of *tablas*, Indian drums, and the occasional drone of a *tanpura*, a string instrument similar to the sitar. The voice slowly overcame all motion in the room.

"*bangri marori sainya nay meri zora zori*"
"My lover cajoled me gently to come to him"
"*khand a ke sar mukut saraja, Radha ke gal dori, se na meri, zora zori*"
"Lord Krishna wears a crown, and Radha, a garland of flowers"

I glanced at Mom. Her head was resting in her hand and her eyes were closed. She looked beatific, consumed by the music.

There was a knock at the door. When I opened it Vikram was standing in the hall, holding copies of the script. He sat beside me on the couch, placing the papers gently at his feet. The three of us listened to what I would soon discover was the soundtrack for *Water*, six original songs composed by India's most famous music director, A.R. Rahman. Rahman had composed some of the best soundtracks in Indian film, working from his small studio in the south Indian city of Chennai. He had composed the music for *Lagaan, Bombay*, and for both of my mother's previous films, *Fire* and *Earth*. He was just starting to work on a musical with Andrew Lloyd Webber, a cross-cultural fusion of music and theatre to open in London's West End, an idea that would eventually become the long-running hit musical *Bombay Dreams*.

My mother stopped the tape player and leaned back in the chair.

"I have some work to do, but why don't you go with Vikram and look at the production office."

I nodded. He handed her a copy of the script, and we moved toward the door.

WATER'S PRODUCTION OFFICE was located in a four-storey building on the banks of the Varana, a small river that ran along the back of the cantt and eventually flowed into the Ganges. The production had rented the top floor and rooftop terrace, while the rest of the building was made up of private residences. Vikram and I walked up the two flights of marble stairs to the office. Above the doorways to the residences were hand-painted *swastikas*, originally an Aryan symbol used by Hindus as a mark to encourage prosperity and good fortune, but later appropriated by Hitler and more infamously recognized as the symbol of Nazi Germany.

The office was still relatively bare in the four weeks of pre-production before shooting. A large plastic calendar was tacked to the wall in the main room showing a breakdown of the pre-production schedule and arrival dates of cast and crew. Red X's, scratched out in felt-tip marker, marked days passed. Three small offices and a galley kitchen radiated off the main room where two computers, a printer, and a photocopier had been set up on brown folding tables. We were a small production, with a budget of $2 million Canadian, about one-thirtieth of the average Hollywood film.

Bob Wertheimer, the film's co-producer, had flown in from Toronto to supervise on-the-ground production needs and to work with local Uttar Pradesh government officials and location managers to ensure all permissions were secured before the shoot began. His voice was now booming from behind the plastic calendar. I had known Bob, as he always reminded me, since I was "a very little girl."

I opened the door to the nearest office and caught Bob's eye. David was sitting opposite him, reviewing the permissions of the state government. Bob smirked, put both his hands on the table, pushed back his chair, and walked over to me, giving me the tightest bear hug ever.

Water was my first experience working on a film. It was also the first time I would be working as a third assistant cameraperson. I had discovered I loved photography when I was seventeen. My dad and I had gone to Turkey for two weeks and I'd taken along a hand-me-down stills camera my uncle Dilip had given me, an old Canon F-1. It was black and heavy and came with an 85 mm lens. I was scared of its weight and the thick glass of the lens, and nervous about my ability to use it. But one evening while my dad and I were wandering through the narrow streets of Istanbul, we came to a makeshift fish market on the banks of the Bosphorus, the wide saltwater strait that separates Europe from Asia. The fishmongers were all men. Rows of small, silvery fish were laid out on flattened cardboard boxes on top of the cobblestones. Their blood had seeped into the cardboard, creating darkened stains behind the rows of small silver bodies. My dad encouraged me to pull out the camera and shoot. I hesitated. Then I noticed the naked light bulbs strung up between poles, white and exposed, illuminating the fish and the reflection of water on the cobblestones. I started shooting and felt an engagement with the world I had never felt before.

Before coming to India I bought a manual on the basics of cinematography. A third assistant's job included loading film and carrying the heavy lens boxes and tripods. I went to a friend of my dad's who owned a camera equipment rental house in Toronto and spent an afternoon loading film. My hands worked slowly in the black portable bag used to protect film from exposure to light.

I would be working under my mother's long-time cinematographer, Giles Nuttgens. They had met in Benares in 1993 while working together on an episode of George Lucas's *Young Indiana Jones* television series. Giles was from northern England and had worked as a BBC film cameraman for eleven years. We had met briefly on the second episode of *Young Indy* that Mom directed and Giles shot in Greece. He was due to arrive later in the evening from London, where he had been working on the most recent *Star Wars*.

My mother told me the idea for *Water* came to her while they were shooting in Benares in 1993. While she sat on the *ghats* on an early morning before shooting, she noticed an elderly woman dressed only in white, descending into the river for morning prayers. A production assistant explained to her that she was a Hindu widow, waiting to attain *Kashi moksha*—liberation from the cycle of life, death, and rebirth, which can instantly be gained by dying in the holy city of Benares.

There was a small office at the back of the building, overlooking the Varana. I noticed a bulletin board tacked up outside the door. Black-and-white photographs of *sanyasis*—Hindu holy men, smeared in ash, with their *malas* or holy beads wrapped heavily around their necks and matted hair—were carefully pinned next to period photographs of women in the 1930s. Small swatches of coarse white cotton and deep indigo silk hung between the photos. Inside the room was a small desk. Behind it, wearing an off-white *salwaar kameez* and speaking excitedly on the phone in Punjabi, was Dolly Ahluwallia, the costume designer.

Dolly got off the phone and introduced herself. We had never met, although I had heard about her through my mother and David. She was warm and gregarious, her long black hair tied solidly into a bun and her thin *dupatta*, or scarf-like veil, dangling just inches from the ground. "Research," she explained, pointing to the bulletin board. The room was full of clothes on hangers. There was a row of *kurtas*, loose cotton shirts, for male extras, a section of aged-white saris for the widows, and a handful of luxurious silk Benarsi saris for Bhagwati, the mother of the male lead character, Narayan. Benares is known for its handwoven silk saris. Weavers work in small rooms off the *galis*. They were usually young men, working on small wooden floor looms by the light of a single naked bulb. They wove for months at a time to produce a single sari. Over the past three months Dolly and her team had shopped in New Delhi, Calcutta, and Benares, putting together a selection of fabric, clothing, and period accessories to make 1930s Benares come alive.

"Come upstairs," she said, walking out of her office.

I followed her into the stairwell and up to the terrace. The afternoon sun was blinding. Damp white saris hung on clotheslines strung diagonally across the terrace. The Varana flowed silently behind the building as local fishermen cast circular nets into the water, silhouetted by the sun. A rhythmic thumping was coming from somewhere on the rooftop. Dolly pulled aside a sari, revealing two of her team members crouching on the ground, beating wet fabric against the marble with wooden paddles. Two large aluminum vats full of water and indigo dye rested on kerosene burners nearby. The dye added a blue tinge to the clothing, reflecting the colour palette of the film—indigo and white.

I COMBED MY HAIR and put on black eyeliner in front of the bathroom mirror. I usually felt self-conscious about the way I looked, but there was a buzz tonight and I felt like wearing some makeup. It was New Year's Eve, 1999, and I felt the millennium's promise of a new beginning. The film offered a chance for me to really be myself, to be beautiful. I was far away from home, school, and the preconceptions people have of you, in my case, the overstudious girl, inaccessible behind the pages of a book.

Bob had invited us to New Year's Eve drinks in his room. The door was open, and music from the film spilled into the hallway. Giles arrived that evening with his girlfriend, Brigitte, who had flown in from Paris to meet him. They sat opposite David and my mother on one of the room's twin beds, drinking and laughing. Giles had a slight build, sharp features, and bright blue eyes. Vikram was standing next to a makeshift bar, where several bottles of vodka, Coke, whisky, and a bucket of ice were on top of the dressing table.

"You're wearing eyeliner," he said.

I smiled shyly and sat on the bed next to my mother and David. Brigitte sat opposite, Giles's hand resting on the folds of her green *dupatta*.

After a little while Vikram crouched near the edge of the bed.

"Some of us are going to the *ghats*. The Dalai Lama is delivering his millennium message from Benares. Do you want to come?"

I looked into his eyes. The party continued around us as midnight approached. I picked up my shawl and followed Vikram.

We walked down an unlit *gali* behind Dashaswamedh *Ghat*, just south of the cremation grounds. A faint orange glow outlined the shapes of people's heads walking in front of us, the only definition among the throng of darkened bodies pushing through the narrow lane toward the river. The sound of feet was swallowed by the heavy sound of bells and chanting, emanating from the hundreds of temples scattered throughout the city. We eventually emerged from the *gali*. The *ghats* descended below us as thousands of people, their faces obscured in darkness, converged in front of the wide black expanse of the Ganges.

A floating platform was moored off the bottom step of the *ghat*. It was the centre of activity. Floodlights had been set up facing the mooring, which glowed amid the darkness of the steps and the cool blue light cast from the halogen street lamps placed along the bend in the river. The platform was covered with a white sheet, and four poles, one at each corner, held a white canopy above it. Orange marigold garlands, the colour of saffron, were strung along the rim of the canopy and wrapped delicately around each pole.

The Dalai Lama sat on a raised dais flanked by Buddhist and Hindu priests on either side. I pulled out my Canon F-1 and began shooting. The Dalai Lama began his address, but we were some distance from the dais and couldn't hear him clearly through the din of the crowd. The next morning we would travel ten kilometres outside of Benares to hear him deliver his millennium message again from Sarnath, where Buddha gave his first sermon. At the base of a giant stone *stupa*, standing in his deep red robes under the sun, the Dalai Lama would speak to a small audience of seventy people gathered on folding plastic chairs. The past century had been one of war and bloodshed. He spoke about non-violence and the growing need for dialogue and discussion in attaining peace. I felt witness to a historic moment. The Dalai Lama's words reminded me of Mahatma Gandhi's vision of non-violence in attaining social change.

Vikram, Giles, Brigitte, and I started to move away from the floodlit mooring toward the darkness of the undecorated *ghats*. Tea candles had been lit by pilgrims and set afloat on the Ganges in small baskets made of dried leaves. We sat close to the water, watching quietly as the candles drifted past us. Suddenly the city erupted with the sound of temple bells ringing in unison, heralding the millennium. Vikram leaned toward us.

"I heard something crazy today. Iqbal, the location manager, said there were rumours in the city that our film is anti-Hindu."

Giles laughed, dismissing it, and we wished each other a happy New Year.

3

Until the camera gear arrived from Canada, I had no real work as third assistant cameraperson. The morning sunlight was falling across the small statues of the gods in my mother's bedroom when she suggested I could do some research on widows to give an accurate portrayal of their lifestyle in the film. She handed me the name of a contact in the city, recommended by her art director, and rushed out to begin rehearsals with her actors. I read the name:

Pinku Pandey
Assi *Ghat*

Pinku lived in a dead-end lane behind Assi *Ghat*. The doors of the houses were covered in layers of peeling paint, and the house numbers were scratched onto their surfaces with white chalk. The unpaved lane was a dusty, light brown clay, like most of the end *ghat* in the crescent curve of the city. Its name was deceptive. The *ghats* stopped just short of Assi, the red sandstone steps disappearing into the clay of the riverbank like an unfinished sentence.

The lane had open sewers on either side, filled with dirty water. I could hear a baby crying behind one of the closed peeling doors and smell the spicy odour of cooking *sabzee*, vegetables. I looked again at the white crumpled paper, and knocked on the last door in the lane.

A man opened it and quickly slipped into the street. As he pulled the door shut, I saw a shaft of sunlight as it fell across an inner courtyard.

"Pinku." He politely introduced himself and shook my hand. He was young, maybe only a few years older than me, but he looked older. He had a thin moustache, carefully trimmed above his lip.

Pinku was his pet name. It was an Indian tradition to give children an affectionate handle. He was a BA student in computer science at Benares Hindu University. A year earlier Pinku had helped a graduate student from Europe complete research on widows in Benares for her master's thesis. I knew nothing about Hindu widows, but he supposedly knew his way around.

As we walked back toward Assi *Ghat* I noticed that he was gaunt and tall, almost awkward. But he moved gently, as if he didn't want to have an impact on the ground he walked upon.

"Come, we're going to visit an old friend of mine." Pinku turned into a narrow *gali*.

We arrived at a metal door behind an open-air pizzeria overlooking the river. Plastic tables were set up with a view of Assi *Ghat*, and Christmas lights were strung up and around the branches of an old banyan tree. The river seemed to flow more slowly here, as if it were a forgotten place in the otherwise chaotic city. I had met a German girl at the pizzeria on my last visit. She was eating an omelet and garlic bread, and wearing a long, flowing *lehenga* and dangly silver earrings. She lived alone in a rented flat behind Assi *Ghat* and had come to Benares to learn the *sarod* from a local music master. She invited me to hear her play. I remember sitting in her small rooftop room as sunlight fell across the floor. Postcards from Europe and faded pictures of the goddess Saraswati, goddess of the arts and learning, were pinned to the doorframe. Her blonde hair fell across her face as she carefully picked the instrument's strings. It was the saddest music I had ever heard.

The corroded metal door was opened by a small woman. Pinku greeted her respectfully in Hindi and then introduced me as a friend doing research on Hindu widows. Sundarbai smiled widely. She was the first widow I had ever seen. She had few teeth and her wrinkled skin fell low over her eyes, giving her a sleepy expression. A maroon-and-white wool shawl was wrapped around her thin body and covered her head. Her lips were wide and swollen, like the mouth of a fish.

Pinku leaned toward me. "She's over ninety," he whispered.

We followed her through a narrow stone passage and passed a small drab courtyard with a rusted hand pump in its centre. It was well kept, with a simple stainless-steel *thali*, or food tray, resting against the base of the pump, shining in the sunlight. The ground glistened from a recent wash. The passage continued past the courtyard. As she walked in front of us, I noticed that her feet were thin and bare against the cold stone.

Sundarbai led us into a room at the end of the corridor. It was windowless and big enough only for a single metal cot pushed up against the damp wall. Pinku and I sat on the ground while she lowered herself onto her haunches. The edge of her worn white sari was visible under the shawl. She pulled the shawl off her head, revealing bone-white hair cropped close to her skull. Sundarbai looked like a little boy, small and vulnerable but somehow defiant. I wondered if I'd encroached into someone's private life.

"Ma," Pinku addressed her formally. "Ma..."

She leaned toward him, slightly deaf.

"How did you come to Benares?" Pinku spoke in Hindi.

She sat quietly with her elbows resting on her knees, squeezing her hands together and sucking on her lips. I had never seen an old woman living this way, her life bound by a stone cell.

"I came here for *Kashi moksha* twenty years ago." She spoke with an alertness that defied her sleepy expression.

Sundarbai leaned past the open door, catching a sliver of light on her withered arm, and pulled aside a blue curtain hanging in front of a low shelf.

"I have his love." She pointed to a small statue of the god Krishna, carefully placed on the wooden shelf, and smiled.

Paint was peeling off the statue's blue belly and his hands were holding a wooden flute to his lips. Krishna, the eighth incarnation of the god Vishnu, the preserver and protector. Krishna, the Hindu embodiment of love and divine joy.

Pinku explained to me that Sundarbai was a Brahmin widow, a member of the highest caste—the priests—in the ancient Indian system of social hierarchy. Discrimination on the basis of caste was now illegal in India, but its social influence continued to permeate people's lives throughout the country. Many still used the system to decide whom they would marry, what they would eat, and how they would mourn their dead. Brahmin widows were more likely to observe the strict rituals of asceticism and purity associated with widowhood, similar to orthodox practitioners in any religion.

I had never been defined by my own place in the caste system. There was only one instance when my position was made clear to me, and that was in the library of my public high school in Toronto. A new student, whose parents had recently immigrated from India, came up to me and said her name was Mehta. She had heard my middle name was Mehta as well. Holding her textbooks close to her chest, she asked me if I was Brahmin. I didn't know what to say, and kept looking at my biology homework, but she seemed genuinely interested and wouldn't leave.

"No. We're Vaisya," the merchant class, I answered.

"Oh," she said, and turned and walked away. She never spoke to me again.

In the cold desolation of Sundarbai's room, Pinku told me that her sons supported their mother. They lived in a town not far from Benares and paid the rent for the room we were now sitting in. Her daughters-in-law would occasionally visit with *dal*, cooked lentils, and *chapatis*, warm flatbread. Pinku had befriended her through them, periodically dropping in to make sure she had everything she needed. Sundarbai was left to spend her days in prayer. She had friends and family and some financial support.

I looked at her, small and thin and old, and then I looked at her room. It was bare with only a few stainless-steel containers stacked under her metal cot. The walls were damp, and the small wooden statue of Lord Krishna was her only constant companion. What I was about to discover was that she was one of the lucky ones.

I thanked Pinku in the *gali* outside the corroded metal door. The wind off the river blew the smell of pizza through the narrow lane. He suggested I visit a widows' *ashram* at the other end of the city, and gave me the name and directions.

"Doesn't the government give them pensions?" I asked.

Pinku laughed, a sad laugh.

"Not really, and even if the BJP did, half the women wouldn't know how to claim it because of their illiteracy."

In India's democracy the Bharatiya Janata Party, or BJP, formed India's coalition government under Prime Minister Atal Behari Vajpayee. They were a strong Hindu nationalist party that had just been re-elected two months earlier. Despite India's diverse population of Hindus, Muslims, and Christians, among others, the BJP envisioned India as a Hindu nation and had recently been accused of turning a blind eye, if not fanning the flames, of communal violence against non-Hindus. Their main opposition, the Congress Party, had been the first party to rule India after independence from the British, under Jawaharlal Nehru and the spiritual leadership of Mahatma Gandhi. Unlike the BJP, the Congress was secular.

VIKRAM AND GILES were waiting on the steps of Manikarnika *Ghat*, the cremation grounds at the heart of Benares. Throughout the day and night bodies burned in the intense white heat of coals; the red and orange fires licked the sky, the flames reflecting in the swollen Ganges. Cremations took place on four large cleared spaces, covered with deep brown earth instead of sandstone. Each space had two funeral pyres on it, with large wooden logs placed in a one-metre-high, flat-top pyramid, big enough to accommodate the human body.

The bodies, fully wrapped in white cloth, were carried to the pyres on wooden biers by the families. The eldest son would start the fire, and after the body had burned, the son and the widow would have their heads shaved on the *ghats* in an act of mourning.

I sat on a stone step and watched the closest pyre. The heat was intense. It had been burning overnight and the body was almost ash. Only the skull, fragile and small, remained. A man walked to the pyre and pushed at the logs with a long pole. The logs collapsed inwards, setting off white sparks that shot toward the sky, fell, and fizzled as they touched the earth. He was a *dom*, or funeral attendant, and an untouchable, the lowest group within the caste system, like leather workers who make shoes and bags out of animal skins. Both communities were unclean because they worked with the dead. *Doms* were always men. They managed the affairs of the dead, selling wood for pyres to mourning families, maintaining them, and collecting a tax on each corpse. A young boy, of perhaps ten, was helping an older *dom* stoke a new fire. The body lay on top, wrapped in a clean white sheet. The boy wore a white *lunghi*, a long cloth tied around his waist, and a ripped undershirt. A cotton rag was wrapped around his head to keep the sweat from his eyes, as he learned his trade.

The scent of camphor mixed with *ghee*, clarified butter, rose from Manikarnika as we walked away from the *ghat*. Camphor was used on the pyres to mask the smell of burning flesh. Behind us huge metal scales groaned under dozens of large wooden logs neatly stacked for use on individual pyres, weighing the cost of death.

The Sunview guesthouse was in a converted mansion high above the *ghats*, overlooking the Ganges. Pinku told me that the manager ran a widows' *ashram* below the main building. Vikram, Giles, and I had come to see if we could shoot some video footage to be used as reference material to accurately depict the lives of these women in *Water*. The production had already rented a private house in the centre of the city, which was slowly being decorated by the film's art department to become our very own widows' *ashram*.

The entrance to the guesthouse was below a curved sandstone archway. A wooden sign was attached to the stone. It read "Sunview Rest" in bright yellow letters. Giles hid the Handycam in his jacket and we walked into the guesthouse. A few rooms opened onto an inner courtyard filled with leafy palms and climbing bougainvilleas. It was bright and peaceful, a quiet place for tourists to stay on a trip through north India. A German couple was having lunch in the dining room—eight tables placed on an open-air balcony that wrapped around the front of the mansion, overlooking the river. The manager was sitting behind a wooden desk off to one side. He was young, in his thirties. The corners of his mouth were stained a deep red from chewing betel nut. We introduced ourselves.

"*Chai*, coffee?" he offered.

When he saw that we didn't want anything, he snapped his fingers and a servant boy standing behind him produced another *paan*, betel nut and spices wrapped in a leaf, from deep within his pocket. He placed it in the manager's hands.

"So, what can I do for you?" asked the manager. He spoke in English.

I explained that we had heard from a friend that he ran an *ashram* below his guesthouse. The air of hospitality disappeared, and he looked at us suspiciously, continuing to chew his *paan*.

"What do you want?" His voice was now harsh.

Pinku had told me that he was a bit of a shifty businessman, but I hadn't thought through how we'd get around him when the time came. I glanced at Vikram and Giles, but they seemed as unprepared as I.

"And, and...we've heard about the good work you're doing and would like to make a donation—after seeing the *ashram*, of course."

It had come out quite naturally, and had clearly struck the right chord. Our host thought for a moment before snapping his fingers again.

The servant boy, a tea towel thrown over his greasy under-shirt, led us past what was left of the German tourists' lunch—half a cup of thick coffee and thin crusts of toast spread with globs of orange marmalade—across the leafy courtyard and down a steep flight of stairs that descended directly outside the entrance of the guesthouse. A widow was sweeping water away from a door at the bottom of the steps. She was bent over a *jharoo*, a hand-broom made of straw and bound with string. In her semi-translucent white sari, with her back curved over the broom, she looked like a shrimp—an inhabitant of a world just below the surface, a world rarely seen.

When I was still regularly visiting India, my grandparents would pick up my parents and me from Indira Gandhi International Airport and we would drive to the south Delhi neighbourhood where they lived. My parents were married in 1973 in a Hindu ceremony in the walled-in front garden of their red-brick house. In all the years I had visited India I had never seen a Hindu widow, but I must have passed them on the streets, in the frenetic neighbourhood markets, on overcrowded buses. There were over 30 million Hindu widows in a country of just over 1 billion. But I never knew. I never noticed.

The widow moved aside as we reached the last step. She looked at us suspiciously. The servant boy pushed open the ratty wooden door, and we quietly filed in. The room was oppressively dark. As my eyes slowly adjusted to the gloom, I saw that we were standing in a single large room below the main guesthouse. Sparse sunlight outlined the shapes of four carved archways that extended to the top of the high ceiling. They were all shuttered except for the one farthest from the door. Narrow shafts of sunlight caught small, floating dust particles. The top slats of the shutters were broken, revealing detailed sandstone filigree latticework on each archway, an intricate series of diamond shapes outlined in sunlight. Someone coughed in the recesses of the room.

My attention was immediately drawn to shapes moving on the stone floor. I saw a woman lying on a thin woven reed mat, turning in her sleep. Beside her another lay sleeping. They must have each been over seventy. The same age as my *Nani* in Delhi, I thought to myself. But my grandmother inhabited a different world. She was a member of middle-class India, with her soft hands, diamond solitaires, and servants. I noticed a widow sitting with her back against the far wall, her legs splayed out on the mat in front of her. She was sifting grains of rice on its uneven surface, periodically reaching into an aluminum container for new handfuls. We walked farther into the room, past the sleeping women. The one who was sifting rice looked up and motioned for us to sit. She got up with difficulty and woke the other two. They all wore dirty white saris and heavily darned shawls. Their heads were shaved. Two had short stubble and one had a close crewcut. The room was freezing, but there was no direct sunlight or heaters to keep them warm.

I introduced us in Hindi and asked what it was like to live below the Sunview. It seemed a silly question as their lives were obviously bleak. The woman with the rice introduced herself as

Gyanvati. She was a Brahmin widow from the north Indian state of Bihar. When her husband died, her children refused to share their father's property with her. To get her out of the way, her sons had brought her to Benares. She had found a place to live below the guesthouse.

"Do you pay rent?" I asked.

She looked toward the door. The servant boy was standing outside, one foot on the bottom step, pulling at the tea towel around his neck. She hesitated, but he wasn't paying attention.

"Yes, we pay. The manager gives us rice every two weeks, but it's never enough." Gyanvati began to press her legs with her hands.

"Some of us work as sweepers in the city to make enough for the rent."

Giles had been recording the conversation on the Handycam, framing her at the far left of the small screen. *Rent*, I thought. The room was crumbling, and fraying mats served as makeshift beds. Each woman had a small cloth bundle stashed in a corner. It was their only property.

The door creaked open and a young woman came into the room. She was wearing a colourful sari and her long black hair was tied into a bun. A little boy ran in after her. She sat next to the others, and the boy collapsed into her lap. She must have been thirty. I wondered who she could be, maybe a maid from the guesthouse? But Gyanvati introduced her as a widow, a recent arrival in Benares. She had come with nothing except her son. Now they both lived here, in this dark room full of dust. The servant boy entered the room. Giles put away the Handycam. I asked Gyanvati if there was anything we could get for them. "Saris. New saris," she said.

We stood up and moved toward the door. I looked back at them and promised we'd come again, but they had already returned to their own world. The young widow was picking at her son's hair, and Gyanvati had gone back to sifting grains of rice. As we climbed the steep stairs, I remembered a description in the *dhyana mantra* of Dhumavati, the widow goddess: "Dhumavati is ugly, unsteady, and angry . . . She is always hungry and thirsty and looks unsatisfied."

VIKRAM AND I WALKED along the *ghats*. Giles had returned to Clarks, and the evening sky was now a deep indigo. Neither of us had spoken since leaving the guesthouse. The *ghats* were empty and dark in the unlit spaces between the halogen street lamps. They seemed to glow in the pale blue light. I thought of the widows, and their social transparency. They were like panes of glass in a solid metal structure. I was glad that the film would help expose their way of life.

Vikram broke the silence.

"I love *Cinema Paradiso*. Have you seen that movie?"

"Yes. I loved it too." Images from the film, about a little Italian boy who falls in love with cinema, went through my mind.

"What else do you like to watch?" I asked.

"Bergman. *Fanny and Alexander, Autumn Sonata*." Vikram lit a cigarette, and exhaled slowly.

We passed beneath one of the many sandstone mansions that rise up from the *ghats*. It was once a princely palace, but now lay in disuse. Its high walls towered above us, the tops of its balconies lost in shadow and covered with overgrown vines. I looked at Vikram. I liked the shape of his nostrils. They were large and elegantly carved. Maybe I could share myself with someone, I thought. Vikram walked toward a metal railing overlooking the river. I stood beside him, resting my elbows on the cold surface.

"I can't believe what we saw today," I said.

He nodded, and stubbed out his cigarette against the cold metal.

"Your mom wants us to take pictures of *galis* tomorrow—possible locations for the scene where Chuyia runs away from the widows' house."

I wanted to spend tomorrow with him, and the day after that. Two boys were playing a game with a stick and ball on the *ghats* below us. They were like ghosts—two black smudges against the pale blue-grey light reflected on the stone. *Pitch and hit, pitch and hit.*

"Come, let's go home." Vikram moved away from the railing.

We found a cycle rickshaw parked in a busy *gali*. It was small and seemed to be made of aluminum, its sides perforated into patterns of flowers and stars. The red vinyl seat was torn and white synthetic stuffing bubbled out of the seams. It was barely wide enough to seat two people. Squished together, we braced ourselves as the driver mounted the bicycle and pushed on the ground with his bare foot to gain momentum.

Benares was teeming with life. Sweet shops lined both sides of the narrow lanes, their glass cases filled with syrupy *rasgullas*, round yellow *ladoos*, and *jalebis*, orange and glassy, frying in shallow vats of hot oil. I could smell the sugar and taste the oil on my lips. The rickshaw had nothing to absorb the shocks. I held on to the collapsed roof and the edge of the torn vinyl seat. The yellow lights of the small shops blurred as we passed them. Vikram talked about movies and Bombay and a trip he'd taken to the Taj Mahal, photographing the nearby Shah Jahan's palace in the morning light as dust floated up into the seventeenth-century Mughal archways. He owned a Nikon. I told him about the fish market on the banks of the Bosphorus, and my hand-me-down Canon F-1. His parents had divorced when he was about the same age as I had been, and he lived with his mother in a small apartment in north Bombay.

The streets became wider and darker as we approached the cantt. The smell of frying sweets was replaced with the fresh, cool smell of *gulmohur* trees.

"I'm writing a film script." Vikram looked out over the darkened colonial residences.

He began to describe the story and told me that he dreamed of directing one day. There was a love scene that took place in complete silence. The couple wouldn't say anything, making love with no sound, only their eyes. I was nineteen, but had never had a boyfriend. My life had been spent running between my parents' houses. I buried myself in my studies as a means of escape. More than anything I wanted to be a part of the world he was describing. I could feel the warmth of his arm against mine in the narrow seat of the cycle rickshaw. Something was opening up in me. It felt wonderfully close, and yet so foreign. The driver pushed on the unoiled pedals, the only sound in the otherwise quiet night.

4

The week before filming began with an arrival and a departure. Nandita Das, who would play the young widow Kalyani, arrived and I decided to move out of Clarks and into my own room. The crew was in their final stages of preparation. Dolly sewed the last touches on the costumes, the art department had almost finished decorating the *ashram*, and the production carpenters finished building several wooden sets to be used on the *ghats*. In the midst of all this activity, the first thing Nandita did was shave her head.

The beauty salon was on the ground floor of Clarks. Nandita arrived with much fanfare. She was beautiful—dark chocolate brown skin, perfect features, and long black hair that fell to her waist. My mother met Nandita while casting for *Fire* in Delhi in 1996. Nandita was an unknown in film at the time, a former sociology major, a teacher, and the daughter of a prominent Indian painter. They were wearing the same *dupatta* at their first meeting, and that shared taste in clothing became the basis of a long working relationship and friendship. She had starred in both *Fire* and *Earth*.

The salon was a narrow room with a counter running its length and a single mirror above it, framed with makeup lights. There were four adjustable chairs. It was oppressively hot, with only enough space for the hairdresser to squeeze back and forth between the clients and the back wall of the salon. Nandita sat in the centre chair, smiling and playing distractedly with her long hair. The hairdresser was Chinese-Indian. She wore a pink smock with metal hairclips pinned to it. Decades of cross-

border migration had led to a substantial Indian population of Chinese descent. The hairdresser looked fully Chinese, except she wore a small gold nose ring and spoke perfect Hindi. She grasped Nandita's hair and clasped it on top of her head with one of the clips. Nandita frowned at herself in the mirror. I waited off to the side with my camera slung over my shoulder.

Nandita's hair started falling onto the linoleum. I began taking photos, kneeling on the floor and aiming at her reflection in the mirror. A fine cloud of mist surrounded Nandita as the hairdresser spritzed her hair to dampen it, snipping away the long black strands. Nandita laughed as her hair fell to the floor. After a few minutes my mother came into the salon. Nandita now had a boy's cut, but she was still sensual, still as beautiful as ever. "Shorter," Mom said, and left to continue rehearsals.

Karma is the Hindu concept that we all have an individual destiny to fulfill, and that one's lot in life is governed by the accumulation of good and bad deeds over previous lifetimes. I wondered about *karma* as I walked through the doors of the Hotel Vaibhav, a small modern building on the opposite side of the cantt from Clarks. After spending a week in my mother's suite I wanted my own room. We hadn't seen much of each other during my stay at Clarks. I was researching for the shoot, and she was busy rehearsing with her actors. I knew she wanted me to stay with her longer, but last-minute preparations wouldn't allow it. Maybe it was our *karma*. I also wanted to stay with the rest of the crew. Other than the lead actors, director, and heads of department, most of the technicians and production assistants, including Vikram and Anurag, were staying at the functional, but not fancy, Vaibhav.

Anurag Kashyap had flown in from Bombay to translate the English script into Hindi. My mother wrote in English, the language she was educated in at Welham Girls Boarding School in north India. The language of British colonization. Anurag was

a fiery, intelligent writer in his early thirties, with large intense eyes and an occasional propensity for whisky. Hot off the Bollywood hit film *Satya*, a movie about the Bombay under-world, he had turned Mom's English dialogue into sparse yet poetic Hindi.

The Vaibhav was a five-storey, office-like block and stood in stark contrast to the grace of the surrounding colonial architecture. The exterior walls were covered in thick brown stucco, and a small café on the ground floor served cold omelets and instant Nescafé coffee throughout the day. There was one small elevator, which crawled up to each floor, and stairs that opened up onto a series of wide marble landings for those inclined to walk. My room was at the end of a hallway on the third floor.

I pulled my backpack along the smooth marble until I was standing in front of my door. It was made of pressed wood, and seemed light and insignificant. But what was behind it would become one of the most significant parts of my life at the time—a room of my own. Two years later, at university in Oxford, I would read Virginia Woolf's *A Room of One's Own* one night in a cold, cavernous library. Her essay on the importance of personal space, access to education, and financial security—all necessary for a woman's independence—would remind me of my first step into that poorly lit room in the Hotel Vaibhav. It would remind me of my first taste of independence, like breathing for the first time, fresh and clean and new.

I never had a room of my own, at least in the sense of a peaceful place where I truly felt at home. I was torn between two houses, a lonely space filled with guilt and with the fear of disappointing my parents. When the court decreed I could live with my dad, I was also granted the right to choose when to visit my mother. I remember the days when I was dropped off at the front door of her pale pink townhouse. There was always a tension in the pit of my stomach that I was going to betray my

father as soon as I walked through the door, that somehow I wasn't supposed to share myself with her. And I knew when I left my mother at the end of the weekend that a sadness would descend over her, cold and impersonal, like the grey carpeting and walls of her rented home. But what was I supposed to do? There was no one to blame, only the great inconvenience of divorce, and the great inconvenience of being an only child. I wished, more than anything, to escape this vicious cycle and somehow break free. *Betrayal*. Why was it a betrayal to want to love both of your parents? I never understood that.

I pulled out the small metal key and opened the door.

The room was tiny, no more than a box with two single beds. The floor was laid with cold brown tile and the walls were painted a yellowy off-white, the same colour as the synthetic powdered custard found next to packets of Jell-O in the supermarket. I stepped in. It smelled clean, like Lysol. There was a large window along one wall with a narrow window seat below it. Placing my bag on the bed closest to the window, I walked over. The glass felt cold to my touch. The room was at the front of the building, overlooking a red-dirt road and a cluster of tall trees. There were no curtains. I watched as the occasional parrot, its sleek emerald-green body streamlined to the wind, flew from branch to branch.

A small bathroom, lined with pale blue ceramic tiles on the floor and walls, was a cool contrast to the yellow room. There was no shower stall or bathtub, only a metal showerhead and a drain laid neatly into the floor. A red plastic bucket and pitcher sat under the sink. My mother had once told me that Indians didn't like to bathe in dirty water, like the still water in Western baths. The bucket was to be filled with hot water, and the pitcher dipped in and poured over one's head while crouching on the blue tiles.

I pulled my clothes out of the backpack and placed them on the bed farthest from the window. A light brown batik sarong served as a bed cover, replacing the dull white hotel sheets with patterns of colourful flying birds and intertwined leaves. My dad had bought it for me on a wonderful trip we'd taken together to Indonesia when I was thirteen. We scuba-dived, climbed a volcano, ate spicy noodles at a roadside *warung* or food stall, and wandered through lush rice paddy fields cut into the hillside. I loved every minute of my time with him. It was easy, and free from the memory of my choice.

My dad always told me that travel was the best form of learning. "I have never let my schooling interfere with my education," he would say in a deep voice, quoting Mark Twain as we walked under the high Indonesian sun.

My father is the descendant of two Russian Jewish families. My *Bubbi*, or grandmother in Yiddish, immigrated to Canada from the Ukraine. My grandfather, or *Zaida*, was born in Canada and grew up in Neudorf, Saskatchewan, a town with wooden sidewalks and one muddy main street. He worked in television broadcasting as an interviewer and weatherman, and was one of the first people to be broadcast on Canadian television, on September 8, 1952. My *Bubbi* passed down her family history to my dad, and he recounted her oral history to me in the form of bedtime stories. My *Bubbi*'s arrival in Canada was connected with tragic circumstances back in her village of Tomashpol, near the sugar-refinery town of Znamenka in rural Ukraine.

At the age of eight my *Bubbi* was taken out of her house into the main square of the town, where she was lined up next to her family, and the rest of the Jews in the village, to be executed by firing squad. It was 1919 and the pogroms against the Jews, led by Czarist White Russians, were in full swing. Miraculously, she survived.

In the early hours of the previous night, my great-grandmother had sent her maid, disguised as an old woman, across the White Russian lines to the neighbouring town in search of help. As the White Russians took aim at the Jewish families, including my grandmother, a flatbed train car attached to a single engine pulled into town. On top of the car, mounted on horses, was a group of Bolshevik revolutionaries. With them was my great-grandmother's maid. The Bolsheviks began firing into the air, the White Russians fled, and my grandmother survived to see her ninth birthday.

After the pogrom they escaped to Romania, where they lived for the next ten years. My father remembered her telling him that she would pick tobacco with her brothers for money, while my great-grandmother, who had been a lady of means, sat at the edges of fields watching her children work. I always imagined my grandmother working the tobacco fields of central Europe, her little child's fingers stained black with tar.

Eventually they reached the Atlantic, where a ship bound for Canada would deliver them to Halifax in the winter of 1929. From there they would migrate to Montreal. My grandfather arrived in Montreal in 1934, and it's there that *Bubbi* and *Zaida* met.

I hung a tie-dyed saffron-and-green *dupatta* above the bare window, attaching it carefully behind the edges of the window frame. It fell softly, turning the cool winter evening light a warm yellow as it filtered into the room. I had never had a connection with my Jewish roots in the same way I had to India. My father's family didn't practice Judaism, and, unlike my mother, my father was born in Canada. I was a generation removed from being a Russian Jew.

The *dupatta* was crinkly, like paper crushed between someone's hands. It was to be worn around a woman's neck, with a cotton *salwaar kameez*, traditional Indian pants covered by a long shirt. But here it was, being used as a makeshift curtain. It was like my relationship with India. The culture was familiar, comfortable even, but I never quite interpreted it the way people who lived in the country did. They would have worn the *dupatta*; I hung it up as a curtain.

I lifted a small aluminum container out of my backpack. It was a little bigger than a shoe-polish tin, deeper, with a light blue label glued to its side. The label was printed with small black lettering, *Oceanus*. I twisted off the metal top and caught four small seashells as they fell into my hand. It was a marbled-blue travelling candle. I had placed a few small scalloped shells, white and pink and dappled brown, in the container so they wouldn't break on the journey. As night fell I placed the candle and the shells on the linoleum-covered bedside table, and got in under the dull white sheets and printed sarong.

The room was absolutely quiet, except for the occasional sound of a cyclist passing in the street below. I lit the candle. The wick began to burn, and the wax melted in a perfect small circle in the centre of the candle's blue surface. The room began to smell fresh and sweet, nothing like the smell of the ocean as the name advertised, but somehow suggestive of the same expanse. I felt comfortable and safe. It was a room of my own.

Lying in bed, staring at the white foam ceiling panels, I began to drift off to sleep. My last thoughts were of the smells of early childhood in the walled-in front garden of my grandparents' home in Delhi—damp earth, *Raat Ki Rani*, queen of the night jasmine, and the smell of burning diesel from the nearby road. How little I knew of this vast country of my mother's birth.

THE NEXT MORNING I found my mother sitting quietly on the yellow couch in her suite. The blinds were drawn, and she was rapidly smoking through a pack of Rothmans. I had come to tell her how location scouting with Vikram was going, but the initial excitement we had felt listening to the soundtrack for the film was gone.

"What's wrong?" I asked.

"I just got a call," she said, attempting to smooth the crease in her forehead with the tips of her fingers.

"What about?" I started to arrange the photos of the cast members on a bulletin board. She said she liked seeing the faces of her characters when she woke up in the morning.

"The location manager just told me that he thinks there will be trouble. He says the Hindus are angry about the film. There are rumours that the film is anti-Brahmin. They say I'm trying to pollute the Ganges."

I didn't know what to say. I remembered what Vikram had said on the *ghats*, but it had seemed so insignificant at the time. The script was beautiful, a love story, a story about three women searching for freedom. Where had this come from?

"Anyway, don't worry," I said. "They can't do anything. You have full permission, right?"

"Yes," she nodded.

Water had the required permissions from the central government in New Delhi. The BJP had swiftly passed the script through its Ministry of Information and Broadcasting. It had been approved with no cuts or censorship. Any foreign film-maker who wanted to shoot in India had to submit the script to the Ministry to be cleared before beginning. The policy arose when French director Louis Malle made *Phantom India* in 1968, a series of documentaries which the government believed portrayed India in a negative light. From then on all foreign filming had to be cleared by the Ministry of I & B.

"Yes, there's nothing to worry about," she said. "The I & B officer who reviewed the script loved it. She said it was beautiful." But my mother's face looked strained as she spoke.

As I left the room she called after me.

"Don't tell any of the crew. I don't want to worry them unnecessarily."

I nodded, and closed the door.

That afternoon I met Vikram in the production office. He was wearing a white cotton shirt and cargo pants. His face was cleanly shaven, smooth, and soft. I wanted to touch it. While he was typing an e-mail at one of the computers, I looked at our production calendar. The days were quickly being crossed off with red marker. We were only a few days away from our first day of shooting. David was smoking a cigarette on the balcony, resting his arms on the metal railing. He seemed lost in thought. Copies of the script were stacked next to him beside the photocopier.

"Ready?" I stood behind Vikram as he finished his e-mail.

"Yeah," he said, grabbing his backpack and pushing back the plastic chair.

We were going to a small tenement in central Benares where *hijras*, eunuchs, lived their lives dressed as women. It was part of our research for the character of Gulabi, a *hijra* who acts as Kalyani's pimp.

Prostitution is an act Kalyani endures because of financial necessity. As a young beauty, she is sent out to support the other widows by selling her body. She has a pure spirit, which she believes remains untouched by her actions. I remembered a line from the script as Vikram and I got into the production car. It was Kalyani's description of how she survived:

"*Padma patram evam bhasa.*"

"Like a lotus, untouched by the filthy water in which it grows."

I HAD SEEN HIJRAS on the streets of Delhi as a child. My grandparents' boat-like Contessa, the Indian version of a Chevrolet Impala, would be idling in traffic when the occasional group of *hijras* would walk between the lines of stopped cars, knocking on windows, begging for money. They moved through the thick brown emission fumes, which hung between the cars like an ephemeral blanket, in a wave of colour. They may have been dressed as women, but they didn't act like women. They danced between the cars, shaking their hips in yellow and pink saris. The material they wore was always gaudy and the blouses short and tight, revealing breasts like tennis balls. I never knew if their breasts were real or if they really were tennis balls. They wore thick lines of *kohl*, charcoal black eyeliner, on the lower rims of their eyes, and scented *chameli* or jasmine buds in their hair.

I was scared of them. They were aggressive when they banged on the windows, and I'd heard stories that if you didn't give them money, they would lift up their saris and flash you—if they didn't curse you first. The memories ran through my mind as the Ambassador came to a stop in the centre of Benares. The streets had narrowed and were filled with people. We got out and walked into the maze of *galis* toward the tenement.

We rounded a corner into an alley that was so narrow, only one person could walk down at a time. The walls on either side were whitewashed plaster and shimmered a translucent blue. The alley had a sickly sweet smell. I looked down at the stones. They were covered in fresh cow dung. Cows roamed freely through Benares and throughout the whole country. As sacred animals in Hinduism, they were protected by law.

We reached worn steps leading down to another alley, which veered off sharply to the left. A woman, her head covered with her sari, walked swiftly toward the river, carrying a small brass *lota* to fill with holy Ganges water. I wanted to tell Vikram that he was right about the rumours in the city, but held my tongue when I remembered what my mother had said.

Stepping down, I noticed a small alcove in the side of a house. It was covered with the same whitewash as the buildings. The plaster was chipping at the edges. Inside was a black stone carving, a plain rounded shaft rising up from the centre of what looked like a shallow bowl. It had been freshly washed with milk, and a few scattered marigold blossoms were placed at its base. I stopped to look more closely.

"It's a Shiv *lingam*," Vikram said.

"A what?"

"A symbol of the god Shiva. This is the city of Shiva."

"I didn't know." I wanted him to tell me more.

Vikram stopped to look. He leaned closer to the lingam, resting his hand on the side of the chipped alcove.

"He's my favourite god, Shiva. The creator and the destroyer. There are thousands of Shiv lingams like this, scattered throughout the city. They say Benares is where he first touched the Earth, where creation began and where it will return in fire at the end of time. Shiv carries a drum for creation, and a trident for destruction. Every image of him shows the Ganges flowing from his head."

I looked closely at the smooth, black lingam. It smelled faintly of sandalwood paste.

"What does it symbolize?" I asked.

"It's his phallus."

"What!" I started laughing, embarrassed.

"No, really. It's his phallus. And the low dish below it has an opening, see? It's a *yoni*, the birth canal and womb. It's the union of female and male, a symbol of creation."

I realized that every stone we were walking on in Benares was holy, each a small part of a constant cycle of creation and destruction. The energy of thousands of years of worship emanated from the worn rock up into my feet. I shivered.

We continued walking. Temple bells echoed through the narrow lanes, signalling the Hindu prayer service. I tried not to look at Vikram's face, but I was drawn to his warm, intelligent eyes.

"Shabana Azmi had her head shaved on the *ghats* this morning," Vikram said.

"Were you there?" I asked.

"Yeah, I took some photos. She wanted to experience it the same way the widows do—publicly—right at the cremation grounds after their husband's body is burned."

Shabana Azmi was playing the hardened, older widow Shakuntala, a woman trapped by her religion and her own bitterness. Shabana was a veteran of Indian cinema, and the magnetic star of numerous art house and Bollywood movies. A member of Parliament, she was a vocal political activist for women's rights and an outspoken opponent of communal violence between Muslims and Hindus. She was also a Muslim woman playing a Hindu widow, something we would soon find out didn't sit well with local Hindus.

"Some journalists want to put the photo on the front page of a local newspaper," he added.

"Great," I said, unaware of the repercussions any publicity would have for us.

The *hijras'* tenement was dark, as if the power had been cut. Vikram and I were led into the low multistorey building by a young *hijra*. She was dressed in a thin red sari and her braided hair fell to the middle of her back. They were expecting us, as the necessary permissions were already arranged by our location manager. As our guide led us up a central stairwell, I noticed that there was no one around. There was only the muffled sound of pigeons cooing from somewhere high above. It sounded as if they were in the water pipes, their song reassuring. Our guide stopped us on the third-floor landing. It was covered in a thick layer of dust.

"Sit down," she said in Hindi.

"Here?" Vikram asked.

"Here," she said, and turned and disappeared into the darkness of one of the corridors, leaving us with only the marks of her bare feet and the fading sound of her ankle bells.

We sat cross-legged in the middle of the landing, and waited. I started drawing with my finger in the dust and counting the spots of light that fell through the meshed landing window. Vikram played with his earring.

Slowly, I began to hear movement: doors creaking, an asthmatic cough, the sound of feet. Then out of nowhere women began appearing from the deep recesses of the corridor and from behind closed doors, ascending and descending the stairwell. They moved in a circle around us. Some sat, others stood, and instantly, we were surrounded.

Vikram and I sat, frozen, as twenty male faces adorned with deep red lipstick and black eyeliner scrutinized us from head to toe. One voice emerged from the crowd, flowery, gliding above the dust and cramped bodies that surrounded us.

"Why are you here?"

The group fell silent. It came from the pouting mouth of a middle-aged *hijra*. Her face was delicate, with only the faintest of lines marking her smooth forehead.

"We're making a film in Benares and one of the characters is a *hijra*. We wanted to know what it's like to be a *hijra*," Vikram replied.

The group burst out laughing.

"I mean ... we wanted to do a bit of research," I added.

The *hijras* became quiet, but we had amused them—two young people naively inquiring about the lifestyle of transsexual males, while sitting on a dusty landing in what looked like the dilapidated Ray Bradbury building in *Bladerunner*.

"We are neither here nor there, but we have each other," she said, addressing Vikram. Maybe she felt more comfortable talking to a man, I thought.

While she spoke, I looked closely at the surrounding faces. They looked like masks, suspended in the darkness. I wanted to reach out and touch their painted skin. Some were young, in their twenties, their tight bodies wrapped in revealing saris. Others were older, and their skin withered beneath the clinging fabric. How had they come here? I wondered. When had their lives led them into this fantastic and bizarre club between genders?

And then I saw her. She was standing across from me, partly hidden by another *hijra*. She was looking directly at me, not a waver in her gaze. She must have been fifty. Her face showed age, and she wore the train of her light blue sari over her head. One eye was deep and black and fathomless, but the other was completely white, the pupil and iris clouded over with a thick opaque film.

"We use the money we earn to stay here. And we just bought a minivan for the home, so now we can travel around. It even has the home's name painted on the side."

The voice of the *hijra* with the delicate face pulled me back into the conversation. Vikram was listening attentively. But when I looked toward the *hijra* with the white eye, she was gone. The other *hijras* nodded proudly at the mention of the van, a celebrated new addition to their lives. *Hijras*, who are considered auspicious, are often invited to weddings and births to sing and dance. Looking at the diversity of faces and ages, I realized that this home, this outsiders' community of men living as women, seemed a lot like the widows' *ashram*. Both communities lived apart from society, falling between the cracks of social definition. Members of one group were neither male nor female. Members of the other were neither daughter nor wife. Yet, unlike the widows, the *hijras* had means. They controlled their own property and income, and even movement, sailing around Benares in a new minivan with the home's name painted on its side.

A hand appeared on Vikram's shoulder. The fingernails were painted a deep copper, chipped away at the edges. I looked behind me and directly into the face of the *hijra* with the white eye. Vikram was terrified and quickly tried to wrap up the conversation. I could feel the *hijra's* interest, but it was in Vikram, not me. It was intense, like lust. I started to get up, but our host insisted that we stay. By that time Vikram was moving toward the stairs. The fingers of the white-eyed *hijra* had slipped off, and she was lost in the crowd. The group moved aside gracefully as we descended the stairwell.

We walked back to the Vaibhav in silence, passing vendors selling handmade necklaces spread out on cloths on the ground. Vikram stopped to look. He searched through the silver and beads, running his hand along the pendants' surfaces. Eventually he reached for one, picking it out from the vendor's selection.

"Here, it's for you."

He placed a small necklace in my hand. It was bronzed metal attached to a black thread—an image of the Sun. He tied it around my neck, knotting the thread just below my hairline. I wanted to give him something too. I scanned the table, ignoring the chunky silver jewelry from Rajasthan, and the rainbow-woven friendship bracelets from Nepal.

"And this is for you," I said.

I placed a brown-beaded wooden bracelet on his wrist. It was simple. Just a string of beads, really.

TWO DAYS BEFORE FILMING I began to work full-time in the camera department. The gear had arrived from Canada and Giles had been regularly meeting with my mother to discuss the look of the film. It was going to be shot on an Arriflex BL5 camera with 35 mm Kodak film stock. We needed to organize the equipment and conduct camera tests to ensure nothing was damaged in transit.

I met Brett Matthews, the focus puller, and Jasmine Yuen-Carrucan, the second assistant cameraperson in the lobby of the hotel. The winter sunlight played against the white marble, and a cool breeze passed through the lobby each time someone opened the twin glass doors. Brett would ensure the film was in focus and Jasmine would take care of the camera body and its lenses. Both were Australian. For the next two months I would train under them, learning about lenses, film stock, loading, and lighting.

Brett was in his mid-thirties. He was heavily tanned with clear blue eyes that shone against his skin. He looked as if he had just led an expedition to the far reaches of Papua New Guinea. Jasmine, in contrast, had an air of elegance about her. She was half-Chinese, half-Australian, and her black hair was trimmed in a short boy's cut. I felt intimidated to be working with them. I had never worked with a 35 mm cinema camera before.

We went down to the basement of the hotel where our gear was stored in an unused banquet room. Chandeliers hung from the ceiling and gilded mirrors lined the red walls. It was a hall for weddings, rich and untouched, like a new bride. Jasmine started lifting the heavy lens boxes and taking them outside into the hotel garden. It was a beautiful day. The full heat of the sun, lost in the marble lobby, now warmed our skin. Brett set up the camera on a large metal tripod as I helped Jasmine bring out the rest of the gear.

"So, you've worked with Giles before?" Brett asked as he attached the camera body to the tripod.

"No, but I've known him for a little while," I said.

They didn't know I was the director's daughter, and I didn't want to tell them.

"I met Giles working on *The Beach*, with director Danny Boyle and Leonardo DiCaprio. Giles shot second unit on it," Brett added, as Jasmine passed him a lens. She stood in front of the camera, holding a card with different shades of grey printed on it.

"Can you pass me a 35 mm lens? It's in that box over there." Jasmine pointed to an open case lined with black foam.

I walked over and knelt beside the case. There were five lenses sitting in it, couched in foam. Each was labelled with a small piece of white tape, the lens length neatly printed on it with black marker. I reached for the 35 mm lens and gently pulled it out.

"*The Beach*. That's so cool. What else have you worked on?" I asked.

Brett continued looking through the camera eyepiece. "Well, I worked on *The Thin Red Line* with Terrence Malick."

I was thrilled. *The Thin Red Line* was one of my favourite movies, a beautiful, poetic exploration of war and human fragility. I wanted to ask him absolutely everything about it.

"What was it like working with Terrence Malick? It must have been amazing!"

"Yeah, well, he's a character. He probes pretty deep, as a director, to get the performances he wants from his actors. I mean, this one time, he spent over an hour with this young actor who was playing a soldier. The guy had to be freaked out in the scene. So Terrence just sat there with him, asking him about his family, asking him about the most painful moment with his family, until the kid was crying and just totally freaking out."

It was amazing, all the individual steps taken to create a final experience on film. I wondered if Mom worked that way with her actors. I looked up at the windows of the hotel. She would be in her room right now, rehearsing.

"So how did you end up on *Water*?" Brett asked.

Pretending to be busy with the gear, I ignored him, but I could feel his clear blue eyes, waiting.

"I...I'm related to a crew member," I said quietly. Both Jasmine and Brett looked at me.

"You aren't Deepa's daughter, are you?" Brett asked.

There was nothing I could say. I could only show them that I was a capable individual in my own right, even if I was working on her film.

"Yes, I'm Deepa's daughter."

But there was none of the judgment that I had anticipated. Instead, Brett and Jasmine continued to quietly do their work.

AFTER WE FINISHED the camera tests I took the elevator up to the lobby. The polished brass doors distorted my reflection. When they opened the lobby was silent and barren, with only one hotel employee behind the reception desk, quietly stuffing guests' messages into white envelopes. Anurag and Vikram were sitting on deep red armchairs near the glass entrance, smoking.

"How's it going?" I sat on the edge of one of the armchairs.

"*Are yaar, chutku,* all is excellent." Anurag spoke in a rapid mixture of Hindi and English, running over his words and leaving me to piece together what was left. Soon after we had met, he began calling me *chutku,* an affectionate play on the Hindi word for "little one." It was what my mom called me.

Vikram smiled to himself, and said nothing.

We sat together in a comfortable silence, a rare moment of peace during the intense preparation of pre-production. Vikram took a long drag on his cigarette, and Anurag rested his head on the back of the plush red armchair. The schedule for the first day of shooting had been printed. I held it in my hands, a single sheet of legal-size paper, neatly folded in the middle. It included the call time for the crew, the list of scenes we would be shooting that day, and a transportation breakdown. Our first day would be in the house that was the set for the *ashram.*

I leaned back against the armchair, resting my head next to Anurag's. Vikram stood up and pulled his camera out of his backpack. I looked into his lens and imagined his eyes behind it. He took a photo of the two of us smiling against the red fabric. They were like my new family, I thought, as Vikram mechanically wound the camera. I felt safe, like I belonged in the company of an aspiring director and a writer. All of a sudden, there were shouts from the street. Anurag stood up. I followed him to the twin glass doors. At the bottom of the circular driveway two hotel security guards were trying to hold back a crowd of more than seventy-five people. They were all women, wearing saris. Some had their hair tied tightly into a bun, others had braids down their backs. Their arms were stretched high above their heads, and each held a wooden rolling pin grasped firmly in her hand. As they shouted, they thrust the rolling pins toward the sky in unison, as if invoking the gods. Vikram and Anurag pushed open the doors and started down the driveway toward the shouting crowd. I watched the women's faces from behind the safety of the glass. Contorted with rage, they were chanting something, while rhythmically thrusting the rolling pins above their heads. I tentatively pushed open the door and walked out. The sound hit me suddenly, like an unexpected swell in the surf, dragging one under and filling the ears with its deafening roar.

"*GANGA MAILE NEHIN KAROGE!*"
"You can't pollute the Ganges!"
"*GANDA PANI GANGA NEHIN SAIHAGI!*"
"The Ganges will not tolerate your dirty *Water!*"

Vikram and Anurag were almost at the edge of the crowd. Some of the women were holding placards above their heads, red-painted Hindi slogans on cardboard. When they saw us, their chanting became stronger. I walked down the driveway toward the crowd. Each step felt unreal, as if I were floating above the pavement, unsure of my own direction.

The guards were having trouble holding back the women. They were using long bamboo poles as a makeshift barrier, but the protesters threatened to break through at any moment. Vikram and Anurag started shouting back at the crowd. By the time I reached the barrier, Vikram had ducked under and pushed himself into the middle of the women. Anurag shouted after him, but Vikram was already trying to break up the protest from the inside.

"Have you read the script? Have you even seen it!" he screamed.

But the women ignored him, waving their rolling pins above their heads.

Vikram was taller than all of them, but I could see that he was being pulled deeper into the crowd. The chanting was so loud it became like white noise, fading into the background. I didn't know what to do. I was scared—scared for him, scared for us. I ducked under the barrier and moved into the crowd. The protesters smelled of sweat. The women's sari blouses were stained with dark patches under their arms. I pushed at their waists so they would move aside. Many of them had deep red *sindoors* painted along the middle parting of their hair—the Hindu symbol for a married woman. The smell of sweat was overwhelming. I reached forward and grabbed Vikram by the arm.

"Come on!" I shouted.

I clutched his shirt and pulled him back toward the barrier. Vikram kept shouting as he followed me, looking back into the angry faces of the women. Rigid faces. Faces with a mission.

The guards raised their bamboo poles, and we slipped onto the other side. Anurag was waiting for us. I let go of Vikram's arm and started walking back toward the hotel. My fingers were red from my grip, and my eyes were burning from the mixture of heat and sweat. The sound of chanting began to fade only long after I walked into the lobby.

DAVID LEANED AGAINST the marble counter. The room was dark, except for the bedside lamp, which threw a warm, circular glow on the wall behind my mother's bed. He looked anxious, his face worn by the news of the day. As *Water*'s producer, he had secured the financing for the film, most of it from Canadian businessman Ajay Virmani and himself. My mother sat on the couch beside my uncle Dilip. He had flown in from Delhi, where he lived with his wife and two young children. Dilip was my mother's only sibling, her younger brother and a world-renowned photojournalist. I hadn't really had a relationship with him since my parents' divorce. Like my grandparents, he had faded into another world, fractioned away like the furniture and property.

"What's happening?" I asked.

My mother was on the couch, resting her head in her hands. A cup of cold tea sat on the table in front of her. There was a thin skin on its surface, hot milk that had cooled long ago.

"It's the Hindu right, the local RSS. They've publicly stated that they won't allow *Water* to be made in Benares. The protesters today . . . are you okay?"

Her voice was tender.

"I'm fine," I said. But I wasn't. I felt this energy building up around us. It was something I had never experienced before.

"Dilip's here to help. He has some influential contacts in Delhi, if it comes down to that," my mother added.

"How do they know what the film is even about?" I asked.

"They don't," David said. "But I think there may be a mole in the office. The local Hindi newspapers have printed distorted storylines and know the characters' names. It's possible someone's leaked the script."

What I had seen today was a blind rage that didn't make sense to me. None of those women could have read the script, and yet they hated it with a passion that could come only from a deep belief in what they felt they were protecting. They were fighting against an idea they didn't even understand. Why?

"Who are the RSS?" I asked.

"The RSS are the Rashtriya Swayamsevak Sangh, the cultural wing of the ruling BJP government," my mother said.

A few years later my knowledge of the RSS and their ideology would be much more complete. The "cultural" wing was one of the largest volunteer organizations in the world. Some argued that it was in fact the BJP who were the political wing of the RSS. It was started in 1925 and followed a strict doctrine of Hindutva, or cultural nationalism, which aimed to keep Bharat, the ancient name for India—as Eire is to Ireland or Caledonia to Scotland— purely Hindu, free from the Muslim influence brought in by the Mughals three centuries earlier and the Christian influence of colonization and missionaries.

It was an RSS follower who assassinated Mahatma Gandhi on that fateful evening of January 30, 1948, as he walked, aided by his two grandnieces, across the lawn of Birla House in New Delhi to a prayer service. And it was the RSS that helped insti- gate the violent communal riots between Muslims and Hindus after the destruction of the Muslim mosque of Babri Masjid in Ayodhya in 1992. The RSS claimed Babri Masjid was originally a Hindu temple and the site of the god Rama's birth, and should therefore be demolished and rebuilt as a temple. They attacked Babri Masjid with sledgehammers and axes, destroying the mosque and leading to nationwide communal rioting, which left 2,000 people dead. The Hindu right had a number of affil- iate groups, including the Vishwa Hindu Parishad and the Shiv Sena, or the army of Shiva. The name referred to Shivaji—a seventeenth-century Hindu warrior-king.

But that evening at Clarks, the RSS were just a group of local housewives protesting with rolling pins. I didn't know then the power of the mob, the power of blind belief.

"We've decided not to shoot in the city tomorrow. We're going to fake shooting Chuyia's head being shaven on the *ghats* in the back garden of the hotel, just until things quiet down," David said.

I walked alone to the production office late that night. The protesters were gone. It was ironic that these married women had no empathy for a film about widows, women who had lost the right to wear the *sindoor*.

The small roadside tea stall at the corner of the lane was boarded up for the night and the dung patties, marked with palm prints, were now gone. During the day a young man sat cross-legged on the small wooden platform, minding his aluminum kettle and pouring out thick tea for local customers. There was nothing tonight, only a light fog coming off the Varana. I felt uncomfortable in the darkness, and quickened my pace. The lights were on in the production office. Someone was working late.

Bob sat typing e-mails in his office. Dolly was just leaving, packing her things into a plastic bag.

"See you at the *pooja* in the morning," she said.

"Yes. I think it's at eight," I replied.

Vikram was at one of the computers. The Polaroids from our location scouts lay on the table beside him.

"Do you want to walk back to the hotel?" I asked, afraid to go alone.

Vikram looked up from the computer.

"Yes. Just give me a moment."

Slumping down in one of the plastic chairs near the photocopier, I tried to sleep, but the bright halogen ceiling lights kept me awake. A halo surrounded them, the way lights glow when you come out of a swimming pool with too much chlorine in your eyes.

"Let's go." Vikram shut down the computer and moved toward the stairwell.

The road from the office to the Vaibhav was curved and unpaved. The dirt was rutted with tire marks. There was nothing on either side except for the occasional bungalow and a public elementary school, barely visible behind thin metal gates. From my room in the mornings I could hear the children shouting and playing. The fog hung thick in the air, lit by street lamps every few hundred metres. We walked close together, unable to see more than a few feet in front of us. It was like moving slowly through thick soup.

"You know, you have train tunnels for nostrils," I said, smirking and avoiding his eyes.

"Very funny, *chutku*." He laughed, and started singing softly in Hindi,

"yeh mahalo, yeh takhato, yeh taajon ki duniya
yeh insaan ke dushman, samaajo ki duniya..."

It sounded beautiful, and a little forlorn.

"What is it?" I asked.

"It's from *Pyaasa*, an old black-and-white Bollywood film by Guru Dutt. It's about a poet whose work is appreciated only by a prostitute. *Pyaasa* means 'the one who thirsts.'"

I had never heard of Guru Dutt or seen old Bollywood films. Vikram began telling me about the golden era of Bombay cinema in the fifties, how Guru Dutt was in love with his lead actress, but remained married to his wife. Bollywood and Indian film was a new world, far beyond the India of family visits to my grandparents' home in Delhi.

"...*yeh duniya agar mil bhi jaaye to kyaa hai...*," he continued to sing.

"This world that pays homage to palaces, thrones, and crowns
This world that's the enemy of humanity
... Even if I could have this world, it's not worth possessing."

"Will you teach it to me one day?" I asked.
"I'll write down the words for you, and the translation."

The Vaibhav lobby was empty when we arrived. There was no one at the reception desk and the small café was dark, closed for the night. We walked toward the stairs. I walked slowly, not wanting our time together to end. Vikram was on the second floor, and I was on the third. We reached the wide marble space between the two floors. One staircase led down to the second floor and another, opposite it, led up to the third. The landing floated between them, serving both, unable to commit to either.

"Well, goodnight." I looked at Vikram. His hair was a mess from the day, but his eyes were clear and kind. I searched his face. He was beautiful. He put his hand on my shoulder, as if saying goodnight, and I turned to leave. But as I moved toward the stairs, he didn't let go, tracing the length of my arm with his fingers until they touched the palm of my hand. I turned back toward him, and he pulled me close. I rested my cheek against the front of his black sweater. My face felt soft against the roughness of the wool. He ran his fingers through my hair and gently held my head. The walls began to blur, and I felt as if I were melting, my body rapidly losing all form. I looked up at him. His eyes expressed a feeling I had never seen before, and we kissed. In that moment I loved everything, and all the divisions I had ever felt in my life closed up like knitted bone.

THE NIGHT WAS completely black outside my window, a comfortable darkness that one can imagine exists only in the depths of the sea—as shapeless and silent. It was eerie after the violence of the day. There were no parrots moving between trees and no sounds from the street below. I sat on the small window seat in my room with my knees pulled up to my chest. My camera assistant's tools were laid out on the bed: a purple fanny pack, coloured felt-tip pens, and my name-tag. *Water: Devyani Saltzman: Camera Assistant.* There was only one light coming from the street below, a naked light bulb strung up outside a small house at the edge of the trees. The house had smooth mud walls and one door. A *charpoy* was placed beside it. I had seen the family early that morning, the sunlight still soft through the dissipating fog. A woman in a *kaftan* was brushing her teeth with a medicinal *neem* stick and spitting into the open gutter that lined the road. Her hair was loose and uncombed. A dog slept under the *charpoy*. I had watched the woman as I drank my morning tea. Her movements seemed so assured and hopeful as she woke to the newness of the day.

5

The crew gathered in the back garden of Clarks at eight the next morning. White sheets were spread out on the grass with bolster pillows laid neatly along their edges. A Hindu priest had been hired to conduct a *pooja,* or prayer ceremony, before filming began. This was a common practice in the Indian film industry, a gathering to bless the crew and the production. The priest was preparing, placing colourful sweets on a silver tray to distribute to the crew as *prashad,* blessings. His forehead was smeared with holy ash, and he wore a thin white string across his chest, identifying him as a Brahmin. Brett had set up our camera on a tripod in the centre of the lawn. It was already covered with marigold garlands, waiting to be blessed. I had spent the morning ironing a new cotton *salwaar kameez,* a gift from my grandmother. It was thin and turquoise, embroidered with delicate white stitching, almost diaphanous. The sun was white and hot on my face, cooled by the occasional breeze. My mother wore a *salwaar kameez* instead of her usual jeans and button-down shirt. I sat down on the sheet next to her, tucking my legs under me.

The last of the crew members seated themselves, and the priest began to recite a Hindu prayer. I covered my head with my *dupatta.* It was light and stiff, still newly starched from the shop.

The priest lit the *havan,* a small wood-burning fire in a square metal container, adding spoonfuls of *ghee* and camphor to the flames as he recited prayers in Sanskrit. The smell of burning camphor mixed with the morning air. I felt lightheaded.

Brett, Jasmine, and Bob watched with curiosity, witnesses to an unfamiliar ritual, as Shabana and Nandita sat quietly, their newly shaved heads covered, their eyes downcast. I pulled at the edge of my *dupatta*, tracing the embroidery with my finger. The heat of the fire created a haze over the gathering. I could just about see Vikram and Anurag sitting on the other side. The priest began to ring a small silver bell, and the world that morning seemed full of possibility, full of the blessings that religion promises us.

"How are you?" I asked Mom, as the priest continued his recitations.

She looked up from beneath her white *dupatta*. "I don't feel so well." Her eyes were puffy from lack of sleep, and dark circles had begun to form below them.

"What happened?"

"We had an emergency press conference this morning at the Press Corp in the city. Anurag and Dilip came with me. We thought if we could clarify the contents of the script, maybe there would be no more misgivings about the film being anti-Hindu."

The priest was now moving around the crowd, placing *prashad* in people's upturned hands.

"What did they ask you?"

"They wanted me to release the script to the public. They said if I have nothing to hide, then I should give them the script."

"Why won't you give it to them, Mom? At least then everything will be okay."

She was quiet for a moment.

"I have no problem releasing the script to the public. There's nothing to hide. But what guarantee do I have that the script won't be doctored by the press or taken out of context to help sell their papers?"

I had wondered what the press would want to do with it anyway. They were journalists, not the RSS. But she then told me that more excerpts of the script had been printed in the Benares Hindi dailies, and they were entirely incorrect, suggesting Kalyani has a cross-caste relationship with a Brahmin priest. I knew little then of the shows the media often likes to stage.

"Also, from the way they were asking questions, I knew that they were out for something. They accused me of setting up the rumours and protests as part of a publicity stunt. The press say we're doing this to ourselves."

She laughed to herself in disbelief.

As an NRI or non-resident Indian, my mother had been accused by some Indian journalists of choosing controversial topics to pander to Western audiences. It was a theme I vaguely remembered around the time of *Fire*—selling India to the West—exotifying, exploiting, twisting culture.

After 250 years of British rule, it was clear that India still had a love/hate relationship with the West, eating up its pop consumer culture while simultaneously hating the idea of pandering to it. McDonald's and Domino's Pizza had opened in the major cities, and even in holy Benares television sets flickered with MTV. Yet an Indian who had gone abroad and was telling stories about lesbians and widows was regarded as selling out. But what if what was being revealed was true? I had seen the widows below the Sunview with my own eyes. I had seen what little they had.

"It will be okay," my mother said. "The press eventually backed off."

The smoke from the *havan* rose in a thin column toward the sky. It was a windless day and it remained almost motionless, suspended in the air. I didn't know that the space between two worlds, two cultures, could be such a painful place for her. I wondered what it was like to be a young, newly married Indian woman in Toronto in 1973, separated from friends and family and everything she knew. I felt it myself at times, adrift between communities, lost without a sense of belonging. It was clear that everything that was happening had much deeper roots than opposition to a story about Hindu widows.

The priest made the final blessing over the camera, and the *pooja* was over.

THE CAMERA TRUCK was parked behind the hotel. It was a long trailer, gutted and fitted with shelves to store lens boxes and equipment. There was a small metal ramp and hand trolley to off-load the gear and take it to the set. Jasmine sat at the back of the truck with the Arriflex camera resting on a box in front of her. The trailer was hot and claustrophobic, stuffed with equipment. I changed from my *salwaar kameez* into work clothes, pants and a T-shirt, and prepared to transport our gear to the garden.

"Come here," Jasmine said. Her Aussie accent was soothing.

I sat down beside her, close to the camera. She lifted a lens out of the case and attached it to the camera body. The Arri was facing down the length of the truck.

"Here, have a look at this." She motioned me to the viewfinder.

I placed my eye on the soft grey pad around the eyepiece, but couldn't see anything. I tried to keep my left eye from fluttering. I pressed against the eyepiece and the frame came into focus. The front of the truck and the driver's seat looked far away, and the walls were wide apart. Suddenly it felt as if there was nothing to feel claustrophobic about.

"It's a 15 mm wide lens," Jasmine said.

I pulled away from the camera and the feeling of claustrophobia returned.

"Here, now try this one." She removed the lens and attached another. I looked through the eyepiece. "Wait a second." Jasmine swung the camera around so it was facing her. Her face filled the frame. I could see her light brown freckles and the edges of her short bangs.

"A portrait lens. 85 mm."

"Thanks for showing me," I said.

"No problem. We all have to learn. Now let's get the gear off-loaded and set up."

THE ART DEPARTMENT had built a wooden platform in the middle of the lawn behind a meticulously kept rose garden. Apple boxes were stacked on top of the platform, and small gas fires were placed on the ground around it. Seated on top of the apple box, dressed in a plain white sari, was Urvi Gokani, the eight-year-old actress who was playing Chuyia. Her sari covered her chest and one shoulder. Widows in the 1930s often didn't wear blouses, one piece of material a testament to their frugality. Standing behind her was a local barber, hired to shave her head as the camera rolled. Manikarnika *Ghat*, the cremation grounds, reconstructed for our safety in a hotel garden.

My mother sat on a black canvas chair, facing the platform. In front of her was a video monitor, attached directly to the camera so she could see the shot as it happened. Chuyia's head-shaving, the ritual that transforms the child-bride into child-widow after her husband's cremation, was one of the first scenes in *Water*. It was my job to make sure the video feed remained connected to the monitor and to run back to the camera truck if we needed anything. My mother wore a blue cotton *kurta* printed with patterns of white-and-yellow flowers. Her hair was pulled back in a tight ponytail. The crew gathered behind the monitor, out of view of the camera.

"It looks like a Sunday brunch on the lawn," my mother said. But it was a tense moment—our first shot.

The barber took Urvi's long black hair in his hand, and held a large pair of metal scissors close to the nape of her neck. Two crew members turned on the gas fires; the bright orange flames were now visible in the background. The camera sat low to the ground, facing Urvi. Giles knelt behind it with his eye on the viewfinder.

"Quiet on the set!" Dylan, the first assistant director, yelled.

The crew fell silent. I crouched beside the monitor, holding the video feed in my hands. We had only one shot at this. Once Urvi's hair was gone, there would be no second chance.

My mother looked at Urvi, her face cast downward, the barber's hand holding her head forward.

"And ... Action!"

With one clean cut, Urvi's long hair fell to the platform. The barber began cutting away what was left.

"Cut," Mom said.

I moved aside as she got up and walked toward Urvi and the barber. She placed her hand on the little girl's head and began telling the barber how to continue cutting, lifting Urvi's head slightly so the camera could capture her transformation to widowhood. She touched Urvi's head gently. It was a feeling I had forgotten long ago. I watched as she held the girl's chin and gave her words of encouragement. Urvi smiled shyly, with complete trust in my mother's direction. I wondered if I had felt that trust once, and searched my memory for such simple moments of joy.

My mother returned to her seat behind the monitor.

"And ... Action!"

The barber continued to cut. Urvi was stoic, as if she had accepted her fate with a child's courage. Fine strands of hair fell along her bare back. They caught on the folds of her small white sari, pieces of a lost childhood. I could see Urvi's mother standing at the edge of the crowd between Shabana and Nandita. Her eyes were closed. She was a Gujarati housewife living with her family in a suburb of Bombay. She watched with difficulty as her daughter's hair was cut. Urvi's hair was now stubble. The barber rubbed water into her scalp as my mother watched the monitor.

As the barber pulled out a flip-razor to begin shaving, sounds started to fill the garden, rolling over the flowerbeds from the direction of the road. I looked over my shoulder, but couldn't see anything. A high white wall surrounded the hotel compound. The camera kept rolling, but the sounds were coming closer and growing louder. One of our crew members went toward the road to check. Urvi focused on the ground as the barber pulled the razor over her scalp, adding a handful of water every so often. The sound was now on the other side of the wall. It was the sound of a chanting mob.

"Cut!" My mother turned and looked toward the road.

Giles stood up from the camera. The voices were clear now, a wall of sound just outside the iron gate.

"*WATER PICTURE MURDABAD! DEEPA MEHTA MURDABAD!*"

"What are they saying?" someone from the non-Indian crew asked. How could they know? I had trouble believing what I was hearing myself.

"They want to kill us," I said quietly.

"What?" Someone was speaking to me, but I could barely hear above the mob.

"They say they want the film dead. They want Deepa dead."

Urvi sat hugging her legs, frightened. Her mother had come and put her arms around her. Aradhana Seth, the production designer, was walking back from the gate. Her face was solemn.

"It's a big crowd. They're burning your effigy, Deepa."

I wondered how we would ever continue. The crew stood frozen in the safety of the back garden, as the chanting grew louder on the other side of the wall. My mother looked at

Aradhana and started laughing. She took a sip of tea a production assistant had brought her in a white china cup.

"What is my effigy wearing?"

"Wearing?" and then Aradhana smiled. "A *salwaar kurta.*"

"Well, it's lucky we aren't doing sound for this shot. Let's keep going."

We continued to shoot. Urvi sat bravely as the last strands of her hair fell, and I watched three hours of work—which would eventually produce two minutes of silent footage—as the all-engulfing sound of "*WATER PICTURE MURDABAD*" filled the garden.

BY THE TIME WE finished shooting, the protesters were gone.

"Mom, can I stay with you tonight?" I asked, as the crew began to pack up. She seemed surprised, maybe since I had pushed hard to move into the Vaibhav.

"Of course," she said.

We walked together along the dirt path that led to the front of the hotel. It was early evening, and her yellow *dupatta* shone in the fading light. As we walked, I looked down at the small grey-and-white pebbles scattered on the ground. I had pushed myself so hard for some sort of independence, insisting on travelling alone when I was eighteen, planning my own trips and choosing the places I would stay. I prided myself on having an innate sense of direction. I was able to find my way around anywhere I went, as if a map of the world were etched in my mind. But walking with my mother that evening, I realized I didn't really know where I was. Two years later, at university, a therapist I would see about the divorce would ask if I felt that innate sense of direction in my heart. "No," I would tell her. "That is a place where I am often lost."

I followed Mom into the hotel room. She switched on the bedside light and went to check her phone messages. The room was overheated, and a layer of condensation had formed on the windows, slick and damp. I sat down on a chair and started pulling off my running shoes.

"Quick, turn on the television." She reached for the remote, the phone still at her ear. "There's a message from David. We're on the news."

The screen lit up, and as the static began to fade, a national news channel came into focus. The newscaster's authoritative voice announced a case of vandalism in Benares earlier today. The sets of Deepa Mehta's *Water* had been burned and thrown into the Ganges by angry protesters, accusing her of defiling Hinduism and polluting the holy river. Footage of our wooden sets were shown in flames on Assi *Ghat* and in the *galis* behind it.

Mom pressed the mute button.

We watched in silence as the flames licked the edges of the film set, like the pyres of Manikarnika. Who were these people? The women at the bottom of the hotel driveway, the man now on television, a saffron cloth tied around his head, shouting in silence, as his arm punched the sky on the pixilating screen.

The phone rang. My mother answered, said nothing, and put it down. The handset clicked as it touched the phone cradle.

"Who was it?" I asked.

She looked tired. Her forehead was creased with anxiety.

"It was David. He just talked with Ajay. Ajay wants to pull out. FUCK! He wants to pull the funding from the film."

I felt sick, a cold sickness in the pit of my stomach, when everything you've known falls apart. I had felt it only once before, sitting with my dad on the seawall in Cannes.

"Ajay wants the crew to meet tomorrow morning in the hotel mezzanine."

Mom began to pull off her gold earrings. I got into the king-size bed and lay with my face against the cool white pillow as she put on her green *kaftan*. She put on small round reading glasses and opened a book across her knees. At moments like these, quiet and alone, I wanted to talk to her, have her understand everything I had felt since the divorce— lost, scared, unloved. But she was deep in an Agatha Christie murder mystery, and the book was as much of a wall as it was a refuge.

Our first attempt at spending time together after the divorce was in Greece where she was on location shooting another episode of the *Young Indiana Jones Chronicles* for George Lucas. We were on location just outside Athens in an arid landscape. The principal cast and crew were having dinner on the terrace of our hotel. The buildings were white, the pool a deep blue, and the people dancing a blur, like the cloudy quality of *ouzo* in everyone's glass. Whether it was the *ouzo*, the stress of trying to relate for the first time, or the pressures of filmmaking, the night only unearthed deep wounds. As we lay beside each other in bed later that night, she asked me why I had chosen to live with Dad and not her. I knew, at the age of eleven, when they divorced, as I knew then, that it was more comfortable for me to be with Dad. Safer. Dad and I would play baseball. He bought me a golden retriever puppy and sang southern spirituals to me at bedtime: *"Swing low, sweet chariot, comin' forth to carry me home."* Mom spent her time reading in bed. Mom didn't like dogs.

We fought until dawn. I eventually called Dad in Canada, despite the six-hour difference. My hands were sticky from crying, and I dropped the phone receiver on my face, splitting my lip. I was thirteen.

The phone rang at three in the morning. I woke from the memories of Greece to hear its shrill tone through my sleep. The Clarks hotel room was completely dark. Mom began to move and grope for the phone. She switched on the bedside light and picked up the receiver.

"*Haan? Haan?* Yes?" I lay still and listened as Mom answered the call. She stared across the room, and then slammed down the phone.

"Who was it?" I asked.

"It was a death threat."

The two feet between us on the king-size bed became clear and focused in the stillness of the night, an unfathomable distance across which to stretch a hand.

"Mom, please take care of yourself." It was the only thing I could say, a thread of concern to momentarily bind us together.

On *Rakhi*, the Hindu holiday celebrating familial ties, a sister ties a thin cotton thread, dyed red, around her brother's wrist—a symbol of the ties that bind. It must be left to fall off on its own, long after the deep red vegetable dye has run and the thread is left a dirty white. My ties with my mother were not as tangible as that, existing only in passing comments of concern.

The phone rang again.

"Wait," I said. "I'll get it."

She placed her hand on my arm as I picked up the handset and put it to my ear. A male voice hurled a slew of Hindi insults across the line. *"Deepa Mehta, you whore, you cunt. You better leave or . . ."* I replaced the receiver with a quiet *click*.

WE MADE OUR WAY to the mezzanine overlooking the Clarks lobby. The morning sunlight filtered through thin white curtains, bouncing off the marble and making the landing glow. Most of the crew were already there: Jasmine and Brett, Dylan, Giles, Bob, Dilip, and Dolly were waiting patiently, speaking in hushed tones. Nandita and Shabana sat next to each other, regal in their short widow's crops. Vikram came in with Anurag. I looked at him and smiled. Attraction is obvious; it shows on the face.

The mezzanine fell silent as David and Ajay walked in. Mom sat down in a wooden chair, and I sat next to her, balanced on the edge of the arm. The sound of shifting papers and polished Hindi drifted up from the lobby. David looked defeated, although he was too proud to show his distress.

Ajay entered the circle and sat down.

He was a short, round man in his mid-forties, with small, stylish Emporio Armani glasses cutting across his full face. He had made his money in a Canadian company, a company he had started working in as a young, ambitious immigrant from New Delhi. He sat before us with his hands cupped, looking down at the floor to avoid the gaze of twenty pairs of expectant eyes.

He eventually looked up and told us that the district magistrate of Benares felt it was too dangerous to continue filming. *Water*, according to the district magistrate, was a threat to public safety. The destruction of our sets and the protests had already caused delays and losses. If they continued, Ajay stood to lose his full investment of $700,000 Canadian.

Ajay adjusted his small rectangular glasses. He felt it would only get worse. He had to pull the plug. His words were spoken with regret. He looked down at the floor. In that moment I felt that he wasn't the cold financier cutting his losses, but a businessman making a hard decision about a project he cared for.

Nobody spoke.

Jasmine's gentle face was filled with remorse. Dylan seemed lost in thought, staring at the sun-filled window. Our adventure had ended on a cold sunny morning in Benares.

"I'll work for free." The words came from Peter, the German second assistant director.

"So will I," Dylan added, looking up.

Within minutes Giles, Brett, Jasmine, Anurag, Vikram, and Liz, our makeup artist, agreed to work for free. As did I. Shabana and Nandita joined them, pledging to put aside their stars' salaries. It was a beautiful moment, a moment of true conviction.

We were a crew working together for a story we believed in, and we weren't going to go down so easily.

Ajay was silent. He rubbed his hands together and looked out the window. As we waited for his answer, I started to feel something building up inside me. It was as if I saw the situation in stark relief for the first time. We were fighting for freedom of expression in a country that called itself the world's largest democracy. More importantly, we were about to lose the opportunity to make a beautiful work of art, a story about a very real group of women and their search for *moksha*.

I got off the chair and knelt in front of Ajay. I told him how important I felt the film was, how terrible it would be if it were shut down. Surrounded by the crew, I begged him not to pull out. It was the first, and only, time I cried over a work of art. My heart was racing.

Ajay agreed to keep his investment in, allowing us to go back and shoot as long as Mom could get re-permission from the Ministry of Information and Broadcasting, and get the assurance of the rss that they would pull back their protesters. We had two days to do it. As the meeting ended David was already on his cellphone booking an afternoon flight to New Delhi.

Two years later, Ajay would tell me that the reason he didn't pull the funding that day was because of the young woman kneeling in front of him, with her impassioned, tear-streaked face. I like to think his compliment was for everyone who was prepared to work for nothing that day. For everyone who passionately *believed*.

I wiped my face and got up from the cold marble floor. Everything felt unreal and precarious, on the verge of change. I thought some ritual or prayer would help us. I asked Vikram and Giles if they wanted to go down to the river, to where people set off floating candles—wishes carried along the steady current of the Ganges.

THE GHATS WERE BATHED in the golden light of early evening. Men and women scaled the stone steps, carrying *lotas*, tarnished brass containers full of holy Ganga water. The priests had begun setting up for *aarti* or prayer service, lighting oil lamps, and setting out small brass bells for the evening rituals. Boatmen rowed their passengers along the river, as tourists took photos of the sunset. Vikram, Giles, and I walked along the *ghats* until we found space to sit on a worn sandstone step at the edge of the water. A young girl pulled up alongside us in a small wooden boat, the sides rotting and patched with tar. She held a basket full of floating candles on her lap. Thin and scruffy, she wore her dirty brown hair in two pigtails and an oversized frock with small red flowers printed on a white background. Cheap metal bangles encircled her tiny wrists. At the age of seven, this little girl was earning her own income and probably making significant contributions to her household. For a few rupees, wealthy tourists and pilgrims got a small basket made of dried leaves, which held three marigolds packed around a white tea candle. Adults bought wishes, and the child took home wages.

I bought a candle, placing two rupees in her small hand. She looked at me with big brown eyes lined with *kohl*, serious eyes. Vikram and Giles bought candles, and the young girl pushed off the step with her oar in search of other customers. We sat close to each other, Giles in a black turtleneck and Vikram in a T-shirt with his backpack slung over his shoulder. The Ganges lapped just below our feet. I held the floating candle in my hands and looked out over the river. We were facing east, and as the sun set low behind us, the undeveloped sandbanks across the river glowed red. I closed my eyes and said a prayer. I prayed for the film not to be shut down, repeating it over and over under my breath. But I was praying as much for the experience not to end as the film. For Vikram, for my first taste of independence. For having a chance with Mom. I lit the candle and set it afloat on the glowing Ganges.

6

After four weeks in Benares, the city felt like home. Vikram and I walked to Assi *Ghat* as life continued in its unchanging rhythms. The devout continued to bathe in the holy river, as *dhobiwallahs* beat the city's laundry against the worn sandstone steps. Nothing fazed the city of creation and destruction. A cold wind came off the water, rushing through the large *peepal* trees and making the small leaves dance.

While the crew waited for Mom to return with re-permission to shoot, sitting idly in the Clarks lobby or in the production office, she would be going to New Delhi, to Jhandewala, the RSS compound and the heart of Hindutva. It would be like entering an IRA compound in a Catholic neighbourhood of Belfast, asking for permission to make a film about a Protestant-Catholic romance. Culture, when embroiled with religion, is a touchy thing.

As we approached Assi *Ghat* I saw the charred remains of our sets lying on the muddy bank of the river, ignored and unnoticed by the flow of human traffic, like a beggar. I turned toward the steep steps that rose from the *ghat*.

Vikram began climbing and sat on the topmost step. Assi *Ghat* was virtually empty. We watched in silence as vendors prepared their kerosene lamps for the evening. Vikram pulled out his camera and pointed it at me. I took my Canon out and did the same, laughing as we took photos of each other. He put the camera down and held it in both hands. I looked at the side of his face, his black hair pulled behind his ear, the curve of his nose. I felt satisfied. With him, I wasn't torn. With him there was no weight, only the lightness of recognition.

"Have you ever read *The Great Railway Bazaar*?" Vikram asked.

"No." I'd never heard of it.

"It's by a writer named Paul Theroux." The afternoon was cold. I wrapped my arms around my knees to keep warm.

"It's about trains. He travelled from London to Japan by rail, flying only when he had to, and then came back on the Trans-Siberian." Vikram held his camera and looked out over the river. There was something distant about him today in the way he looked at me and then drew his eyes away.

I thought of trains. The way they rumbled along the rails. How inside them there was no other world, only the distance covered and the scenes outside the window—the fading light on a field, the outskirts of a city, a woman moving along a country road with firewood balanced carefully on her head. Removed from everyday life, the world below the rails became even more real.

"I'll get you a copy," he said.

The copy he bought me—a paperback with an orange spine—would be signed by Theroux a few years later in Blackwell's bookstore in Oxford. When I would arrive at the book signing, I would find myself the first one there. Theroux sat behind a small desk wearing a tweed jacket and thick-framed glasses, looking bored. When I shook his hand, I noticed a small blue tattoo of a flying bird between the web of his thumb and forefinger. I would ask him what it meant, but wouldn't remember his answer.

As we watched the river from Assi *Ghat*, Mahesh Bhatt, an eminent Bombay film director/producer, was introducing my mother to a local Delhi TV man who knew how to get in touch with the RSS. On an early morning in February, they travelled by car through Delhi to show the RSS the script and to try and get their assurance that there would be no more trouble.

Later, my mother told me that the fog was thick, lining the streets of the city. Damp and grey. Jhandewala, the RSS compound, was where K. S. Sudarshan, the head of the RSS, and the offices of Seshadri Chari, editor of the RSS mouthpiece, *Organizer*, was based. The car pulled up in front of the main gate of the compound. Wrapped in a thick shawl, Mom walked through the entrance with Dilip and Anurag and onto a driveway flanked by sports grounds. On either side old men and boys were practising their morning exercises. They were dressed in matching khaki shorts and white shirts, the RSS uniform, and swung *dandas*, wooden sticks, in a synchronized, militaristic pattern. There were no women on the grounds.

The main building was forbidding. The shouts from the exercises and the sound of wood hitting wood echoed through the corridors. The morning exercises, with their perfect form and visual uniformity, reminded Mom of the German youth leagues of the Third Reich. Hindutva, like any political-cultural belief system, is strongest when indoctrinated at a young age. The small boys practising in the morning fog were learning early.

Sri Aurobindo, one of the forefathers of Hindutva in the nineteenth century, felt Hinduism suffered a weakness—an *effeminacy*—that led to India's subjugation by both Islam and England. He argued that Hindus needed to return to masculinity, to the justified violence of the *Kshatriyas*, or warrior caste, in order to survive. Jyotirmaya Sharma, author of *Hindutva: Exploring the Idea of Hindu Nationalism*, suggested that "political Hindutva's self-perception today is one of aggression, machismo, virility and militancy." Jhandewala, with its cold architecture and army of men, seemed to embody this perfectly.

Mom, Dilip, and Anurag were led upstairs into a hall with a long table and were told to wait for Mr. Sudarshan. The sound of the exercises drifted up from the grounds below. Mom was expecting to meet a monster, the man behind the protests in Benares and possibly darker displays of Hindutva across the country. Without his support of *Water*, the protests would continue and Ajay would pull the funding from the film. But the sixty-something man who entered the room wearing glasses, a heavy brown shawl, and a saffron balaclava with an opening for his face, didn't run at her with a fiery *trishul*, Shiva's trident and a symbol of Hindu nationalism. He walked up to her and quoted a passage from Dante's *Inferno* in perfect Italian.

Sri Mr. Sudarshan sat down and told her not to have pre-conceptions about the RSS's ignorance. An aide brought in coffee and *amla*, a gooey paste made of a bittersweet fruit poached in sugar.

"Why did you make a film like *Fire*? It's not what our culture is about," he said in a calm, measured voice.

Sri Mr. Sudarshan sipped his tea, as the sound of the *dandas* reverberated through the hall.

"The Ganga is very precious to us," he added, changing the topic.

"Have you read the script for *Water*?" Mom asked.

Sri Mr. Sudarshan placed a copy of the script on the table.

"Where did you get that?" she asked. Only one script had been submitted outside of the production, and that was to the Ministry of I & B.

Sri Mr. Sudarshan replied, "After all, whose Ministry is it anyway?"

And then the head of the RSS, the cultural wing of the BJP government and the leading force of Hindu nationalism, said something amazing.

"It's a very good piece of work. There are just some things that are offensive to us."

Sri Mr. Sudarshan suggested there would be no more problems if she worked with Seshadri Chari, the intelligent, forty-something editor of the RSS magazine, *Organizer*, to make some small changes to the script. The tension of the morning burned away like the winter fog.

They worked in Chari's small office in the Jhandewala compound until four the next morning. Dilip, Anurag, Chari, and his secretary went through the script with Mom, detail by detail, arguing terminology late into the night. In the end there were two main changes the RSS required. One had to do with the character of Kalyani. She was originally named Janaki, another name for the Hindu goddess Sita. It was offensive to use the name of a goddess for a widow-prostitute. Mom changed the name to Kalyani. Secondly, the RSS insisted she remove an old saying about Benares that they felt insulted the city and its holy men. "*Raand saand seedhi sanyasi. Inse bachay to bhogay Kashi.*"

> "Widows, bulls, *ghats*, and holy men
> If you can save yourself from these,
> For you awaits the liberation of Kashi."

In the early hours of morning, the changes were made and the RSS officially supported *Water*.

THE BUILDINGS OF RAJ DELHI sat heavy and regal in the early morning light. The mammoth sandstone façade of Rashtrapati Bhavan and the Indian Parliament shone despite the Delhi dust. British architect Sir Edwin Lutyens had designed the buildings as the seat of the empire in India. Rashtrapati Bhavan had been the viceroy's palace and was now the president's residence. Small stone Britannic lions guarded its entrance, vestiges of Empire catching the early morning light. It was one of the few neighbourhoods of Delhi that had wide boulevards, having felt the neat touch of urban planning. The only people on the roads were the morning sweepers, gathering the previous day's dust in the gutters. After a sleepless night of minor changes to the script, they pulled up at Shastri Bhavan, the Ministry of Information and Broadcasting.

Mom was greeted by the officer who had originally passed the script through the censor board. Together with Chari, representing the RSS, they met with Arun Jaitley, the minister of I & B.

As their meeting continued in the heart of New Delhi, I walked past the entrance to the Sunview guesthouse, avoiding the courtyard, the slick manager, and the boy with the tea towel. The steps down to the widows' *ashram* were slippery with dew. I could see the Ganges, tepid and swollen, over the wall surrounding the guesthouse. Under my arm I held a plastic bag full of brand new white saris.

No one was sweeping that morning, and the thick wooden door was shut. I knocked gently. "*Aajao.*" A faint voice told me to come in. The door opened with difficulty.

Without the midday sun, the filigree archways were even more faintly outlined in the darkness. Near the far window the grey morning light illuminated the shape of a woman's head— Gyanvati. I placed the package on the floor in front of her. The plastic crackled as it touched the cold concrete. "*Saris, ji,*" I said respectfully, fulfilling the promise I had made with Giles and Vikram a few weeks earlier. Gyanvati looked at me, surprised. She pulled out the thin white material and felt the cotton between her dirty fingers.

I looked around the room. The young widow and her son weren't there. But there were others, new women I hadn't met when I first visited. More than I remembered. One with thick-framed glasses was chanting morning prayers, holding wooden prayer beads between her wrinkled palms. Her lenses looked like they were made out of the bottom of a Coke bottle, unusually thick and uneven. The widows started coming over to see what had arrived. They got up from their woven mats with difficulty, bracing themselves on their knees. I stood to leave as the elderly women began to unpack the saris. I had hoped to bring a little relief to their poverty, but as I left I heard them fighting over the cheap pieces of white cloth. There wasn't enough.

LATER THAT MORNING, in New Delhi, Seshadri Chari presented the minister of I & B with assurances that the RSS was happy with the changes. There would be no more disturbances, and we were given the government's written re-permission to shoot. But as they left the building, Chari stopped Mom in the stairwell leading out of the Ministry. He said only one thing.

"Deepa, keep this in mind. A good general knows when to retreat."

But she was already moving down the stairs, his words lost in the excitement of receiving re-permission.

7

The street was silent when I opened my eyes. Not even the sounds of the parrots could be heard. The yellow *dupatta* hung down and touched the edge of the wooden window frame, filtering the early morning greyness. I looked at my alarm clock. It was seven and the Vaibhav was dead. *One more hour.*

The polished tile was cold to my feet. It glistened like wax as I walked to the washroom and turned on the tap. The water was frigid. I shivered and looked at my face in the mirror. For the first time in my life I smiled to myself with confidence. We were going to make the film. Benares had given me something, a sense of strength and freedom, an alternative to a previous life. I never wanted the feeling to end.

My purple fanny pack full of assistant's gear lay on the window seat, ready. When I lifted the curtain I saw the small naked light bulb glowing from the house below. It dangled on its thin black wire, bare and exposed. The woman in the *kaftan* wasn't awake yet. I pulled on jeans and a T-shirt and went downstairs.

Vikram's hallway was dark. The thin wooden doors were all firmly shut. But a thin strip of yellow light shone below his door, and I could hear movement inside. I knocked gently and he pulled it open.

"Are you ready?" I asked.

"Let's go." He closed the door behind him, avoiding my eyes.

Our crew call was for eight a.m. in the lower lobby of the hotel. The morning was cold, and everyone was wearing thick fleeces and jackets when we arrived. Mom sat with Dylan and Giles, talking about the shots that were planned for the day.

Peter, the German second assistant director, sat on a couch, drifting in and out of sleep. There was a line of minivans waiting to take us to our *ashram* set in the centre of town. They sat, idling outside the lobby in the morning fog.

I knelt next to Mom when she had a moment alone.

"Are you excited?"

"*Haan, meri jaan.* Yes, my darling," she said affectionately. It was the first time I had heard her relaxed in weeks, but she looked exhausted. Her wavy black hair fell over her grey sweater and her blue *dupatta* had slipped down her arm. She pulled it up and looked at me.

"You okay?" She glanced at Vikram.

"I'm fine."

Smiling, she put her hand on my head. It was soft and light and small, smaller than my own.

The crew waited patiently for the go-ahead to leave. The outdoor lights had been switched off and dim sunlight started to fill the lobby. The minivans waited. Everything was ready to go. David walked into the lobby, followed by Iqbal, the location manager. They walked past me to Mom.

"Why aren't we leaving?" I asked.

"There's been a delay."

I looked at him in disbelief. He had his cellphone in one hand and a piece of paper in the other.

"I'm so sorry . . . ," David addressed the crew.

"There is a rumour that a mob of 10,000 people are protesting on the *ghats*. Until we confirm this, I can't jeopardize your safety."

And so our day started with an apology. For the next six hours we waited in the lobby as time drifted by. I once heard that without expectations, without desire, one never felt pain. But without expectations, how could one feel pleasure? Vikram, Dylan, and I ate breakfast in the hotel restaurant and waited. Mom, David, and Iqbal had disappeared.

Vikram looked at the plate as he ate. I felt bound to him in the struggle to make the film, as much as I had exploring the *galis* and sitting on the dusty floor of the *hijras'* tenement. But something had changed. He pushed at an omelet with the edge of his fork.

At two p.m. David came back and told us that the 10,000-person protest was a hoax. He had sent someone to the *ghats* to find only twelve protesters. Meanwhile, the Uttar Pradesh government had placed a rapid deployment force—200 police officers in blue camouflage uniforms—outside the gates of the hotel, for our protection. There were also anti-riot squads armed with water cannons, smoke bombs, and tear gas. They lined the street with their backs to us, guns in hand.

"Come on! We're going!" David rallied the crew.

Tired of waiting, the crew finally began moving toward the vans. I jumped to my feet, and piled into a red minivan with Brett, Jasmine, and Giles. The driver turned on the ignition, and we started to move toward the wall of police officers.

But the entrance of the long circular driveway was blocked, as if our protectors were in fact our captors. I pressed my face against the window and felt the vibration of the engine against my skin. Slowly, the army of officers began to move, climbing into waiting police Jeeps. They were going to accompany us. It was then that I saw the news cameramen, moving in and out of the sea of blue uniforms, their large grey cameras balanced on their shoulders. We drove through the streets of Benares in convoy, out from under the shade of the leafy *gulmohur* trees, past the shopkeepers looking out from their narrow stores crammed with sweets and rice and loaves of white bread.

Our arrival in the city was charged and chaotic. The streets were swollen with traffic, and our minivans and the police Jeeps clogged the side street that led to the widows' house. Families had come out of their homes to see what was happening, and children leaned over the edges of the flat rooftops. We had already lost more than half a day of filming.

Giles slid open the minivan door, and we moved quickly up the narrow alley to the set. Police pushed against the side of the van, in an effort to protect us, but I couldn't see any protesters among the crowd.

The house was built around an open courtyard. It was filled with camera and lighting equipment, silvery metal stands, and thick black cable. Khaki-clad officers stood on the roof, looking down on us as we worked. I helped Jasmine move a box of filters to the small corner room where we would be shooting. Nandita was already in costume, a simple white sari. I noticed a female officer kneeling in the courtyard, her hair pulled back tightly under a deep green beret. She was showing Shabana how to grind grain on an old stone hand-mill, which sat disused in a corner of the courtyard. She moved the wooden shaft back and forth between her palms. The sheaves of grain were crushed between the two rough stone disks, as her fellow male officers looked on.

"You're in the shot!" Dylan yelled at the police.

They were fascinated by the filming—a brief touch of Bollywood in their ordinary lives. They cowered in the corner obediently, celebrity forever stronger than politics.

No one would have known that day that the shutdown of *Water* was not about permission from the central government, re-permission, or democracy. In all likelihood, opponents of the film probably cared little about widows, if they were aware of them at all. It was about the blind pursuit of an *idea* of Indianness, an idea that required that anything that challenged it, threatened to fray its perfect borders, be cleansed and destroyed. In a country with so much exclusion, poverty, and difficulty, an idea was perhaps the only pure thing worth pursuing. And the preservation of that idea was as much about creating a self-serving image as creating one that would export well.

When Indian director Satyajit Ray made *Pather Panchali* (*Song of the Little Road*) in 1955, depicting life in a rural Bengali village, a famous Bollywood actress criticized him for glorifying India's poverty. Why did he want to show the negative side of India? He could use his time to make films about India's great industrial progress. Why not make a film about dams instead? It seemed to me that India under the BJP was in the midst of a similar purification campaign. Pavan K. Varma, a writer and member of the Indian Foreign Service, said "all nations indulge in a bit of myth-making to bind their people together." *Water* was one of the casualties of maintaining that myth.

The Uttar Pradesh police officer carrying the single piece of white paper arrived on set after we had completed only two takes. He wore a dark green beret and lightly tinted glasses, and was flanked by several officers. He handed the sheet to Mom as she sat on the low ledge that framed the courtyard. Shabana and Aradhana looked over her shoulder to see what it was.

"The U.P. government has ordered the film to be shut down. It's a law-and-order situation." Shabana read the letter aloud to the crew.

The courtyard fell silent.

"It's from the district magistrate of Varanasi," the officer announced.

"But there's no stamp on it, nothing official..." Aradhana looked at the officer who had brought the letter.

The police who had been loitering around the set began to gather around the officer with tinted glasses. Mom held the paper with both hands.

"We need a letter from the district magistrate with a stamp and succession number. Once it comes, we'll see," she said.

I tried to move closer to her, but was blocked by the police. Giles got up from the camera, and Nandita came out of the room in her white widow's sari. I could hear the police Jeeps idling in the alley as the faint sound of temple bells floated in from the *ghats*.

"Ma'am, we don't need to give any explanation. We've got an order," the officer said, resolute in the company of twenty armed officers.

"You will receive more information later," he added.

"What law-and-order situation! There never were 10,000 protesters. We checked and there were only twelve protesters! Twelve!" Shabana fumed.

But the officer wasn't shaken, nor was he aggressive. He continued to calmly do his duty.

"Ma'am, a man just jumped into the river. He attempted suicide in protest. Now you must please leave immediately."

It was true. A local member of the Shiv Sena had tied a rope to his waist, a stone to the other end, and rowed himself out onto the Ganges. The Indian TV stations had captured it as he threw himself over the side. What they didn't see, or chose not to see, was that when the cameras were gone, he pulled himself out of the shallows, only to do it again as soon as someone else was looking. We found out later that he was a "professional suicider," if there is such a thing, paid by the Hindu right. He had once been hired to jump off a bridge. The suicider survived both attempts, of course, although he was making a show of it in the local hospital.

Buying a political act was not unusual, especially in a country where so many have so little. I had heard a week earlier about a group of village women brought to Delhi to show support at a political rally. They didn't even know who they were supporting, but were promised running water and a sewage system in exchange for their presence.

The officer stood firm.

David flipped open his cellphone and tried calling the production office and our local lawyers. Dilip got on the phone to

Delhi—to the people who had reissued permission less than twelve hours earlier.

"My phone's dead." David pressed at the keys.

"Mine too." Dilip flipped his shut.

Every crew member with a cellphone tried to call out, but the phones had been jammed. Without a channel to the outside world, there was only the rule of law in a small rectangular courtyard in Uttar Pradesh. Why did the story being enacted within its confines pose such a threat to the state, enough of a threat to precipitate pre-censorship?

"Come. Let's go." The officers started to herd us toward the alley and the idling police Jeeps.

David looked at us and nodded.

"What about our equipment?" he asked the officer who had brought the order.

"You can get it later."

Mom leaned against a courtyard pillar. She looked neither sad nor angry, but possessed the calmness of one who has accepted her fate. David whispered something into her ear, pulled her up, and ushered her, Shabana, and Nandita into a production van. If safety was a real issue, he didn't want to take chances with the three most prominent crew members. Before leaving, my mother looked at the officers.

"It's a dark day for democracy," she said, and followed Shabana into the alley.

As the courtyard emptied, I helped Dylan, Giles, and David shut the equipment cases. I didn't want to leave. Black lens boxes lay scattered across the grey concrete of the courtyard. We were the last people on the set. I worked slowly, deliberately, as the remaining officer watched and waited.

"Go on." David put his hand on my shoulder.

"But I don't want to leave." I think I knew then that we were never coming back. The feeling passed through me like a cold wind through the trees of Assi *Ghat*.

The officer ushered Giles, Dylan, and me out of the entrance and down the narrow alley leading to the street. A white police Jeep was waiting at the curb. The walls on either side of the alley were crumbling. I could feel the dampness through the red brick. It was the same desolate coldness as the widow's room where Pinku had taken me a month earlier, as lonely and as fragile.

The officer shut the back door of the Jeep. There were still no protesters on the street, only the questioning faces of local residents. I huddled next to Giles and Dylan. The windows were covered with a thick black metal mesh. I watched as the street in front of the widows' house receded behind us. The mesh fused and blurred in my eyes until the world was one small black spot.

David stood on the rooftop of the widows' house as the last of the convoy pulled away. The crowd of Benarsis who had gathered to watch the white police Jeeps resumed their evening activities. The eighteen-year-old son of the house was standing beside him.

"Do you understand this?" David asked, as the last Jeep turned north toward the cantonment.

The eighteen-year-old replied without hesitation. "There are a lot of men in this country who want to keep women down."

WHEN WE ARRIVED at the hotel, white Ambassadors were parked in front of the lobby, scattered on the driveway like mechanical rabbits about to be released at the dog races. Aradhana and her art department team were squeezing into one as the police Jeep dropped us off. Brett and Jasmine were in the back of another, their faces partially obscured by the reflection of the evening sky. Anurag came toward me, his eyes wild. Vikram was behind him. His green rugby shirt was stained with sweat.

"Come on, *chutku*! We're going to the district magistrate's office!" Anurag pulled me toward one of the cars.

"*Chutku*...." I felt Vikram's hand on my shoulder. It dissolved into my back as soon as it touched. "There's something I have to tell you."

But I was already being pulled into another car, the sound of the engine drowning his voice, the fumes erasing the shapes of our bodies against the growing darkness.

The Ambassador pulled away and joined the convoy, a line of white moving slowly through the darkened streets. The seat creaked and moaned at every dip in the road, the springs weak under our weight. The trees of the cantonment were like a wall outside the window, dense and entangled.

The district magistrate's residence was a colonial bungalow, curved and lined with cream-coloured columns. We pulled into the dirt driveway, the yellow beams from the headlights of our Ambassadors cutting across the façade. The crew climbed the steps to the verandah and entered his office.

Inside was a desk covered in green and red files, and piles of paper. On the wall behind it was a faded tourist poster advertising the pleasures of Uttar Pradesh. We occupied his office, ignoring the pleas of his underlings. A few of us sat on scattered chairs, while the rest crouched on the deep green wall-to-wall carpet. I crouched against the back wall as Shabana, Nandita, and Mom sat on three chairs placed close to his desk.

A small man walked in. His short black hair was parted to one side and a moustache covered a large part of his face.

"Everyone, meet Mr. Alok Kumar, district magistrate of Varanasi," Mom said loudly, pointing at the slight figure in a grey sweater. He was under the authority of Uttar Pradesh's BJP chief minister.

The crew began slapping the desk, the floor, the walls. The sound echoed past the columns and onto the verandah outside.

The DM's desk vibrated with the noise, but Alok Kumar remained cool.

"Tell the truth if you want the film stopped! We will not run!" Shabana shouted.

The room erupted again. A lackey, who had come in bearing a tray of glasses of water, nearly stumbled as he tried to place it on the desk. Alok Kumar dryly repeated the words of the police officer. Everything had been done for our own safety and protection.

"The protester was being protected. Your own position was being protected," Mom snapped back.

"This is about freedom!" she added, looking directly into his small eyes.

I felt proud of her. But I also remembered the words of the RSS editor: "A good general knows when to retreat." It was clear that we were dealing with greater forces than we realized.

But impassioned statements fell on deaf ears. The district magistrate found ways to circumvent any responsibility for the shutdown. He explained that the order had come directly from the chief minister of Uttar Pradesh, Ram Prakash Gupta. Still, we refused to leave. After more than an hour of our sit-in, he made us an offer. He would consider reissuing the permits after a two-week cool-down period, but he knew very well that our finances would not last that long for a permission that may never materialize. Even if it did, the re-permission of the central government seemed to carry less weight than the paper it was written on.

Anurag jumped at the district magistrate, his arms flying, his eyes enraged. Vikram held his shoulder and gently eased him back down into his chair.

"Control yourself, behave yourself." The district magistrate pointed his finger at Anurag, like an incensed schoolteacher.

But it was over. Uttar Pradesh had shut its doors.

The Indian media were waiting on the verandah. National news channels and the government broadcaster, Doordarshan, flocked around Mom as soon as she exited. She looked into the lights from the cameras and the reporters' waiting microphones.

"They stopped our shooting because it was supposedly for our protection from the thousands of people protesting against the film. But our crew went there, and there were only twelve people protesting!"

Pavan K. Varma was right: "All nations indulge in a bit of myth-making to bind their people together." Someone had gone to great lengths to ensure that *Water* didn't challenge that myth.

I moved past the cameras to one of the waiting cars. Vikram got in beside me. The back seat was dark. I leaned over to kiss him, but he pulled back.

"Devyani, there's something I have to tell you."

I felt as if something seized me and dragged me far away, away from Benares, and back to a lonely childhood.

"I have a girlfriend."

The Ambassador rumbled along toward the hotel, the windows black, the driver's head silhouetted against the boot of the white car in front of us. I felt the softness of the seat fabric between my fingers. It reminded me of lying in a field of grass. But I knew, you see. I knew all along. My mother told me he had a girlfriend at the beginning of the shoot. I had just lived in hope, indulged in my own form of myth-making. If the Hindu right could create an India with no poverty, no ugliness, no widows, why couldn't I create a world that included love?

I FOUND MOM on the rooftop terrace of the production office later that night. She was alone. The Varana was still and black, as if asleep. Dolly's saris were gone, leaving the terrace bare and empty. I went and sat next to her.

"I'm so sorry."

She sat, frozen. Her face seemed greatly aged. It was a mask of sadness, an expression I recognized and hated, mostly because even now I didn't know how to make it go away.

"I love this script. It's your best work, Mom."

She smiled weakly.

"Vikram told me he has a girlfriend," I said.

She looked at me, and her eyes were filled with empathy. She, too, knew what it was like to love and to lose. For a fleeting moment I thought maybe we weren't that different after all; both passionate for that which we cared for, and yet both so vulnerable to that passion. But the thought passed quickly, replaced by a growing anger as I looked at the expression on her face. No, I didn't want to be a part of that sadness anymore.

"Some of the crew are going to Nepal. I want to go with them."

She nodded.

"David's putting Shabana, Nandita, and me on a plane in the morning. He says they may find a way to arrest us if we stay. I'm going to Madhya Pradesh and West Bengal to see if we can do this in another state. But the security is going to be tight, so it's best if you don't come," she said.

Both states were run by non-BJP governments. Madhya Pradesh was Congress and West Bengal was communist. Their invitations were as much a gesture of generosity as a potential political lever against the central BJP government. We were a pawn in a much larger game.

"What about Vikram?" she asked.

My feelings of doubt temporarily burned away.

"It doesn't matter if he doesn't love me back. It felt good just to love." Although I said it with complete conviction, I knew I was lying to myself. Deep down I wanted him to love me back, a secret seed of hope.

Mom looked down at the Varana. There was an abandoned lot beside the building, full of scrub and overgrown grass and cow dung. Smoke was coming from a small bonfire on the lot. It didn't smell of wood. I leaned over the edge of the terrace. David was below us, the orange flames illuminating his face as he carefully placed copies of the script into the slow-burning fire.

I **E-MAILED MY DAD** before leaving the production office for the last time.

Dearest Dad,

A sad day in Indian history and a sadder start to the twenty-first century. *Water* has been shut down by the state government, and we wrapped this evening, having completed two shots. I'm heartbroken, but also know that this film WILL be made at some point, but maybe not in this place. For a city I love so much—my favourite in the world—it is hard to see it in anything other than darkness. People are crazy, and the politics of this country reflect that. I love you very, very much. I'm planning to go to Nepal for a few days with some of the crew. Then to Delhi. Then let's see.

Love,
Devyani

8

I was packed and ready to leave before anyone else, waiting in the lobby of the Vaibhav in the early morning before the sun rose. I left my room the way it had been when I arrived, the window bare once again. Nine of us had rented a van, escaping the reality that had engulfed us in Benares. I convinced Vikram to come, delaying his return to Bombay by a week. I was still nursing hopes of something beyond friendship. Many of the crew members had travelled all the way to India just for the film. Rather than leave with a bitter taste in their mouths, a number of them decided to travel. So in the early hours of the morning, the day after the shutdown, the crew dispersed, scattering across north India.

Dylan helped place the bags into the van. The morning was cold. We shut the door and turned on the heat. Benares faded behind us, and with it the memories of New Year's on the *ghats*, wrapped in orange light from the prayer candles, and the sweet shop *galis* with their smell of sugared oil. I was surprised how quickly memory erases what it doesn't like—the widows in their world below the surface, the protesters chanting "*Water picture murdabad!*" and the state police with notification of our shutdown. I looked for the woman in the *kaftan*, brushing her teeth under the naked bulb, her long black hair flowing down around her shoulders, but the *charpoy* was pulled up against the house, and the light was turned off.

The leafy trees of the cantt gave way to the low-lying, disorganized suburbs of the city as we drove north toward the India–Nepal border, 200 kilometres away. It was the transitional space between urban and rural, excited by rapid growth, but still clinging to the rhythms of a slower pace of life. Children ran half-naked in front of their whitewashed houses, among chickens and pigs, while their fathers switched on morning television, greeted by the energized strains of Bollywood's newest hit song. I pulled my shawl around me and used it as a pillow against the window of the middle seat. Mom would be flying to Delhi in a few hours. I pictured her face, both sad and impassioned after the shutdown. Dylan, Peter, and Archana, who had worked in the production office, slept in the seat behind me, their heads resting on each other's shoulders. Four office production assistants were squeezed into the remaining spaces.

Vikram was looking out the window and listening to his headphones in the seat in front of me. I stared at the back of his head, willing him to turn around, yearning for a connection that was slowly starting to fade, like the memories of Benares, like the vegetable dye in a *rakhi* bracelet—washed away from an intense red to a parched and meaningless white. I closed my eyes, waiting for the doubt to pass.

We arrived at the Nepalese border at sunset. The landscape was flat and dusty. There was a faint chill in the air, the slightest suggestion of the Himalayas. While our visas were being issued, we ate in a small border *dhaba*, a makeshift restaurant. Rows of tables were covered in pink plastic tablecloths and flanked by lawn chairs. Thick vegetable curry was simmering in an oversized aluminum vat. The sky had turned a deep orange, exaggerated by the yellow dust kicked up by Tata trucks, waiting to cross the border to transport their precariously balanced goods.

Everyone's faces appeared faded in the orange light, like in an old photograph drained of its colour. Vikram was loading film into his Nikon. I pulled out my camera and photographed him, his face downturned, focused on the camera, the background of the street and the border crossing a blur of orange, and a single ray of sunlight, refracted in the lens, cutting across the image.

I had never travelled to Nepal, although I had come close to its borders when I was a child. My great-aunt, my grandfather's older sister, owned an apple orchard in the northern state of Himachal Pradesh amid the pine-covered foothills of the Himalayas. Maya auntie lived alone in a simple, two-bedroom house, a world away from the bustling social life of middle-class Delhi. The house was at the top of a hill, and the orchards lined the gentle slopes below.

I was seven and on a road trip with my grandparents, who took care of me while my parents were still together and busy working on a documentary. Maya auntie grew Macintosh apples, bright red and waxy. I don't think I picked any, but I do remember putting them in a cooler to keep for the long drive back to Delhi. The paths through the hills were covered in pine needles, and the mountain air was clean like glass. Every morning I would run down to where the workers lived, dressed in Indian clothes like the orchard workers' daughters, and help feed and milk the cows.

As we drove toward the mountains, I felt I was picking up scraps of my childhood from the landscape, fragile fragments of memory that had been eclipsed by darker days. We slept on the road, arriving in Pokhara at four the next morning.

Pokhara was dead in February. It was the off-season, cold and quiet. I opened my eyes to streets lit blue-white by a full moon. I looked groggily at the shuttered storefronts, the hand-painted signs advertising incense, *momos*, thick Nepalese dumplings, and mountain gear. My eye was caught by one sign in particular. It hung above a restaurant, and its broad painted letters read "The Enlightened Yak."

Built along the shores of Phewa Lake, the town was seven hours west of Kathmandu. At an altitude of 900 metres it was the major base point for treks up the Annapurna Mountain circuit. We found a clean, simple guesthouse in the centre of town. I shared a room with Archana. There was no hot water in our room, so we borrowed from Vikram, carrying the steaming buckets along the terrace as the water splashed and spilled over the sides.

I went out onto the terrace early the next morning. The summit of Annapurna was visible in the distance. The tenth highest peak in the world, it rose to 8,000 metres. Only the tip was visible, white and glowing in the morning sun. The fresh air and clear blue sky seemed to dissolve the uncertainty of the past weeks. I was sure that Mom and David would find an alternative location in Madhya Pradesh or West Bengal. I didn't even know where they were and didn't think about it, really. I pushed the painful image of my mother's fallen face and the film's demise out of my mind and absolved myself of any responsibility. Instead, I clung to my hopes about Vikram, forever the empress in her invisible clothes.

We decided to take a three-day hike to Gorapani, literally "white water," a small mountain village with views of Annapurna. It was a well mapped-out trail and didn't require a guide. We passed through small Nepalese villages, where the dirt path would become temporarily paved with cobblestones.

My backpack was heavy. The trail slowly wound up through the valleys and across small icy mountain streams, the white-tipped Himalayas looming above us on either side. We spent our first night in a small rest house, just off the trail.

The rest house had six bedrooms and was made of rough grey stone. There was no insulation and no heating, and the space between the stones was filled with mud and straw. It overlooked a valley covered in fine stalks of yellow wheat that rustled delicately each time the wind passed between the mountains.

Vikram, Dylan, and I sat in the small dining room attached to the rest house. We were alone except for two Australian travellers writing in their journals. I looked to Vikram for a glimmer of what he had so readily given me in Benares. But he and Dylan were busy laughing, sharing a joke. I got up and went to bed.

The room was freezing and dark. The walls were made of the same rough stone, and there was a thin glass window that seemed haphazardly placed into it. Frost was inching across the thin pane. I lit a candle and placed it next to the window. There was one small single bed and two thick wool blankets, like a monk's cell. Not knowing anything about conserving body heat, I did what I was told the next morning was the worst thing to do. I put on all of my clothes—two layers of pants, socks, an undershirt, a long-sleeved shirt, a yellow Gore-Tex jacket I had borrowed from someone, and a wool hat from Peru—and got into bed.

The darkness comforted me despite the cold. I lay awake, looking at the bright moon through the small windowpane, thinking about Vikram on the other side of the stone wall. Although still wrapped in the warmth of hope, I could feel its edges beginning to thin and fray and age from overuse.

I thought about how everyone has his or her own life, like individual threads that navigate the universe. And how each person follows and directs that thread through time and space. Vikram would return to his life, his rituals, rhythms, and habits, just as I would have to return to, and face, my own. The memory of sitting alone on the subway, commuting between my parents' houses, made me shrink. Our time together was a moment of crossing, that's all, I told myself.

Someone I would meet years later would call it "bordering" someone. He believed we come close and share and love and experience, and then move away. I fell asleep wondering if we travel through someone as much as we do through a place, crossing their invisible borders the way we cross the invisible lines of geography.

GORAPANI WAS AT the top of a steep incline, a few thousand metres above sea level. We approached at dusk the next day, when there was still a faint glow of light in the air, but the sun had already set behind the mountains. Two Nepalese archers were practising on the outskirts of the village. They drew their bows back and aimed at a round target fifteen metres away, releasing their arrows in unison. I couldn't see the snow-capped peak of Annapurna as we walked up through the small dirt and stone streets of the tiny village. There was a light layer of snow on the ground and icicles hanging on the eaves of the roofs. As they melted, drops of ice water slid down their length and fell into the fresh snow, catching the evening light in their clear, thinning bodies.

It was only when we turned out from the small muddy streets into a clearing at the edge of town that the Himalayas became visible. A valley was spread below, and the Himalayas were a wall of fire in front of us, closer than I could ever have imagined. Annapurna burned, glowing deep orange and magenta as her snowy sides reflected the setting sun. The range drifted in and out of view as low-hanging clouds moved through the valley.

It was February 14, Valentine's Day. A few years later, in 2003, members of the Shiv Sena would attack card shops selling Valentines, burning red paper hearts and intimidating store owners until they pulled their stock from the shelves. The Associated Press would report the leader of the Shiv Sena's words at the time: "Valentine's Day is against the ethics and culture of Indian society."

We spent that evening around an open hearth in the common room of the guesthouse. The walls were lined with wood and strung with Nepalese prayer flags. We took turns having a shower in a stone bathroom, which could be entered only by going outside and walking a few feet through the snow to a low tin door. There was no light inside the room, so we bathed by candlelight, washing quickly and running back to the common room to dry our hair by the open fire.

I sat on one of the wooden benches beside the hearth, running my fingers through my wet hair. Dylan and Peter laughed with the Nepalese owner, ate *momos*, and listened to the Bollywood songs played on a little plastic tape deck. In a few days they would also return to their own threads of life. Dylan to Budapest, and Peter to Berlin. I still felt beautiful when Vikram came over and sat beside me. Smiling, I rested my head against his shoulder.

"He's a very noble guy," Peter said, as we walked back down the trail toward Pokhara the next day.

He said it with sympathy and concern, glancing at Vikram, who walked a few metres in front of us. I knew he was referring to Vikram's girlfriend. I moved ahead, trying to hide my feelings.

Old Nepalese women sat with their grandchildren on the small stone steps of village houses. Their faces were broad and beautiful, lined like fractured china. I thought of the widows and of how different their lives were. Unlike them, these old women lived in their homes, surrounded by their grandchildren and family. The children ran up to us when we entered the villages and left as soon as we reached the last house at the edge of town. I wondered where I would go when everybody left. Back to my father's house in Canada, to my grandparents in Delhi, or to my mother, searching for an alternative location somewhere in India? My own thread of life seemed elusive and uncertain. The mountains remained silent, offering no advice.

Our van was waiting to take us to Kathmandu where we would spend a night before flying back to India. Most of the production assistants would be returning to their homes in

Bombay, while Dylan and Peter would stop over in Delhi before flying back to Europe. In a few days this would all feel like a surreal dream, I thought, a simple punctuation mark in everyone's lives. I looked at Vikram walking in front of me and felt a heaviness begin to form inside.

The hills and rivers on the drive to Kathmandu appeared ugly to me, and the sweet *chai* and roadside food tasted like paper. Kathmandu was crazy and overpopulated. Children ran around the main pagodas of Durbar square, amid peddlers, popcorn vendors, and backpackers. My dad had told me about Kathmandu. He travelled there as a young hippie filmmaker in the early seventies. He ate hash brownies on Freak Street, once the centre of hippie life in the city. The way he had described it, I imagined a muddy street, lined on both sides with dilapidated tenements housing Western tourists strung out on heroin and hash, the heavy smell of incense mixing with the sickly sweet smell of vomit from those tourists who had OD'd.

I dragged Vikram out the night before we left to find the place. Freak Street was now a small, neatly paved road lined on both sides with brightly lit shops advertising cellphones and Bollywood hit singles, punctuated by the occasional vegetarian restaurant. I figured that small piece of my father's history would have to remain in my imagination.

When we boarded the Indian Airlines plane the next day, I found myself uncomfortable between closeness and distance with Vikram, oscillating between despair and a delirious façade of having a *good time*.

But there was still affection between us. When we took off for Delhi I felt peaceful, sitting in the seat next to him. And when he pointed out the window to Mount Everest, dark and regal in the fading evening light, and told me her real name was Sagarmatha—the head of the sky—I felt the same warmth as the night on the Vaibhav landing.

"Can I come hang out in Bombay?" I asked hopefully, feeling I knew where I wanted to go for the first time since the shutdown.

"Sure," he said. But I couldn't tell if he spoke as a friend, or more.

9

I bought a train ticket from Delhi to Bombay two days later, having stayed at my grandparents' house long enough only to wash my clothes, arrange for the ticket, and get an update on my mother. She was tired, but otherwise safe, as she travelled through Madhya Pradesh. I had last visited the house just before New Year's and it had been a few years before that since my last visit. It was both familiar and uncomfortable, the place where my parents were married more than twenty years earlier, and where I had spent so much of my childhood.

My *Nani* and *Nanu* were keeping vigil in the television room in the front of the house. They watched Doordarshan and Star TV, as they broadcast *Water*'s shutdown across India and Mom's attempt to revive it in other states. The news had made the BBC and Canadian press, and caused a rallying of international artists for freedom of speech. George Lucas and the *Young Indiana Jones* team had taken out a full-page ad in *Daily Variety*, the film industry trade newspaper, pledging their support to Deepa Mehta and the crew of *Water*.

As the film quickly became a national issue in the media, my grandparents prayed for their daughter's safety. They also knew the uncertainty of working in film. My grandfather had been a film distributor and owned two movie halls from the 1950s through the 1970s. My mother grew up in Amritsar, a small city in the northern state of Punjab, bordering Pakistan. The theatres were called Ashok and City Light, and my mother would go for the noon show and stay through the afternoon show as well, sitting in the private box adjacent to my grandfather's office, enjoying the free Coke and ice cream the manager would give her.

My *Nani* leaned forward, her arm resting on her sari. She covered her mouth with her hand as she watched the news. I loved them both very much, but something in the house reminded me of a missing piece in my life, unresolved and jagged. I wanted to leave and avoid everything that both comforted and constrained—the slightly musty smell of our dark green living room, the small front garden where my parents were married, and the servant who had known me since I was born and still brought me steaming morning *chai* in one of my *Nani*'s white china cups.

Vikram confirmed his invitation, and after exchanging e-mails, said he would meet me at Bombay Station. The train left at ten p.m., an overnight express that arrived in Bombay at nine the next morning. Before I left, my *Nani* put her hands on mine and told me how concerned she was about my mother. She was so exhausted after Benares. I squeezed her soft hands, and went to get my bag.

My grandparents' driver dropped me off at New Delhi Station. Wearing a blue cotton shirt, embroidered with mirror work, I tucked myself into a lower berth seat beside the tinted train window. My backpack, significantly lightened but still cumbersome, barely squeezed under the seat. The journey would take me through Rajasthan and the southern tip of Gujarat, arriving in the western state of Maharashtra at daybreak. I had never taken the train to Bombay, and hardly knew the city. But most of the journey would be invisible anyway, lost in the darkness of night.

A businessman and his family sat on the opposite berth. The mother held her baby across her lap, rocking it gently with both of her hands as her husband chewed *paan*, which crept, deep red, out of the corners of his mouth. He read a Hindi-language newspaper. I couldn't see any references to *Water* on the thin black-and-white sheets. It was already becoming old news to the national Indian media, replaced by a political scandal, a caste-related murder, or a flare-up in Kashmir. The Indian public's attention span was as blissfully short as the average North American's. I rested my head against the tinted glass. It seemed to be peeling at the edges, as if someone had stuck an appliqué sticker on the window, and the glass wasn't tinted at all. I fell asleep as the train sped through sleeping states I wouldn't see.

The conductor moved through the car, shouting for passengers to place their breakfast orders. I opened my eyes to bright sunlight streaming in through the window. The sky outside was vast and clear, the landscape almost desert, scattered with only a few low-lying shrubs and rough yellow stones. Maharashtra. We were considerably farther south than Delhi, approaching the Arabian Sea on the west coast of India. There was no trace of the winter fog I had become so used to in Benares.

I ordered a vegetarian meal and the conductor returned a few minutes later with a stack of trays balanced on both arms. He passed two to the couple opposite me, the baby awake and crying between them, and handed me a tray which I placed carefully on my lap. It was covered with a thin yellow omelet, buttered white bread, *sabzee* or vegetables, and flat *pooris*—fried unleavened bread. The *pooris* were wrapped in a plastic bag lined with condensation.

As we neared the outskirts of Bombay, I pulled out a small fabric toiletry bag from the top of my backpack, and walked down the narrow corridor to the washrooms. The space between the cars rattled as if it would fall apart. As I put my hand on the sliding door, I noticed a man out of the corner of my eye. He was sitting in a little recess, no bigger than a broom closet, on a mountain of white linen, folding. Thin and intensely focused on his work, he piled and sorted the hundreds of sets of sheets used by passengers the previous night.

I locked the washroom door behind me and balanced the small toiletry bag on the edge of the sink. The toilet was open and I could see down to the ground, a blur of movement below the train. The sound of the wheels on the rails filled the small room. I closed the seat and the sound was muffled. The room rocked back and forth, repetitive and reassuring. I looked at myself in the small glassy mirror. My hair was a mess from sleeping, and my shirt crumpled. I carefully smoothed them both down and brushed my hair with my fingers. Pulling out a small bottle of perfume from the bag, I covered the smell of sleep and sweat, and splashed my face with cool tap water. The light coming through the frosted-glass window filled with shadows as fields were replaced by the buildings and slums on the outskirts of the city. The world felt light and new, like a white sheet drying in the sun. *He is waiting.* The train began to slow. I looked in the mirror one more time, and smoothed my eyebrows with a wetted finger.

The compartment was unusually calm when I returned. There were no passengers pushing for their luggage, no conductors running through the corridor doing last-minute checks, pinning back the synthetic blue curtains that separated the sleeping berths. The couple sat quietly, their baggage beside them, the baby blissfully asleep on his mother's lap. The husband was reading a morning newspaper. I sat and looked out the window as the city grew around me. Low Art Deco apartments were painted in pastels, open balconies hung with thin paper lanterns shaped like five-pointed stars, tall palms bent under their drooping foliage, and there was a hint of humidity—the simplest suggestion of the sea.

The tracks began to converge and collect as we entered Bombay Central. I pulled out my backpack and crossed my legs. The train came to a stop in the station, and I stepped off the car.

The platform was bright and busy under the cover of a vast plastic roof. I felt myself floating through a sea of passengers in light cotton saris as the ends of their floral *pallus*, or sari trains, caught the sunlight. The crowd fell away into waiting black-and-yellow Bombay taxis, and I saw Vikram standing at the end of the platform. Life, after all, just a series of connections.

He was smiling and wearing a Rolling Stones T-shirt. The beaded bracelet I had given him was on his wrist. I smiled back in my blue mirrored shirt. So this was belonging.

"Hi," I said, shyly.

"Hi." He helped me pull off my backpack, placing it on the dusty platform. I looked at him for a moment, the curve of his nostrils and the familiar warmth of his eyes. And then he stepped aside.

"This is Ishika." Standing in front of me was a small, pretty woman. I knew it had to come. I just hadn't expected it to come so quickly.

My vision blurred.

"Let's go." Vikram ushered us toward a waiting taxi, carrying my backpack over one shoulder. The three of us sat in the cramped back seat, with Vikram in the middle.

I stared out the window and tried not to cry as the taxi drove along the Bombay freeways. They talked between themselves and I avoided their eyes, realizing my fool's journey. We had to drop Ishika off at a photography studio, where she was an assistant, before heading to his house. When the taxi stopped and she kissed him goodbye, I closed my eyes. *See you later. Nice to meet you. Smile.* We exchanged polite goodbyes, and as she got out of the car I wondered how we could live with such duplicity.

The drive to Andheri West, the suburb in north Bombay where he lived with his mother, was uneventful and quiet. His apartment building was at the end of a shopping street lined with ice-cream parlours, restaurants, and clothing stores. The taxi stopped in front of a complex of four brown concrete high-rises.

We walked across an empty parking lot, through a small dark lobby to an elevator.

He pulled back the iron gate in front of the elevator door. An electronic version of a Christmas carol started playing as soon as the gate was open—"*Dashing through the snow.*" The Muzak stopped as soon as the gate was shut. We stood in silence as the elevator ascended. Four feet away and a world apart.

His apartment was comfortable, with a living room, kitchen, two small bedrooms, and a bathroom. A wall of windows in the living room looked over a wide expanse of undeveloped marsh-land to the north. The windows let in the breeze and lifted the light cotton curtains, carrying with it the occasional smell of sewage from below. I looked down to the street, yellow and dusty. A few squatter settlements lined the open drain that bordered the marsh. It was a lonely view.

Vikram put my backpack in his bedroom. "I'll take the couch," he said. I went into his room. It was narrow and plain. A single bed was pushed against the wall. The shelves were lined with books and foreign films—*La Dolce Vita*, Kieslowski's *Blue*, *Cinema Paradiso*—some of my favourites. Film was my second language, even before Hindi. Sometimes I felt it expressed life more succinctly than spoken or written language ever could. Images of life in motion. *Money into light.*

It was the common culture both my parents had raised me in, beyond being Jewish or Indian. We celebrated the funding of my mother's first film as a family around our dining table more seriously than we would have celebrated the Jewish Pesach or Passover, or Diwali, the Indian New Year's. My dad bought champagne, and I photocopied one-dollar bills and put them in the glasses. It was the film that would eventually take us to Cannes and the divorce.

But film was also the shared language that allowed them to meet and fall in love in 1972. My dad, a young documentary filmmaker, was shooting a film on the Canadian High Commissioner to India. And my mom was a twenty-one-year-old cinephile and an editor for the *Junior Statesman* newspaper in Delhi. I was named after the lead character in *Mamta*, a film my mother had seen forty times in my grandparents' theatre in Amritsar. The manager gave her a Cassata ice cream on her fortieth screening. *Mamta* was about a mother separated from her daughter. *Mamta* meant "a mother's love."

Vikram came in. "Do you want to see some photos from Nepal?"

I nodded.

We looked at colour slides of the mountains projected onto his smooth white closet door. Annapurna, the morning sky, the Himalayan range on fire. And then there was one of me, in the lobby of our hotel in Kathmandu, looking sad and serious. Everything I hated about myself. I looked at Vikram casually flipping through the slides. We were both children of divorce, yet he didn't seem to show any of the insecurity and self-doubt I felt. But then, who knows? We all deal with pain in different ways.

"I have to go out later to pick up some stuff, and then we can meet up with Ishika."

"Okay," I answered. What else was I going to say?

Vikram went into the living room to turn on some music. I sat on the narrow single bed and looked at photos of his life, of him and her, their arms wrapped around each other. I started to feel a growing sense of desperation. I had been wrong about this thread. My trajectory lay somewhere else, with someone else. I sat with my hands on my lap, as if waiting at a bus stop for a piece of life to come by and take me away.

"Come into the living room." Vikram was standing at the door.

"Okay," I said. It would become my false mantra.

The living room was peaceful, filled with the breeze from the marshland and the light from a small yellow lamp. The sound of a gentle guitar came from two black speakers resting on the floor.

"It's Bob Dylan's 'Blood on the Tracks.'" Vikram stretched himself out on the couch and closed his eyes. "It's my favourite album."

I had never heard Bob Dylan before. His lyrics caressed the room.

"They sat together in the park
As the evening sky grew dark,
She looked at him and he felt a spark tingle to his bones.
'Twas then he felt alone..."

I waited for that bus to take me away. I looked at Vikram, his eyes shut, the smoothness of his face. Was this the painful transition to friendship?

"The song's called 'Simple Twist of Fate,'" he added, without opening his eyes.

I followed him that evening as we picked up his things and met up with his friend for dinner before meeting Ishika. We ate curried crab at a brightly lit restaurant in downtown Bombay. The crab was served with metal crackers to break the shell. In the middle of dinner, amid their comfort with each other and the sound of cold metal cracking shell, I started to cry and ran to the restaurant bathroom before they saw my tears.

Behind the closed bathroom door I thought of Mom searching for a place to make the film. I envisioned her on the banks of the Narmada River in Madhya Pradesh. She would be looking at Maheshwar, a temple town with its own *ghats*, although much smaller and less grand than Benares. I let the tears fall into the sink, and wondered if she was doing any better in her search for fulfillment than I was in mine. I wiped my eyes with toilet paper and went back downstairs.

Vikram and I said goodbye to his friend and moved in and out of taxis on the congested Bombay streets before we finally met up with his girlfriend.

I followed them into an autorickshaw. I couldn't speak and, instead, watched the Bombay streets pass by. They were alive and vibrant at night. The lights of Marine Drive flashed by, night vendors were selling pineapple and tropical fruit by gaslight, couples walked on Juhu beach, and children emerged from the frayed cardboard and corrugated iron of the slums. The Arabian Sea smelled of sewage. I focused on the smell, trying not to notice as they chatted and kissed.

We dropped her at her home and headed back to Andheri. The door to his mother's bedroom was shut. We went into his room and watched Kieslowski's *Blue*. I sat on the bed. Vikram pushed a chair up against the closet, behind me and out of view. While Juliette Binoche mourned her dead family, increasingly consumed by grief, I secretly hoped he was looking at me, not the screen. But when the movie ended he went into the living room, and I went to sleep feeling desperate and alone.

The phone rang in the early morning. Vikram came in in his pyjamas.

"It's your dad."

I pulled myself out of bed and went into the living room. The phone was sitting on the couch where Vikram had slept. He left to shower, giving me privacy.

"Hi, Dad."

I could feel something about to break inside of me, spurred by the familiarity of his voice. I rushed at him in French, poorly spoken, Canadian high school French. With all of its formal grammar and lack of conversational ease, it was our secret language. I poured my heart out, hoping Vikram couldn't hear or understand.

"I'm moving into Anurag's apartment." Anurag had given me an open invitation before leaving Benares. My dad agreed it was for the best.

Vikram came into the living room after his shower. His mother was awake and making breakfast in the small kitchen. The smell of ground coffee and heated milk filled the apartment. The curtains moved gently in the breeze, sucked back like when you pull your cheeks in after eating something bitter. When I told them of my plans to spend a few days with Anurag, Vikram's mother insisted that I stay. "This is your home," she said.

Vikram was silent.

I PACKED MY BAG and moved into Anurag's apartment later that morning. Anurag lived with his wife in a nearby complex. They were on the sixth floor, in a comfortable one bedroom with large arched windows and a hanging swing on the small, crescent-shaped balcony. He let me in and fed me *dal* and *chapatis*. I felt at home under the protection of a big brother. They had converted their narrow TV room into a bedroom, throwing down a thin futon and pillows. When they went to work, I sat alone in the room and spent the day watching the tenants on the other balconies, or looking across the concrete parking lot at the palm trees in the distance. They were still a faded green-grey, waiting to be washed clean by the monsoons.

An old woman came out onto the balcony below and almost diagonal to Anurag's. She wore a printed sari pulled over her long white hair. I watched as she walked to the edge of the railing in her bare feet, closed her eyes, and raised her cupped hands from her chest up toward the sun. The dust that blew up from the parking lot didn't seem to affect her. She raised her hands several times, as if offering her heart, completed the *surya namaskar*, the sun salutation practised in Hinduism and yoga, and went back inside, closing the sliding glass door behind her.

I woke up the next morning feeling heavy. The weight I had fought for so long had returned. I decided I needed to get out of the apartment and visit the city. I needed its vastness and life to help erase memory. I took an autorickshaw to Andheri Station. Commuter trains rushed back and forth between the suburbs and downtown, between Andheri in the north and Churchgate Station in south Bombay.

The station was bustling with rush-hour commuters. The platform filled and refilled with people, the constant ebb and flow of arrival and departure. I walked up and across one of the congested pedestrian bridges as local female labourers, their saris pulled up between their legs, carried heavy bundles on their wiry arms. They spoke a rough Marathi, as the muscles in their legs strained and pumped under the weight of their load. I waited on the platform with the labourers, middle-class housewives, and Muslim women in full black *burqa*. When the train to Churchgate pulled in, I pushed forward with the women, squeezing into an already packed "ladies only" compartment.

Rows of plastic handles were suspended from the ceiling. I held on to one and watched as women shifted to find space, their bodies and faces silhouetted against the open compartment door. At Bandra Station the compartment emptied enough for me to find a seat. An old woman stood across from me. She was thin and poorly dressed. Her face was dark and lined from the sun, and two small gold nose rings hung from her nostrils. With one arm over her head, she held on to a metal bar. In the other she held a blue plastic bag filled with empty bottles. She was sleeping as she stood. A woman wearing a pink golf shirt whispered to her friend, pointed, and laughed at the old woman. She slept throughout the ridicule, resting her face on a withered arm. After a little while I stood up and gave her my seat.

The train pulled into Churchgate Station, and I followed the flow of human traffic out onto the street. Downtown Bombay was bustling with life. Office towers and hotels flanked the vestiges of British colonial architecture—Victoria Terminus with its domed roofs, and Flora Fountain, carved out of white stone in the middle of a roundabout. More than anything I wanted to be lost in the flow of life.

Near Flora Fountain men and women ran in and out of the small shops that lined the ground floors of Bombay's buildings, following their lives with a smooth continuity. I felt out of place. Either I moved too slowly or too fast, but something in my step lacked synchronicity. I walked along the stone sidewalks, searching in vain for somewhere to go. I tried desperately to feel like a tourist, to feel anything except the emptiness. But the sun was too hot, and I began to sweat until dark patches formed under my arms. Spotting an art gallery, I tried to cross the street, but a wave of black-and-yellow taxis rounded the corner, making me jump back onto the curb.

I leaned back against a wrought-iron fence.

The voices of college students talking and laughing drifted through the bars from the grounds behind me. Families picnicked on the Oval *Maidan*, as couples strolled across the green—women in light, flowing saris, men in short-sleeve cotton shirts and leather sandals. I thought of all the times I dreamed of being close to someone, of belonging.

The bars dug into my back. I realized I was standing on a street corner in a city I didn't know, waiting for someone to come for me, to save me. Life that evening was like looking through the fence I was leaning against, unable to reach the other side.

I held my commuter train ticket in my hand, smudged and torn, Vikram's map to Andheri, a list of phone numbers, and a bus schedule, tokens of my innate sense of direction. But they seemed useless now.

My heart.

"*No,*" I would tell the therapist.

"*That is a place where I am often lost.*"

ANURAG'S FLAT WAS DARK when I returned. I switched on the small overhead light and went into the narrow kitchen for a glass of water. They had left dinner on the counter, *sabzee* and *dal*, kept warm in a small metal tiffin carrier, and *chapatis*, wrapped in a cloth napkin and placed in a round plastic container.

I ate standing, picking at the *chapatis* and listening to the low buzz from the halogen lamp. Desperation moved through my body like a slow-acting drug. I began to feel numb and tingly, my forehead cool. The sensation moved down my arms to the tips of my fingers. I was chasing a lost cause, but I couldn't stop. I had seen despair before and didn't want to go back to it. I picked up the phone. The halogen hummed in my ears.

I dialed Mom on her cell.

"Mom?" The reception was weak. "Where are you?"

"I'm in Bengal, on my way to Calcutta. We just saw a possible location."

"What happened with Madhya Pradesh?"

Her voice was silent on the other end of the line. A strange, hopeless silence. And then she told me how, while waiting for the plane back to Delhi, a letter had been delivered to her by an armed soldier. It was from Uma Bharati, the BJP opposition leader in the Congress-led state. It was printed in Hindi, a polite warning not to do the film in Madhya Pradesh.

"It was too close to what happened in Benares. I didn't want to risk it again," she said.

But I could hear in her hopelessness an unnerving desire to continue fighting for what she wanted, despite the RSS editor's words. But then I knew that desperate drive for something you loved but could not have. I had it in myself. After hanging up, I sat alone in Anurag's apartment, cradling the phone in my hand. I began to dial.

"Hello, Vikram? Do you want to come over and hang out for a bit?"

My palms began to sweat.

"Great, see you soon." I put down the receiver.

I ran to the bathroom and washed my face, placing a fine line of *kohl* in both my eyes. *He had liked that in Benares.* I rushed into my room and straightened the pillows and futon. *The window.* I pulled open the sliding door to the balcony. The evening breeze, *pavan* in Hindi, rushed past the swing and into the room. *Pavan*, that's what my parents were going to name me if I had been born a boy. I remembered that now. Funny how memory works. I dug into my backpack for clothes. Mirrored shirt, *no*. Black pants, *no*. I settled on an indigo wraparound skirt from a store in Delhi and a simple grey T-shirt. I went out onto the balcony to wait, full of the expectation I had spent the day trying to kill. What had they said? Without desire, there is no pain. But feelings don't die an easy death.

An autorickshaw turned off the main street and pulled into the parking lot below the balcony. Its single headlight shone toward the darkened building. I watched as Vikram got out and paid the driver. He glanced up toward the light from Anurag's apartment. I stepped back into the shadows so he wouldn't see me.

In that moment all the love I knew and could remember was with this one person—in the space between us, in the tenderness of a kiss on the Vaibhav landing, in the click of a camera shutter on Assi *Ghat*. In friendship. In first love.

The doorbell rang.

"Hi." I opened the door.

"Hi." He was standing tall and lanky in his rugby shirt and cargo pants.

"Come in." I moved aside to let him pass. He went into the kitchen and opened the fridge.

"Do you want something to drink?" he asked, one hand resting on the fridge door.

I nodded. And while I started laughing and telling him about all the great museums I had visited, he poured two rum and Cokes. It was that painful place, standing on the edge between friendship and love, lost in your own awkwardness. Vikram walked into my room and looked out over the balcony to the faint outline of the trees in the distance.

"The monsoons will wash the dust away soon..." He sipped his rum and Coke. "...the leaves will shine."

I looked at him longingly.

We sat on the thin futon and drank in awkward silence, the breeze brushing gently past the swing.

I leaned over and kissed him.

And he kissed me.

"I love you," I said.

It was the first time I had said it to anyone. I looked into his eyes, at the curve of his nose. *Expectations.*

He looked back into my own waiting eyes.

"I love you very much, but I'm not in love with you," he said. "I love somebody else."

Expectations.

I went out onto the balcony and sat on the swing. I held my face in my hands and stared out through the iron railing. Vikram came over and rested his arms on my knees. I rocked back and forth, studying the marble floor.

"There will be others." He spoke quietly.

"No, there won't." I refused to believe that. Didn't that somehow diminish everything I felt for him? My eyes clouded up, and then I felt the weight of his arms lift from my knees and saw the blur of his body move past me and out of the room. The door shut quietly, and with him the possibility of happiness seemed to slip away. *A simple twist of fate.*

10

Vulnerability often makes you want to run away. I had a queasy feeling in my gut the next morning, of having been too open, of having risked too much in pursuing Vikram. Somewhere on the other side of the country my mom was feeling the same way in her pursuit of the film.

Although the Hooghly River, flowing from the Himalayas into the Bay of Bengal, was of the same waters as the Ganges, changing its name only when it crossed the state border, Calcutta was different from Benares. The West Bengal government was Communist-Marxist, not BJP. Yet, there had still been problems, leaving no safe place in India to shoot *Water*.

Because of the media exposure and violence surrounding the film, the only way the West Bengal government felt *Water* could be safely completed was near the town of Barrackpore, in the confines of a police camp on the banks of the Hooghly. There had been protests as well, both for and against the film. A procession of sex workers had walked the streets of Calcutta with black cloths tied around their mouths, symbolizing the suppression of free speech. Ironically, they were misinformed that *Water* was about prostitution and that was the reason why it had been shut down. Between the politicians, media, protesters, and, in this case, supporters, misinformation seemed to be the rule of the day. My mother politely declined the invitation to shoot in West Bengal.

In early March, only a day after talking with her on the phone from Anurag's apartment, Mom returned to Delhi where my grandparents checked her into a small private hospital in a leafy neighbourhood. She had suffered a severe asthma attack, compounded by exhaustion. She curled up in a hospital bed, vulnerable and spent, protected from the outside world by nurses and doctors and an IV inserted deep into her vein, the cold needle justifying her escape.

I wanted to curl up and do the same, surround myself with starched white uniforms and the reassuring smell of antiseptic. To escape Bombay, to escape the geography of pain. Although Mom had politely declined West Bengal, the chief minister, Jyoti Basu, invited her back to Calcutta to receive a token award for conviction in freedom of speech. She asked me to meet her there. Two days later, after she recovered, I left Anurag's apartment, went to Bombay's domestic airport, and bought a one-way ticket to Calcutta.

Sitting in my narrow economy seat on Jet Airways, I looked down as the arid deserts of Rajasthan and Gujarat slowly turned into the green lushness of West Bengal. Calcutta, on the opposite side of the country from Bombay, bordered the Bay of Bengal and was closer to Burma than to New Delhi. Bombay sat on the coast like a painful point in memory. The city by the sea. I willed it to wash away.

As the plane landed I felt an emptiness in my body, as if the India we were travelling through was not real, but an illusion, a shadow of the country I had known as a child. I would be going back to Canada in a week, and my mother would follow a few weeks later. I would return home to my life with my dad, far away from the world I had seen with my mom. And when she returned, we'd see each other a couple of times a week until I left for university in England at the end of the summer.

Mom was waiting for me at Calcutta Airport. I picked up my backpack from the carousel and walked out of the gate into a crowd of waiting friends and relatives. Bengali surrounded me, a language so soft and curved, it seemed to ease the pain of rejection. The state had provided her with a government car, a white Ambassador with curtains on the windows.

"Hi, Mom." She hugged me. When I put my arms around her, I could feel the fragile outline of her ribs.

The sky was brown as we drove through evening congestion into Calcutta. Scooters and cars were stuck in traffic jams all the way to the centre of town. We sat in silence. I didn't know what to say to make her feel better, so I said nothing at all and looked out at the billboards advertising Coke and Samsung televisions.

The buildings around us were heavy and dark, not the city of the gleaming white Victoria memorial and the colonial British residences that I had envisioned. The British East India Company had landed on the banks of the Hooghly in the seventeenth century. But this was not the Calcutta of the Raj. This was the India of cellphones, cars, pollution, and the constant drive for upward mobility—a drive that sponsored corruption and poverty, political game-playing and violent nationalism. There were more advertising billboards lining the highway than I had seen even in Bombay.

We arrived at Laudon Street at dinnertime. It was in the centre of the city, just off bustling Park Street, the original shopping promenade of the British. But Laudon Street was quiet, most of the houses and apartment buildings darkened behind high white walls. My mom's first cousin, Anil, lived with his wife, Rupa, two of my favourite cousins, and my great-aunt Nirmal in a comfortable apartment on Laudon Street. Our government Ambassador stopped in front of their driveway, and we walked up the dimly lit stairwell to their apartment. The air felt damp and smelled of soot.

Nirmal auntie opened the heavy wooden door.

She was shorter than me, round and full, with one of the warmest faces I knew, though partially hidden behind large glasses. Her expression was permanently benign, a woman of grace who took pleasure in taking naps in her simple blue bed-room and making sure everyone was well fed. She was my grandmother's sister-in-law and one of her best friends. A beauty queen at seventy-six.

"*Aajao, aajao,* come in." Her chiffon *dupatta* fell lightly over one shoulder.

The apartment was cool and peaceful. Low lights in the living room outlined two couches and folk art on the walls. Rupa ran an artists' co-operative that bought craft work from rural Orissa and Bengal to sell in their Calcutta store.

Rupa and Anil greeted us with worried faces and hugs. We sat in the low-lit living room late into the night, recounting what had happened to the film and sipping whisky soda the way Anil's parents and Mom's parents would have at 2 Circular Road, the joint household my mom grew up in in Amritsar.

Joint households and extended families were so far removed from the way I was raised as an only child of divorced parents. Only a generation earlier *Nani, Nanu,* my mom, and uncle Dilip shared a house with my *Nanu*'s brother and his family in Amritsar. Anil and his parents would visit in the winters. On those winter afternoons Nirmal auntie and my *Nani* would have tea together while the *channawallahs* would sell spicy chickpeas at Company Bagh, and the *Granth Sahib*, the Sikh holy book, would be recited in the Golden Temple far away, in the inner city.

It was in Amritsar in 1919 that General Edward Dyer ordered the massacre of peaceful protesters in the early days of India's struggle for independence from the British. The crowd met in a walled-in garden, and had nowhere to escape when the British opened fire. The official estimate released by the British government was that 379 men, women, and children died under machine-gun fire, although historians suggest the figure was at least twice as large. Those who survived did so because the soldiers and officers ran out of ammunition. The massacre was immortalized in Sir Richard Attenborough's film *Gandhi*. Two blocks away, at the Golden Temple in 1984, Prime Minister Indira Gandhi ordered Operation Bluestar, sending the Indian army into the Golden Temple to flush out Sikh separatists fighting for an independent Sikh homeland, Khalistan. This assault on the Golden Temple led to Indira Gandhi's assassination by her two Sikh bodyguards, and in retaliation for her death there was brutal violence against Sikhs across India, concentrated in Delhi where Hindus and Muslims went on a rampage, killing 4,000 innocent Sikhs over three days.

And we call ourselves a non-violent nation. As I sat in the dimly lit living room on Laudon Street, I began to believe that India was a nation ruled by thugs. The word "thug" came from the Sanskrit *sthagati*, meaning thief or villain. Thugs would rob and kill travellers and perform religious rites in honour of the goddess Kali, Hindu goddess of destruction. "Thug," it was an Indian concept.

The next morning, after Nirmal auntie had fed us a filling breakfast of *bhurjee*, Indian scrambled eggs made with tomato, onion, and green chilies, Mom and I went downstairs to be taken to the awards ceremony for conviction in freedom of speech. Waiting beside our Ambassador was an open Jeep occupied by four soldiers carrying AK-47s.

"Mom, what's happening?" I asked, frightened. I thought we had left this all behind.

She looked at me, hemmed into something far beyond her control.

"The government insists, for our safety."

I felt protected by her in that moment, and remembered when I was four or five we had walked up the icy stairs of our home in Toronto, the Canadian winter biting at our backs, when I slipped and fell backwards down the stairs. She fell, too, and broke my fall, landing on her back on the cold brick path. Her black coat spread out beneath her like a blanket, slowly gathering flakes of snow. I don't remember if she was angry with me, or happy that I wasn't hurt. It seemed that most of our relationship had to be reconstructed through fragmented pieces of memory, like shards of glass, some reflecting light, others opening deep wounds.

Our driver turned into a sports stadium in central Calcutta, followed by our armed escorts. The West Bengal government had arranged for the awards ceremony to take place on the main field. Our hosts led us into a small anteroom. A table was spread with *samosas*, Bengali sweets, and cheese sandwiches made with Britannia bread. Journalists nibbled at the food, their press IDs hanging loosely around their necks. When we walked in, Mom was immediately surrounded by the Bengali media and questioned about what she would do next. I don't think she even knew.

"Devyani, there's someone I want you to meet," Mom said, breaking away from the nibbling crowd.

She led me to a middle-aged woman wearing a sari. Her black hair was tied neatly into a bun, and she wore diamond solitaires in her round earlobes.

"This is Aparna Sen." I shook her hand politely.

Aparna Sen had starred in *Teen Kanya*, a Satyajit Ray film I loved and admired. She had been a young teenager in the black-and-white beginnings of Indian humanist cinema. Satyajit Ray, a Bengali director, was one of the fathers of modern film and a recipient of an Oscar for lifetime achievement. He started making films in the 1950s. He tackled issues about everyday Indian life, from drought and its effects on farmers to the hardships of a poor family growing up in rural Bengal—human issues, without the gloss of Bollywood. It was a tradition *Water* would have been a part of.

Calcutta had been the heart of India's intelligentsia during the freedom movement from the British. It was where the first

Indian newspapers had been published discussing the oppression of colonial rule, and where revolutionaries gathered to participate in the "Quit India" movement. I was reminded of the great artists and writers who had gathered in the city to discuss politics, publish manifestos, and plan India's freedom from the British. It was ironic now to be in a room full of Bengalis, talking about freedom from their own fellow Indians.

I reached to shake her hand again, but an official ushered us to the main stadium. Mom was being led to the door. I moved across the room and out of the way as the crowd began to funnel toward it.

"Mom, I'll stay here." I felt shy and out of place.

"Come with me."

Something in her face, in the redness of her eyes, told me she needed me. It was an expression I wasn't used to.

The official led us up a narrow ramp into the darkened stadium. Floodlights lit a platform in the centre of a cricket field. I sat beside Mom at a long table covered with a white tablecloth. We were flanked by writers and filmmakers who were also receiving awards for their belief in freedom of speech. I could see only the outline of people in the stands because of the photographers' flashing strobes, white and blinding. The stadium seemed to be half-filled.

WE ARRIVED BACK at Laudon Street as evening fell over Calcutta. The sky was a deep blue against the stark colonial whitewash. Park Street was crowded with hawkers and shoppers. Young boys sold magazines and offered shoe-shines out of little wooden boxes, while Bengali women with large round *bindis* stopped to buy the latest issue of *Stardust*, Bollywood's premiere rag magazine. Stardust—that's what all of this already was. What felt like a catastrophe to us was nothing in the daily traffic of Indian life. A film was chewed up by politics and the media, and spat out, unrecognizable and forgotten—dust over a country that had so much more to deal with. We left our armed escorts on Laudon Street, and walked down the darkened driveway to Anil's apartment.

Nirmal auntie had dinner waiting on the dining room table. She sat with us as we ate off the checkered oilskin tablecloth. The table and walls were covered with small diamonds of light, thrown from the woven cane lamp hanging from the ceiling. Reassuring patterns like auntie's occasional interjections, "*Arey baccha, theek hai, kya karen?*" "Children, it's okay. What to do?" She may have been speaking to Mom, but I felt she was speaking to me too.

We ate the rest of the dinner in silence, as the sounds of the street floated through the window. There was nothing left to do. There was nothing left to fight against, and it left an empty hole in both of our lives. Rupa arranged for us to meet Soumitra Chatterjee, another star of Satyajit Ray's movies, knowing we were both fans. It would take us out of the house and occupy our time.

Soumitra Chatterjee had played Apu, a soft-spoken twenty-year-old writer with a slightly hooked nose and sensitive, shining eyes, in *The World of Apu*. It was made in 1959, the last film in a trilogy Ray made about a boy growing up from birth to manhood in West Bengal. The second film in the Apu Trilogy won the Golden Lion at the Venice Film Festival in 1957. Chatterjee was an icon, the Marcello Mastroianni of Indian cinema, and the man I wanted to marry when I was a kid.

We waited for him at a small table in the outdoor café of the Tollygunge Club, as men in golf shirts and white spurred shoes played at the adjoining golf course. It was one of Calcutta's most venerable establishments. I was too nervous to drink the English tea served to us in white china cups.

And then he arrived, the man I wanted to marry, the quintessential sensitive soul. He was sixty-five years old now, a grandfather with greying hair and thick glasses. He was a tall man, neatly dressed in a shirt and chinos. But despite his age, he had retained the beauty of Apu. The same slightly hooked nose and sensitive, shining eyes of the young man he had played more than forty years earlier. I almost fainted.

Mom and I listened as Soumitra Chatterjee talked about his relationship with Ray. Chatterjee was sixteen years old, from a town 70 kilometres outside Calcutta, when he saw *Pather Panchali*, the first film in the Apu Trilogy. It changed his life, and he went to an open audition for the second film. He was too old for the part, but Ray was impressed and remembered him when casting for the adult Apu in *The World of Apu*. Their working relationship as leading man and director would last thirty years and include fifteen films.

Between sips of tea he explained how most of his current roles were limited to Bengali soap operas. A few days later I would notice a poster on a lamppost advertising one of the soaps. Chatterjee's face appeared in the midst of several others. A melodramatic Indian family. The quality of the poster gave his skin a greenish tinge. Seeing Apu that way seemed to give me a glimpse into the future of Indian cinema—its increasing tendency toward the cheap.

Before leaving, Soumitra Chatterjee politely inquired about *Water*, mentioning what a travesty the shutdown was. At a loss for words, we appreciated his concern and said our goodbyes respectfully. Rupa took a parting photo of the three of us together. I watched as he walked gracefully across the club lawn and got into a small white car.

We drove along the shaded driveway of the Tollygunge Club, the Jeep with armed Bengali soldiers following close behind.

"What would you like to do?" Mom asked.

"I don't know." I looked out the window.

In a few days we would go our separate ways. We had come from Canada at different times and our return tickets were on different airlines. She would return home alone, with an unfinished film.

"Let's go to Shantiniketan," she said. Her eyes lit up momentarily. "Then we can get away from all of this bullshit."

Shantiniketan was about two hundred kilometres northwest of Calcutta. It was a small town and the home of Rabindranath Tagore's university. Tagore was a Nobel laureate and a master poet of the early twentieth century. He was a friend of W.B. Yeats, and an educator. His father had started the university in 1863 in rural Bengal. It was supposed to be beautiful, and Mom knew it would take us away from Calcutta and, hopefully, far from the political fray.

Shantiniketan. It meant "abode of peace."

HOWRAH STATION WAS FILLED with floating dust particles. They were suspended in shafts of light that stretched down to the station floor from windows high up in the rafters. Pigeons flew between rafter and ledge, streaking the walls white as the sound of train whistles filled the large, open space. Howrah, one of India's largest train stations and a central hub in one of the world's most extensive railways, was dotted with sleeping families and beggars. A scruffy little boy stood in one of the shafts of light, his hands holding on to an iron fence, one foot raised. He reminded me of when I stood on the street corner in Bombay, listening to the laughter of college students on the other side of the fence. He was also drawn to a world he couldn't reach, waiting for a piece of life to come and take him away.

Although we wanted a peaceful getaway, the West Bengal government insisted that our armed escorts accompany us to Shantiniketan. We were led across the station platform by a small group of khaki-clad officers. People turned and stared, and moved out of the way. The officers led us to a trailer that sat next to the platforms. The blinds on the windows were firmly shut. An officer, his AK-47 slung casually over his shoulder, opened the door.

The room was cool. A small air conditioner was attached to one of the windows. It was furnished with a desk, a few plastic chairs, and a poster advertising the Eastern Railways, the train line that ran between Delhi, Bengal, Orissa, and Assam. We were greeted by a railway official with a handlebar moustache, who insisted we stay inside and make ourselves comfortable. I wanted to go buy a newspaper, but the official wouldn't let me leave. Mom sat on a plastic chair with an armed guard on either side. Not the holiday either of us had expected.

The Shantiniketan Express departed at midday. We boarded the train with our guards, who stationed themselves at either end of the car, while we sat together in a second-class seat. Mom was quiet. She looked out the window occasionally, then tried to sleep, as the armed officers, their backs perfectly straight, stood sentry in the small space between the cars. I could see one of our guards through the narrow glass door that separated the carriages. He was young, his gun slung over his shoulder. Every time he looked back at us, I felt afraid for our safety. Was the threat of violence against my mom so real?

I looked out at the dense green paddy fields and lush palms of rural Bengal. It soothed my fear of being surrounded by men with guns. We passed small houses made of mud and thatch. They were built around still pools of water, covered with thin lily pads. I imagined that these were the villages where Ray had shot *Pather Panchali—Song of the Little Road—*fifty years earlier, their green richness immortalized in black-and-white film.

Shantiniketan was a small, deserted town. There were few cars, and the main transportation appeared to be cycle rickshaw. Mom and I were free to take a rickshaw to our hotel, while our guards followed in an open Jeep. The earth was a deep yellow. The wind moved gently through the trees as rural women bathed and washed their clothes in streams surrounded by lush vegetation. We had been transported to another India. A silent place.

The hotel was an incongruous structure on the landscape, a new cement-block building in the middle of a field beside a stream. The pale marble lobby was empty, but the manager came out to meet us regardless, dressed in a black suit and tie. It was likely that the West Bengal government had informed him of our visit even before we left Howrah. Mom and I followed him down an empty corridor. Far away from the sounds of film sets, protests, and Bombay traffic, the stillness felt close to death.

"Here you are, ma'am." He smiled and opened the door to our room.

His voice dripped with hospitality, syrupy and false. The extremes of behaviour I had encountered continued to confound me, from the violence of the women with the rolling pins to the submissive grin of the manager.

The room was bare. Warm afternoon light poured through the windows onto a double bed made of cheap imitation pine. It was like a cardboard box, everything insubstantial and wafer-thin.

I put my backpack down on the bed. There was a loneliness to the place, made more acute by the lack of city noise. The only sounds were the faint trickle of the stream outside the hotel gates and the women's voices as they washed their clothes on the rocks. I looked out the window at the landscape of rural India, silent and natural, as if only recently shaped by earth and rain. Maybe peace is more painful than we really think. There's room in peace, and room allows time for reflection. But often we don't want to see our reflections. Mom pulled out a mystery novel and began to read.

"Mom..." I looked across the desolate room.

"Hmmm?" She didn't look up from her novel.

"I'm so sorry about all of this."

Looking at photos with Mom. Toronto, 1981.

Mom and Dad. Montreal, or possibly New York, 1970s.

Mom on set with her Rothman's cigarette.

Producer David Hamilton.

The ghats. Benares, 1999.

Protesters burning Mom´s effigy.

The bombed-out shell of the Regal cinema. Jaffna, Sri Lanka.

The set of the ghats in Sri Lanka.

ABOVE: *Lisa Ray, "Kalyani," on set.*

CENTRE: *Manorama, "Madhumati," smoking a Gold Flake between scenes.*

BELOW: *Seema Biswas, "Shakuntala," and Sarala, "Chuyia."*

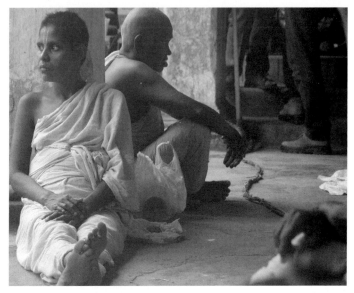

The Sinhalese widow extras resting between shots.

Director of photography Giles Nuttgens.

The crew at work on the set of the ghats.

Dylan (left) and Vikram preparing for the final scene at the train station.

With Mom after the Belfast International Film Festival in Northern Ireland.

I felt our time together ending in this lonely room. In three days I would be home in the bitter Canadian winter. Who knew if we would all meet again? If Mom and I would ever work together? This had been our first real chance.

"What can we do?" Her voice was like a scab over a wound, already dry and hardened.

"Let's at least go out," I said. The room was feeding our collective depression.

A single cycle rickshaw was parked in front of the hotel. The driver lay stretched out across its length, with his feet resting on the handlebars. How he survived, I don't know. He was thin and friendly, and offered to take us on a tour of Shantiniketan and the university. The town was so small that within minutes we were on the wide, dirt roads of the university. Large trees dotted the grounds and shaded the streets. Tagore had advocated outdoor teaching, and classes often met under the benevolent shade of one of these trees. It was a holiday and there were no students, adding to the silence.

We rounded a corner and came to an open-air theatre. Folk art was painted on the side of its clay walls, broad brown strokes of primitive figures and cattle. The sun had begun to set, casting a warm orange hue through the deserted campus. It was the colour saffron, the Hindu colour of strength and also the colour of the RSS and Hindu right. I had heard a few journalists at the Calcutta stadium talk about the "saffronization" of India, referring to growing Hindu nationalism. I don't think either Mom or I had realized its true force.

The rickshaw came to a stop in front of a simple white bungalow. It looked like an administration office for the university, maybe where Ray had come to register as a visual arts student a half century earlier. He had studied at Shantiniketan for a few years before moving into advertising, and then film. The rickshaw driver turned around in his seat.

"Go, go. Tagore Museum." He gestured toward the building with his arms. Neither of us jumped at the opportunity, tired and ready to sleep indefinitely, but he seemed enthusiastic. We climbed down from the rickshaw and walked into the building. There was one main room on the ground floor, open and wide. It smelled musty, of old letters and damp wood. The room was divided by glass display cases holding photographs, books, and yellowed papers. Small white stickers, curling at the edges, were printed with explanatory text, in both Bengali and English.

The dust had settled on the tops of the low cases, but every glass panel had been freshly cleaned. Mom wandered through the displays, as I stopped to look more closely at a black-and-white photo of Tagore. He had a long white beard and intelligent eyes. A white sticker noted that he was on a visit to Japan. He seemed to be wearing a robe, maybe a kimono, and was standing outside with the hills of Kyoto behind him.

I remembered that he had written the national anthem of India, "Jana Gana Mana," and that my *Nani* had taught me to play it on the harmonium when I was six years old. I still remembered the tune and the opening lines of the song.

That evening when we returned to the hotel the syrupy manager told us that he had arranged for a group of tribal musicians to perform folk songs for us in the garden. We agreed to join him after first going to the room to wash up.

Mom and I walked down the long deserted corridor. Without the lights of Calcutta, the Bengali night was thick in its darkness, suffocating. The only sounds were the quiet of the stream and the drone of cicadas. Mom opened the door to our room. Our last refuge in India, a place of peace. But there was no peace in her. I could see it in the dislocation of her gestures, the frequency with which she lit a Rothman's cigarette. And with me there was the desire to appease, to heal, to take away the growing weight I saw in her. We sat in silence on opposite sides of the room, her on the bed, me on the couch. Still waiting for that little piece of life to come and take us away.

THE GARDEN LAY behind the empty hotel, a flat expanse of grass, devoid of flowers. The manager had spread two white sheets on the ground, one for the musicians and the other for the two of us. The night had turned cool. We wrapped ourselves in shawls. The manager flicked on a garden lamp and the lawn was flooded in chilled grey light. Four men, dressed in white cotton *dhotis*, plain sarongs, *kurtas*, and turbans walked across the grass and seated themselves on the white sheet in front of us.

The night filled with tribal rhythms, smooth in their rural roughness. The hands of the *tabla* player grazed the drums' skins with the flat of his palms and fingers. Was this Indian culture then? I wondered as the singer's eyes closed in ecstasy. The pure, traditional India that the RSS and Hindu right fought so hard to preserve? Maybe. There seemed to be no room for anything else that might challenge their definition.

The stars shone bright in the Bengal sky. We both knew that night that *Water* was dead. Uttar Pradesh had thrown us out, Madhya Pradesh and West Bengal were unable to guarantee our safety, and the central BJP government was too closely tied to Hindutva to support the film. It was a marriage only growing stronger, blossoming and basking in mutual love like smug newlyweds.

India had rejected us. And like rejected lovers, we would nurse our wounds.

Oxford
2000

11

The phone call came three years later.

I woke up in the dark, to the sound of rain falling lightly on the trees outside my window. The phone rang again. I got up from my green futon and reached for the switch on the small desk lamp. The room was chilly and damp—an early spring morning in Oxford.

"Hello." My voice was thick and groggy.

"Devyani..."

"Yes."

"It's Mom."

It had been a while since we'd spoken. She was busy working in Toronto, and I was finishing my degree in England. The Isis, the stretch of the Thames that runs through Oxford, flowed below my dorm room window, flooded from the heavy rains. It ran frigid beneath the Folly Bridge, and past the Head of the River Pub, toward London.

"Mom?" I turned on the small electric heater beneath the windowsill. Outside the sky began to lighten to a pale grey, vast and blank, like distances untravelled. The sound of metal beer barrels being rolled along the cobblestones drifted up from the laneway behind the pub. It was a poor connection, but her voice seemed excited on the other end of the line.

"We're going to make *Water*! The film is happening."

And then the line went dead.

IT HAD BEEN A LITTLE more than three years since we left the deserted solitude of Shantiniketan. I had returned home to

Canada and to my dad's house. My mom returned a month later, in April 2000, defeated and depressed. All of a sudden the safety of Canada seemed too small after everything I had seen in India. And when Mom returned home, my life was once again divided, a division I had no taste for after having felt what it was like to have a room of my own, with my yellow *dupatta* and a candle that smelled like the ocean.

When *Water* was shut down I found out that I had been accepted at Hertford College, Oxford, to read a degree in anthropology, sociology, and biology. It was one of Oxford's smaller, more intimate colleges. It would provide me with food, housing, and access to the university community. I spent the summer preparing to go, knowing that it was the only way I'd be free from feeling torn within my own family.

My mom accompanied me to England. My dad wanted to come and settle me in, but I told him that I wanted to go with her. He had just moved in with his girlfriend, who had two grown children of her own. I felt a distance growing between us, and anger that he had separated me from half of my family. He was initially upset, but had slowly begun to realize that I needed my mother as much as I needed him. We took a black cab from Heathrow, stuffed with duffel bags. The driver was Indian and gave us his phone number, offering to be of service if I ever needed a hand. I knew no one when I arrived on a cold fall day in October 2000.

Mom settled me in over three days, and then got a cab from the street corner next to the college. I felt a strange sadness when she left for London, and watched as her face in the back window receded on the unfamiliar street. The colleges glowed a dim golden orange as their sandstone façades reflected the afternoon light. The small curved streets and medieval buildings invited me into a world far away from anything I had ever known. A world free from my own history, an ocean's separation from my parents.

There was a university bulletin board on the street corner. I began reading to distract myself. A brisk fall wind blew across the fronts of the colleges. A young woman came and stood next to me. We stood beside each other for five minutes, looking at the board, pretending not to notice each other. She looked Indian, and was equally lost. Eventually she introduced herself as Maria, a Christian from the south Indian state of Kerala, studying English at another college. She became my closest friend.

I spent the winter of my first year walking to classes through the barren beauty of Christ Church Meadows, a grassy field where cattle could graze in the centre of town. The winter cold left a light frost on the edges of the tall meadow grasses, bending them ever so slightly under the weight of the snow. The workload was heavy, and I found myself struggling. Painful memories surfaced for the first time in my life. But it was Maria, with her short black hair, tomboyish good looks, and affectionate smile, who would pull me out of my past and the memories of *Water*.

She would sneak into my college residence, bypassing the security codes, and leave handwritten notes tacked on my door. She taught me how to cook Indian food in her windowless residence kitchen, carefully dicing onions to fry in vegetable oil with pre-packaged *masala*, spices. Each student was assigned a kitchen cupboard. She labelled hers with a piece of tape, "*Devyani and Maria.*"

Together we went to buy second-hand bicycles. I found a blue-green bike with half-size wheels and named her "*Pearl*" because she reminded me of the sea. Maria bought a mountain bike, which was stolen a few weeks later. There was a rumour that bikes stolen from Oxford were sold in Cambridge, and vice versa, making for a constant exchange between the age-old rivals.

While I studied for my first-year exams, Mom began to write *Bollywood/Hollywood*, her first comedy starring a Canadian–Indian actress named Lisa Ray. She sent me the script, and I told her I didn't like it. But when the film was made I loved it, and realized that I had been wrong about the script. Mom sent me a CD of photographs from the set. I felt a tinge of longing, looking at the smiling faces of the crew. I had yet to be with her when she completed a film.

If I wasn't wandering with Maria, I would sit in the Bodleian Library, still and silent, surrounded by bound volumes resting permanently under the stone canopy of the library's arched ceilings. They had sat there for centuries, touched by a thousand hands, some dead and gone, others yet to come.

I chose to work in the Indian Institute one day, a reading room devoted to South Asia. It was famed for its view of Oxford's dreaming spires. I didn't know readers had to be working on South Asian material. When the librarian, an old Englishman with thinning white hair, found out I was reading about the physiology of the kidney, he asked me to leave. I began to gather my papers.

"You aren't, by any chance, Indian?" he asked.

"Yes, partly. Why?"

"Well, then, you can stay." He said it quietly, under his breath.

It seemed to me a strange form of reverse racism.

It was with Maria's companionship and my own space that I finally began to see where I had come from in my life up until then. As the end of my first year approached, I realized I didn't like what I was beginning to see. Something had always bothered me. It ate at me from deep inside, but was invisible to most of the people around me. But when I was sitting at the pub, surrounded by friends, pint glass in hand, that something pulled me away from where I was. Away from the barman taking orders, away from the laughter and the sounds of the kitchen until my experiences were like varnish, clear and meaningless, a coating over something much more substantial beneath. While passing the Oxford counselling service on the way to class, I told Maria that I might want to see someone to talk about things.

One year after leaving India, I had a breakdown and was on the verge of failing my exams. No longer able to hide behind the identity of being a top student, I was forced to face feelings I had buried long ago as an eleven-year-old. I remember lying in my dorm room, staring at a fragment of deep blue sky from my single first-year bed beside the window. It was clear and cold, like a piece of Persian tile placed carefully behind the turrets and peaked slate roofs of the college.

I watched as the pigeons sheltered themselves under the grey metal eaves, their heads tucked under their wings to protect against the British damp. Small trees grew between the gaps in the slate, no more than saplings, their little leaves fragile and exposed. I lay there as the minutes of my alarm clock ticked away, unable to get up.

The weight had finally consumed me. It held me in the pit of my stomach, a force so strong I missed all of my morning classes. Instead, I stared at the layers of cream-coloured paint on the ceiling above my bed, unable to turn over. The pigeons woke and flew away, and the sound of students unlocking their bicycles and going to class filled the courtyard below my window. I willed my mind to explain what was happening. But it had no answers, oblivious of the inexplicable heart.

Maria arrived in the evening, wondering where I had been. She opened my unlocked door, only to find me in bed, unable to speak. It had been ten years since the divorce. I realized I had never spoken about it with anyone. When I tried to tell Maria what was happening, my voice stopped in my throat, frozen, like an invisible barrier had been lodged in my windpipe—a fine piece of glass sliced into muscle and skin. I called my parents in Canada. A few days later they were on a plane to England.

I lay in my narrow bed and waited. Waited to be held, waited for a piece of my childhood to revive itself like a rose after winter. They would take me away from Oxford when they came, the way they had taken me out of grade four at an all-girls' school in Toronto after I refused to go. They had been fighting then. I'd hidden under my bed, holding on to the bedpost for dear life. If I went to school and left the safety of that dark square space between the floorboards and mattress, they might not be together when I got home. I had to stay and make sure that didn't happen. The fragment of sky outside my window turned blue to grey to white, and back to blue again. A tile glazed so shiny I could touch it.

"Mutzers."

My dad came into the room and sat on the edge of my narrow bed. It was night, and the sounds of the college bar came up loud and noisy and laughing from the courtyard.

"Mutzers..."

He called out my nickname, a gentle bastardization of the Hindi *choti*, little one. Choti became chutz, and chutz became mutz. The Yiddish influence, perhaps.

I opened my eyes.

"Your mom's waiting downstairs. We came on the bus from London together."

They had sat together, side by side, on the itchy red synthetic seats of the Oxford Tube, an express bus service between the city and the university. And they had talked about me. They had talked about me as parents are supposed to talk of their children, perhaps for the first time.

With their encouragement and support, I decided to see a therapist to talk about the weight. The three of us met her in a small English cottage on the Iffley Road, on the edge of town, where the glowing sandstone and stained glass turns into the low-income housing and immigrant shops selling rice, halal meat, and phone cards to Pakistan. We were invited into a small dollhouse room, everything miniature and floral print. While we sat for the exact forty-five minutes allotted to us, surrounded by big yellow roses swirling on the walls, I told them how I felt during the divorce and its aftermath.

I had been carrying a heavy crystal ball my whole life, and more than anything I wanted to let it go and see it shatter on the ground into a million pieces. Shatter beyond recognition.

They listened with difficulty, aware for the first time of the extent of the weight. I had hidden it so well under top marks and my innate sense of geographical direction. It's strange how one event in the past can manage so much of one's life in the present.

They stayed with me for one month. My mother stayed a little longer, and then returned to their own lives in Canada, their responsibilities, their friends, their work. Mom and I hadn't really discussed my choice to live with Dad. The topic was too raw, and we both avoided it. It was a hidden sliver that kept threatening to work itself to the surface, an irritant that never seemed to go away. I decided to stay in Oxford and continue my degree.

Maria let me stay in her room on the nights I felt too afraid to be alone with myself. Her room was basic and minimal, with a single bed and a prefabricated desk unit. The only decorations were a bulletin board with photographs of her college friends in south India, wearing silk saris and smiling, and a poster of John Lennon above the bed. On those nights she slept on the carpeted floor with only a thin sheet spread beneath her. My mom and dad would call me periodically to see if I was okay. It was the first time they communicated with each other in reaching out to me. With Maria's support I was able to catch up on the year's work and pass my exams.

I began to make new friends: Gautam the Gujarati-Brit vegetarian who read Gandhi, and Colm, the northern-Irish Catholic with whom I went to a 1920s prohibition ball. We spent the afternoon searching a second-hand clothing store that specialized in costumes for the Oxford summer balls. I found a pair of flying goggles and a silk scarf, and went as Amelia Earhart. Colm went as an Irish gangster with a Tommy gun. There was Laurence from Paris, who taught me how to make crêpes, and John, an American exchange student with a love for Walt Whitman.

Mom came to visit during my second year. She bought food at the local Sainsbury's, cooked in Maria's kitchen, and slept on my floor on a mattress.

I spent many hours over my second year reading social anthropology in the libraries and bookstores of Oxford. My introductory anthropology text was called *Other People's Worlds*, a soft-cover book by a local anthropologist named Joy Hendry, who specialized in the anthropology of Japan. I liked the idea that there was a discipline that allowed one to enter other people's worlds. It reminded me that I had already made my first steps into that discipline when I descended into the widows' *ashram* below the Sunview guesthouse in Benares. I began to fall in love with anthropology, and the study of rites of passage became a minor obsession. Along with my sessions in the rose room on Iffley Road, and friendship, it was my way through.

My anthropology tutor, an Englishwoman who did her fieldwork among the women of Gujarat, conducted her classes from the living room of her house in a residential north Oxford neighbourhood. My favourite days were when I rode Pearl up to the quiet streets away from the centre of town, the sky always moving between rain and shine.

The Bemba of Africa have a ritual for when a girl comes of age. It's called the *Chisungu*, and they talk of it as "growing the girls." I mulled over the Bemba, and a famous anthropologist's argument that all rites of passage involve three stages: separation from one's old state, a liminal period where one is without definition, and a reincorporation into society in a new form. The Bemba left their village as girls, performed tasks in seclusion to help them "grow," and returned to their community as women. The process fascinated me.

Growing the girls.

Somehow those meetings brought me closer to understanding something about myself, and what I was going through an ocean away from my parents and the life I had known. The separation of the Bemba girls was painful but necessary. I wanted to be an adult like them, and never go back to the little girl torn between two houses.

At the end of my second year Maria graduated. Her degree ended a year earlier than mine and she returned to south India to work as a teacher. I missed her terribly, and felt alone once again, left to create something from its bare beginnings like when I had first arrived in England. It reminded me of Mom and me, piecing together our relationship like torn cloth.

As my final year approached Mom followed *Bollywood/ Hollywood* with an adaptation of Pulitzer Prize–winning author Carol Shields's *The Republic of Love*. Both films were made in Toronto. *The Republic of Love* explored the loneliness of twenty-first-century urban life. It had no Indian themes and no Indian actors. Mom's visits to India were rare now, and then only to be with my grandparents in Delhi. India at the millennium was her painful point in memory, something she willed to wash away. The need to complete *Water* was like a piece of torn clothing she wore close to her skin, despite outward appearances of grace and dignity. She carried it through *Bollywood/Hollywood* and *The Republic of Love*—both conscious steps away from the heavy memories of Benares.

I had dealt with *Water* and Maria's departure in the same way—by immersing myself in the familiarity of film. A friend passed on an advertisement he found in one of the student newspapers, announcing the establishment of an International Cinema Club. They were looking for people to be part of the committee.

The meeting was in a musty common room in the university club. I was the youngest person there. Most of the men and women worked for the university in the libraries and as tech support for university Web sites, or they were post-doctoral students working in one of the many labs buried in the basements of Oxford buildings. I joined the committee that night and rediscovered my culture, rooted in film before anything else.

We programmed eight films a term, screening a DVD projection every Thursday night in a lecture room in the Engineering Department. Lecture notes with formulas and diagrams from material sciences were always left scattered on the banked seats from the last class of the evening. Within an hour the room was transformed. The hard lines of the podium and sterile grey walls softened as images from Buñuel and Chinese cinema filled the front of the theatre. *La Dolce Vita*, *Y Tu Mamá También*, and *Blowup* were just some of the films that graced our lecture room screen. Within a year I was vice-president, and then president, organizing mini film festivals and guest lecturers for our growing membership. I invited Mom to come and present *Earth* to the film club as my time at Oxford drew to an end. She stood in front of the audience and I introduced her. But however close we were becoming, I still felt the weight of my choice between us.

THE PHONE RANG a few minutes later.

"Mom?" I could hear her voice now, faint, but clear.

When her phone call woke me, I was in the midst of preparing for my final exams. Two years' worth of material loomed over me and in two months I would sit for seven three-hour exams. Notes were stuck to the walls of my small dorm room by the river. Flow charts and mock exam questions hung precariously with round globs of Blue-Tack. There was no way I could leave now.

But I knew I had to go. *Water* was an unfinished piece of my own life. Maybe it had less to do with the film than with her, with all the things left unsaid between us. I watched as the rain continued to fall lightly on the surface of the river. Students rode their bikes across Folly Bridge, plastic shopping bags covering their seats to keep them dry.

"When are you making *Water*...and where? In India?" I asked, excited, and so afraid of being left out.

"After your exams are finished..." The line crackled.

"In Sri Lanka."

Sri Lanka

2004

12

From the window of the small propeller plane Adam's Bridge looked like a floating rib in the deep blue body of the Indian Ocean. The 29-kilometre-long geographical strip of land that connected India and Sri Lanka was no more than a sandbar, a wasteland, and the route through which anthropologists believe early Hindu Tamils migrated from India to Sinhalese Buddhist Lanka thousands of years earlier. It was a migration that would lead to a violent twentieth-century civil war between the minority Tamil population in the north and northeast of the island, who believed they were oppressed by the majority Sinhalese in the south. Sri Lanka was seventy-four percent Sinhalese and eighteen percent Tamil, and the rest of the population was made up of small Muslim and Christian communities. The tension began building during the 1950s, post–Sri Lankan independence from colonial rule in 1948. In 1956 the Sri Lankan government passed the Sinhala Only Act, making Sinhalese the official national language, and immediately began to exclude Tamils from positions of power. In the 1970s, two more acts of legislation continued to cause Tamil unrest. One limited Tamil numbers in universities, and the other placed Buddhism as the foremost religion of Sri Lanka.

The twin propellers of Lion Air flight 702 from Colombo, Sri Lanka's capital, to the northern city of Jaffna hummed through the cabin. I looked past Mark Burton, our new American executive producer, to Mom. Her hair was neatly straightened and her face beamed. She sat on the other side of the aisle talking with Asoka, a representative of Film Location Services Sri Lanka, our local guides and producers. With a little more than four weeks left before shooting, we had the time and the opportunity to fly north.

It was March 7, 2004, eleven months since we spoke on the phone in Oxford, and four years since *Water* was shut down in India. I had arrived in Colombo two days earlier, at three in the morning when the sky was still filled with stars. I had never been to Sri Lanka, and it was the first thing I noticed. One could rarely see the stars in Delhi. Colombo was on the west coast of the island, and the tropical heat wrapped around me in the airport, a building open to lush palms and fragrant frangipani trees. There was none of the cold white marble of north India.

The road to the hotel was lined with one-stop supermarkets, their shiny cash registers and multiple checkout aisles visible through polished plate glass, Honda motorcycle dealerships, and furniture stores selling puffed-up couches. Even in the middle of the night Sri Lanka appeared, at least on the surface, a less poor country than India. It also had a population of about twenty million, one-fiftieth the size of India's one billion.

I wondered if our time together would be peaceful, or once again haunted by politics and personal history. I looked back out the oval window at Adam's Bridge. The double layer of plastic reflected the South Asian morning sun, dusty and warm. It was unbelievable. We were on the verge of embarking on a journey I believed dead for so long. The world rarely afforded second chances. The excitement and anticipation I felt came from deep inside, from a small box labelled and safely stored in the recesses of memory, its contents full of both pain and pleasure. Our passage was geographical as much as it was the passage of time. A narrow strip of land away from India. Close enough to see the bleached coastline of the south Indian state of Tamil Nadu, far enough to hopefully guarantee our safety.

The BJP were still in power in India under Prime Minister Atal Behari Vajpayee. And as we flew toward Jaffna, the Tamil capital in the north of the island, they were in the midst of one of the most expensive and elaborate political campaigns India had ever seen—the India Shining campaign, estimated at a cost of US$100 million. India's general elections were in two months. Their main opposition was the secular Congress Party, under the leadership of Sonia Gandhi. On May 12 the world's largest democracy would vote.

But we couldn't take the chance that a new government would come into power. Hindutva and the RSS were still going strong. Only two months earlier original historical manuscripts were burned at a research library in Pune, Maharashtra. The Bhandarkar Oriental Research Institute was attacked by the Sambhaji Brigade, a Hindu right group who believed that the American professor using them for research for a book on the seventeenth-century Hindu king Shivaji was misrepresenting Indian history. Oxford University Press had to withdraw the book from the local market.

Sri Lanka was the perfect alternative location. The lush foliage and rivers could pass for rural India without the threat of the Hindu right. In the years after we had returned to Canada, Mom had searched for alternatives to India when she discovered Sri Lanka boasted a small, efficient infrastructure for film production.

The money had to be raised from scratch after the losses of Benares. David and Mom had to buy her script back from Ajay, who owned the rights as part of having financed the first attempt to make the film. In the end it was the Canadian government, through Telefilm Canada, a film funding body, that provided the largest investment in the project. Their decision to support *Water* was the beginning of a new way for Canada to support its artists. Telefilm's mandate would only allow them to fund films made in one of Canada's two official languages, French or

English. Recently the policy was extended to include Aboriginal languages. This narrow criterion ignored the reality of the country. Canada is a country of immigrants. Although they required that we shoot an English version of the film alongside the Hindi, they supported *Water*, a film set in India, beginning to embrace a new definition of what it meant to be Canadian.

David had spent the summer at his computer, working and reworking the budget. He found the final piece of funding through Mark Burton, a Los Angeles–based producer, who introduced him to Doug Mankoff, owner of Echo Lake Productions, with whom David formed a partnership to close the funding gap. Financing independent film was like sewing a quilt. Instead of piecing together squares of cloth, David sat late into the night in our basement in Toronto, the only light from the glow of his laptop, sewing together pieces of funding.

Our budget, $5.7 million Canadian, would allow for only forty-five days of filming, a short schedule in an industry where the Hollywood average was ninety days. Despite filming outside of India, a sliver of land away from the political fray, the crew would be required to sign a confidentiality clause, forbidding them to speak about the film to any media. Also, we would no longer be making *Water*. Language elicits memory, and there was no room for risk. Before leaving for Sri Lanka, David suggested that Mom change the name to *Full Moon*, an innocuous, almost silly-sounding title that hopefully nobody would question.

The small propeller plane began its slow descent into Jaffna. The land below the window was arid and desolate, more like a savannah than the rich tropical lushness I had seen in and around Colombo. We had been warned not to go. Jaffna was one of the bases of the LTTE, the Liberation Tigers of Tamil Eelam, or the Tamil Tigers, who had been fighting a guerrilla war against the Sinhalese government and Sri Lankan army for an independent Tamil state in the north of the island.

If secession ever occurred, the state would be named Eelam, Tamil for "precious land." Although there had been a formal ceasefire since February 2002, negotiated with the help of Norway, war had raged in the north and northeast of the island for almost thirty years. There were over 60,000 dead on both sides, over 300,000 internally displaced persons and many more refugees scattered across the globe. Sri Lanka's future was about to take another turn. In less than one month, on April 2, Sri Lanka would vote for a new president. The two main candidates had very different views on the war. Chandrika Kumaratunga, the incumbent president and head of the People's Alliance (PA), took a hardline position against the Tigers, while Ranil Wickremasinghe, head of the United National Party (UNP), and prime minister under Kumaratunga, was instrumental in reviving the peace process with the help of the Norwegians.

The plane touched down on a narrow strip of ashen tarmac. The memories of Benares were still with me, but they had changed with time and experience. The rawness had faded, and the experiences had combined with my love of anthropology to give me a new perspective on what had happened—that national identity and nationalism are complex, and people will go to extreme lengths to define it. It was a perspective that I would soon find had relevance for Sri Lanka.

I stepped down onto the runway. It sizzled in the heat. Although only morning, the sun was relentless in an empty blue sky. There was almost nothing near the airstrip, only two mottled puppies playing in the red earth and a dilapidated bus, waiting off to one side. The flight attendant, a young Sinhalese woman with chocolate skin and pretty features, told us that the bus would take us to a terminal. Friends and relatives would meet us there. The bus was badly rusted, as if no one bothered with maintenance. I stepped up toward the driver. A yellow banner with gold fringe hung across the front windshield. In the centre was a small altar with pictures of Hindu gods and goddesses.

I sat down next to Mom on a narrow plastic seat. She wore her round Lennon sunglasses and looked out over the deserted fields surrounding the airstrip. She wasn't smoking in an effort to be healthy before beginning to shoot. I was proud of her. Tamil music blared over the sound system. The language was so different from Hindi. It was round and hard, each syllable like a red rubber ball bouncing off the ground.

The bus pulled off the airstrip and onto an uneven dirt road. The trees and shrubs on either side baked in the sun. There were no houses and the land was perfectly flat. I turned to look at the rest of the passengers. Other than Mark, Asoka, Mom, and I, they were mostly older Tamil men and women. The women wore saris, round gold earrings, and nose rings. The men wore cotton shirts and sarongs. They had ash freshly smeared across their foreheads from a visit to a Hindu temple before leaving Colombo—a daily ritual of blessing, like Holy Communion. It was still morning, and the sweat of the day had yet to wash it away.

The bus turned sharply off the dirt road and into a clearing. The terminal was the first building I saw in Jaffna, a low, white-washed bungalow with a slanting corrugated iron roof. Parked on the red earth beside it were two UNHCR (United Nations High Commission for Refugees) Jeeps, the only white and pristine things on the landscape. Everywhere else men and women were dressed in deep combat green and shin-high black boots—the Sri Lankan army. The civil war had spurred one of the largest exoduses of refugees from South Asia. At its height, in the 1980s, hundreds of thousands of Sri Lankans from in and around Jaffna had fled to the U.K., the U.S., and Canada.

My only knowledge of war came from books and movies, but I guessed that airports were one of the most important things to control in warfare. The Tigers had bombed Colombo International Airport and the adjoining military airbase in 2001. Eleven aircraft had been destroyed, and the nine Tamil Tigers who had executed the attack were killed. One of the stipulations of the ceasefire was that the Sri Lankan army, made up of mostly poor young Sinhalese men and women, would occupy and police Jaffna. Hindutva seemed light in comparison.

It was Sunday, and after we were met by Asoka's driver in his minivan, the ride toward Jaffna felt like a Sunday drive. There was the same quiet, sunny stillness as the minivan ambled along narrow rural roads. Only as we neared the city did another layer of the landscape become apparent. Countless shelled buildings lined the road from the airport, their colonial façades pockmarked with bullet holes. They looked like pieces of crumbling cake.

A young soldier flagged us to a stop. His post was surrounded by chain-link fence wrapped in barbed wire. It was the first of a handful of army checkpoints. A female soldier stood near the hood of the van, gun in hand, while another soldier opened the sliding door. I didn't feel intimidated when he looked at us, Mom and I sitting side by side in the back seat. It didn't feel like it did on the Shantiniketan Express, Mom silent and despondent, me afraid for our safety as the Bengali soldier looked at us through the glass compartment door. I was nineteen then, twenty-four now. And the hard truth I had to tell myself was that this wasn't our war. The dark brown eyes set deep in the Sinhalese face weren't looking to protect an idea of India. They were looking for Tigers.

The soldier shut the door and waved us past. As the minivan neared Jaffna, signs of civilian life, almost non-existent on the road from the airport, became visible. Young girls rode bicycles along the edges of the pavement, one hand on a handlebar, the other holding a black umbrella to shade themselves from the sun.

We passed a grove of trees bound with yellow police tape. There was a hand-painted sign nailed to one of the thin trees— Tamil letters and a skull and crossbones.

"Asoka, what's that?" I leaned forward toward the passenger seat.

"Did you see the Danish crew on the flight?" he asked.

"No."

I hadn't noticed the Danish de-mining crew who had flown in with us, and had no idea when we landed that the north and northeast has an estimated two million undetonated land mines. We turned a corner and passed a large bungalow. The blue sign hanging over the door was in English and Tamil, with a faded white dove painted in one corner. It was a factory producing prosthetic limbs.

"Just don't walk off the roads," Asoka advised, as the mini-van continued into the city.

There was an army bunker on every street corner in the centre of town. Sri Lankan soldiers huddled behind sandbags, with only their eyes and the barrels of their guns visible through the bunkers' narrow slits. We passed small shops on the side of the road. Their walls were made of woven palm fronds, dried a yellow-brown, and they had thatch roofs. The buildings that still stood were old and scarred by bullets. There were no neon signs, no new cars, no Honda dealerships, and no one-stop supermarkets with shiny glass windows. Jaffna was an hour's flight away from Colombo, but we had travelled back in time to the Ceylon of fifty years ago. Other than the construction of a new library—a strange neo-colonial structure that seemed to rise grandly out of a deserted field—the city was almost devoid of infrastructure. No one invests in a war zone.

Mom asked if there was a market we could go to. Asoka talked to the driver, and we pulled to the side of the road in front of an open-air market. I tentatively walked in and among the rows of vendors, aware that we were the only tourists I had seen since arriving in Jaffna. But the women selling bananas and vegetables laid out on blue tarpaulin on the ground just smiled and asked where we had come from.

I bought a wooden *hopper* maker from a man wearing a colourful sarong and plain button-down shirt, the uniform of most men I would see in Sri Lanka. I had heard someone mention *hoppers* before I arrived, but had no idea what they were. I thought they were fried string beans. But like rice, rotis, potatoes, and tortillas, *hoppers* were just the accompanying starch in the Sri Lankan diet, round, thick pancakes cooked in a wok-like pan and served with curry or *dal*.

Asoka took us to lunch at one of the only guesthouses left in Jaffna. The drive took us past empty fields, the tall grasses parched and flattened by the wind.

"All of this used to be built up," Asoka said, looking out over the fields.

I began to notice the foundations of buildings, swallowed by the yellow grass. It had once been the centre of town; now, it was a wasteland. The driver pulled to a stop.

"Look." Asoka pointed out the window toward one of the barren spaces. In the middle of a field, surrounded by broken concrete, was a building. Only its façade was left standing, riddled with bullet holes and the gouges left by shellfire, so you could see the field behind. The remnants of a sign clung to the building like a child to its mother. The Regal, once Jaffna's only English-language movie theatre. Benares had taught me about the fragility of freedom of speech. Jaffna taught me that war was the ultimate silencer.

Our van pulled up to the white colonial guesthouse. It was a bungalow with a curved verandah, black-and-white-tiled floor, and planter's chairs. The guesthouse reminded me of the district magistrate's residence in Benares, and the night we had spent protesting on its floor. It also made me aware of Sri Lanka's own colonial history, shared, in succession, between the Portuguese, Dutch, and British, unlike India, which was ruled almost exclusively by the British for more than 200 years. The guesthouse was British colonial, the last European rulers of Ceylon. They left in 1948, one year after Indian independence.

A half-dozen dishes of food were spread over the dining room table just inside the verandah. The curries were spicier than anything I had ever tasted, spicier than Indian food. Mom, who always reached for raw green chilies when we ate in Benares, made no motion for them now. The cook, a middle-aged woman wearing an apron, invited us to lie down in one of the rooms after lunch. She escorted Mom and me to a large room in the front of the house. Asoka and Mark went out onto the verandah to smoke cigars and drink shandy. For a moment we were reliving a piece of colonial history in that British bungalow in Jaffna—the men going out to smoke while the women retired from the midday sun.

The room was airy and sparse. Other than twin beds and a dressing table, there was no decoration among the high ceilings and whitewashed walls. A rickety wooden fan spun slowly on the ceiling. Mom lay down on the bed nearest to the door. I looked out over the verandah as Asoka and Mark sipped their drinks. Neither of them really knew what had happened in Benares. They knew through reports in the BBC and *Daily Variety*, through word of mouth. But neither knew what we knew, the visceral fear that accompanies seeing something die. I lay down on the other bed.

"Mom?"

"Hmmm?" She lay on her side with her eyes closed. The fan blew strands of hair gently across her face.

"Do you think I'll be okay?"

I had felt this before, a panic that rose like a wave in moments of silence, or when I was alone with her. It was like an addiction. I craved my mother's reassurance. But the hit would never be enough. Can one be addicted to soothing words?

"Yes, you're fine." She didn't open her eyes, her own senses dulled by the repetition of my question.

I turned over and looked at the long white curtains. They almost touched the cracked tile floor, suspended, with just a few inches between them. *A few inches between them.*

I closed my eyes and tried to sleep.

Asoka knocked at the door. The sun seemed less harsh as it shone across the tiles. Mom was already up and putting on her sandals.

"Come, I'm going to take you somewhere you'll find interesting," he said.

We piled into the van and drove through Jaffna's residential neighbourhoods under the mid-afternoon sun. It felt less intimidating than the centre of town. There were fewer bunkers at the intersections, and the houses were either new or didn't bear the architectural scars of war. Most of the homes were bungalows, surrounded by low garden walls. The houses began to thin out, and we were once again driving across a flat, dry, rural landscape. The driver pulled off the main road onto a long driveway. In the distance was a large wrought-iron gate painted a burning white. It came into focus as the van drew closer. The gate was more than three-metres high, and the shape of two large rifles were worked into the design, one on either side, mirroring each other in perfect symmetry. Behind it were hundreds of rows of gravestones, baking in the afternoon sun. The Tamil Tiger cemetery.

I pulled open the sliding door and Mom and I stepped out onto the gravel. The gates were open, and the only signs of life were two men in a small guardhouse behind it. Asoka led us through. There seemed to be no problem; we were the only ones there.

Countless graves of cadres who had fallen for Eelam lay in immaculately maintained rows. The gravestones were low and simple, painted a washed-out blue. They were the graves of both men and women. After the loss of nearly 20,000 soldiers in the 1990s, the LTTE started conscripting women and children to fight for the cause. They were trained in guerrilla warfare, side by side with the men.

As I walked through the rows I wondered if the bodies were cremated. They were Tamil, and mostly Hindu, and would have gone through a ritual similar to what I had seen at Manikarnika *Ghat* in Benares—wood and camphor and *ghee*.

I knelt next to one of the headstones, flat and smooth. The grass was soft beneath my knees. These people had died for an identity greater than their individual selves. They had killed and died for an "imaginary homeland," an idea of a nation that didn't exist—an Eelam, their "precious land." Sri Lankan and Indian nationalism seemed to work on the same principles. Maybe all forms of nationalism did, regardless of culture.

The Tiger flag flew from a metal pole near the gate. Its imagery was both frightening and determined—a red-eyed tiger emerging from a ring of bullets, two rifles crossed behind it, all on a deep red background. Mom wanted to get one to take home. I understood her desire. Other than being strangely beautiful, it was a symbol of the lengths people go to for a nation. But the guards refused. The sun was beginning to dip in the sky, and our flight back to Colombo would be departing soon. But Asoka had one more idea of how to find a flag.

We drove back to town and into the small grid of streets of a residential neighbourhood. A woman carried a bag full of fruits and vegetables home from the market; a bunch of bananas threatened to fall onto the dusty road. The driver pulled up in front of one of the houses. The wall in front of this one was higher. Asoka told us to wait in the car, opened the door, and disappeared behind the wall.

We waited in the van as the engine revved beneath us. In a way we were the ultimate voyeurs, moving through a wounded world behind the safety of Plexiglas. After a few moments, Asoka stuck his head out from behind the wall and waved us in.

The gate opened into a garden courtyard. Mark held his digital camera. Asoka motioned for us to come into a small room off the garden. It was poorly lit, and there was a wooden desk at the back of the room. A man in a dark green uniform greeted us and invited us to sit on three plastic chairs placed under the window. The room smelled musty, although it was neatly kept. There was care in the simple placement of the chairs and the desk, as if someone wished to create a clean public face. Through Asoka's translation, we were welcomed into a political office of the Liberation Tigers of Tamil Eelam.

As Asoka explained to the cadre that we were a film crew from India and wished to take back a Tiger flag, I thought about how the south Indian state of Tamil Nadu was one of the main sources of Tiger support. The Tigers had set up training camps and safe houses in the state, and the Tamil community was supposedly a major source of financial support for the movement, like the Tamil diaspora in other countries, including Canada.

I looked around the room. Mom sat with her legs crossed and Mark played with his camera, but didn't take photographs. There were posters on the wall. Each one carefully framed behind a thin sheet of glass. There was an image of a cadre in green uniform with a thick moustache that dipped below the edge of his lips. The photo was of Velupillai Prabhakaran, the founder of the LTTE. After a few minutes Asoka turned to us and apologized. It wouldn't be possible. The cadre behind the desk seemed genuinely sorry not to help; they just didn't give out flags to passing tourists.

As we stood to leave, a young female soldier walked in from the garden. When she noticed us she stood shyly in the doorframe. Her body was thin-boned and small, no more than five feet. Her dark green army pants were cinched tightly to her waist by a black canvas belt, and her black hair was arranged in two braids pinned to her head. I looked at her eyes, warm and soft against her even brown skin. But it wasn't her eyes that I remembered vividly. She was wearing sandals, and when I glanced down I was shocked to see that her right leg was made of plastic.

13

The Colombo Plaza Hotel was like an oasis after Jaffna. The cool marble lobby, an atrium filled with plush settees and colourful oil paintings of tropical birds, spoke of a wealth that the wartorn north never had a chance to develop. A marble fountain trickled just inside the entrance, the water lit from lamps submerged just below the surface. Two little Sinhalese girls, dressed in matching pink frocks, sat on the edge of the fountain, whispering to each other and dipping their fingers in the water. Sinhala was different from Tamil. Michael Ondaatje described the round, symbol-like letters of the alphabet as "washed blunt glass which betray no jaggedness." The little girls' whispers reminded me of his description.

The hotel would be our home over the next two and a half months. It was in central Colombo, facing Galle Road, the main highway from Colombo to southern Sri Lanka. We were a few doors away from the prime minister's residence and across the street from the Indian Ocean. It was much fancier than Clarks, where we had stayed in Benares. It also housed our production office—five converted rooms in the old wing of the hotel. Mom had a suite on the eighth floor. Unlike the Vaibhav, I was going to stay in an apartment building attached to the hotel, sharing it with five production assistants. The crew had already begun to reconvene, and people would continue to arrive until we started shooting twelve days later.

Not everyone had made it back. The cast had changed almost completely since that day when Mom, Shabana Azmi, and Nandita Das protested in the district magistrate's residence in

Benares. Mom met with Nandita in the living room of my grand-parents' house in Delhi. But it had been four years since Benares, and although she was still an unequivocal beauty, she no longer possessed the deep innocence needed for the charac-ter of Kalyani, the beautiful young widow. Neither did Nandita possess the age and experience needed to play the embittered character of Shakuntala, the middle-aged widow hardened by a life of self-denial. Nandita fell between the two, and Mom's deci-sion not to cast her cost them their friendship. Kalyani would be played by Lisa Ray, the star of *Bollywood/Hollywood*, who had taken time off from drama school in London to do the role.

Mom also felt that Shabana's high profile might endanger the secrecy Sri Lanka offered, and one of the conditions of getting the script back from Ajay, and receiving a bond guarantee, was not to cast her. Ajay had the Indian rights for distribution and feared her presence in the film might scare off Indian exhibitors. Shabana was in the media spotlight, not only as an actress but as a political activist and former member of the Indian parliament. Instead, Shakuntala would be played by Seema Biswas, a fine actress from the northeastern Indian state of Assam, whose roots were in theatre. Seema had starred as Phoolan Devi, one of India's most notorious female bandits, in the art-house film *Bandit Queen*.

We walked past the fountain toward the elevators, tired after our day in Jaffna. A man in a white shirt stood next to the pol-ished brass doors. As soon as we approached, he pushed the Up button. Mom stood with shopping bags in her hands, kitchen-ware from the market in Jaffna. I looked around the pristine lobby, the polished elevator doors, the faces, South Asian but dif-ferent from the familiarity of India, and felt a sense of peace associated with the film that I'd never felt before.

The elevator door opened, and Seema stepped out. We had not met formally. Mom put down her shopping bags and intro-duced us. *Full Moon* would be the first time they would work together. I shook her hand. She was beautiful, a small woman in her mid-thirties with strong features, dark brown skin, and eyes that flashed with honesty and an incredible depth of spirit. Bollywood had never really given her a break. She was always cast in supporting roles, but never a leading woman in an industry obsessed with fair skin and model good looks.

"A pleasure to have met you, Seema*ji*." I instinctively used the honorific *ji* when we said our goodbyes.

Mom and I got into the plush elevator.

"I have something to show you upstairs." She smiled excitedly.

"What?"

But she just smiled, and for a moment I was transported back to Benares and the excitement I felt when she played A.R. Rahman's music for the first time, sitting on the yellow couch in her room.

I thought of Seema's non-Bollywood beauty and training in theatre as we walked to Mom's suite at the end of the corridor. She came from a very different background from the actor who was to play Narayan, a young romantic idealist and Kalyani's love interest. Mom had been at a loss about casting Narayan. The solution came from my grandmother.

Nani found him on a Bollywood movie channel beamed into the dark green living room of their Delhi home. She had been sipping asparagus soup at dinner in front of the television with my grandfather when a music video for the film *Jism* came on. A handsome man looked longingly at a beautiful woman as they chased each other across a perfect white sand beach. *Jism* means "body," and the film was in fact an Indian rip-off of *Body Heat*. Although the actor was clearly a sex symbol, *Nani* saw some sensitivity behind the muscle. She suggested Mom consider him for Narayan. John Abraham, a rising Bollywood star and former male model, was cast a week later.

Mom opened the door to the suite. It was spacious, a corner room with a living room, dining room, and a view of the sea. I could see my apartment from the large plate-glass windows. It was strange to be standing in a different country, at a different moment in history, but in a way repeating yourself. Giles would be arriving in a few days, fresh from shooting *Bee Season* with Richard Gere and Juliette Binoche in California, and then I would join the camera department once again. A job I had left unfinished four years earlier. I was excited to work with him as third assistant cameraperson, but then some part of me felt past all of that.

Mom switched on the lights in the small dining room. It was completely filled by a round wooden table and four chairs. The lamps from the room were reflected in the large glass window.

"I found her." Mom stood near the round table.

"Found who?" I was staring at the window, preoccupied by the reflections in the glass.

"Chuyia."

She motioned me toward her. On the wall dividing the living and dining room was a bulletin board.

"I got my assistant to put it up while we were in Jaffna."

It was the same thing I had helped put up in Benares, a dull brown bulletin board with a cheap wooden frame. But it was more than that. It was her world of characters made alive through images. Seema, Lisa, and John—Shakuntala, Kalyani, and Narayan—were pinned carefully next to reference photos of Benares. The prayer ceremony on the *ghats*, images of women bathing in the Ganges in their saris, and the *galis*, alive with the flow of human traffic. They were colour photocopies from photography books, the work of photojournalists such as Steve McCurry and the late Raghubir Singh. It was like looking at the blueprint of a world that didn't exist yet. I felt overwhelmed, a powerful bittersweet happiness. We had lost something four years ago, but we were on the verge of gaining something new.

"This is Chuyia." Mom pointed to a poor-quality colour print-out of a little girl. She was laughing, her eyes squinting in the sun. She wore a summer dress with thin straps, and two pigtails fell over her small brown shoulders.

"Her name is Sarala." Mom beamed.

I had watched Mom scan videotape after videotape of auditions before arriving in Sri Lanka. A casting director in Bombay had interviewed countless little girls and sent the tapes to Canada, but none of them had been right for the role. Urvi, who had played Chuyia in Benares, was now twelve years old and too big for the part. Chuyia, the eight-year-old child-widow, had to embody the innocence of a child and yet be full of life—the antithesis of what a Hindu widow should be.

Sarala was from a suburb of Galle, four hours south of Colombo. Mom had seen her in an audition tape of twenty girls made after a Colombo-wide casting call. But when Sarala arrived in Colombo for the audition, they found a shy little Sinhalese girl who spoke only Sinhala, and no Hindi or English. Sinhala had completely different linguistic roots from Hindi. It was much closer to the languages of south India with their Dravidian roots than the Indo-Aryan languages of north India and Persia. She entered the hotel room and sat quietly, flanked by her mother and aunt, two long braids falling over her red dress.

Mom was disappointed, but since Sarala and her family had driven four hours to see them, Mom decided to test her with one of Chuyia's harder scenes, when she is left at the *ashram* by her *Baba*, or father.

Sarala listened to Mom explain the scene through a Sinhala translator. Direction through translation; it was a crazy idea. But as soon as the translator finished, Sarala immediately stood up, grabbed his legs as if he were *Baba*, and began crying, telling him not to leave her. She spoke in Sinhala, but language seemed inconsequential. She possessed the spirit of Chuyia.

Sarala and her mother had already moved into an apartment on the floor above mine. While I admired her small face on the print-out, she was in the midst of learning the Hindi script phonetically with the help of a tutor. It was a language she had never spoken, but when her tutor, Kay, asked her why she found it so easy, Sarala credited her love of Hindi film songs. Chuyia was found.

I said goodnight to Mom and walked back to the apartment. The lobby was nearly empty. Two men in suits sat on the settees and talked while a local band crooned Celine Dion songs in a cocktail lounge just off the lobby. Tealights lit the dim lounge. The lead singer wore a sequined red chemise, her brown hair cascading down her back. There was no one in the bar as she passionately hit the high notes of "My Heart Will Go On." I felt bad for her, singing without an audience. The waiters stood politely at attention, but looked like they had heard it one too many times.

The apartment had three bedrooms, a kitchen, and a living room with a balcony. The production assistants hadn't arrived yet, and the apartment was empty except for me and my mother's new assistant, Vasant. Vasant and I were the same age, and good friends. I had met him first in Delhi, where he studied literature at Delhi University before doing a second degree in politics at Cambridge. He loved film, and wanted to direct. He had the energy of a ten-year-old, enthusiastic and eager to please. I could talk with him, and we chose bedrooms next to each other.

But the apartment was dark when I opened the door. Vasant was probably working late in the production office, making changes to the script. Mom had mentioned wanting to simplify the script. *Simplify. Shed.* Thin the dialogue and let the images speak for themselves. It was as if she were letting go of the thin skin of sadness she wore below the surface, peeling it away layer by layer.

I switched on the hall light and went into my bedroom. It was the biggest room in the apartment. It had a large closet, bathroom, and two single beds, each with its own bedside table and lamp. I would be sharing it with Avani, the young woman who would take care of the cast in the assistant director's department. She would be arriving from Delhi in a few days. I had convinced Vasant that the girls needed the bigger room. There was no real reason why. I had just liked the bigger windows, with the view of the driveway curving in from Galle Road to the lobby and the green landscaping that framed it.

I turned on the small bedside lamp and closed the curtains, shutting out the world from the empty, impersonal room. I placed a few things on the bedside table to create a sense of home. There was a photo of my mom and dad, happy and smiling with their arms around each other. It was taken in the early 1970s, on a street in Montreal, or possibly New York. I placed it in a simple silver picture frame, the only photo I had of them together. I also had a small silver statue of the god Shiva that my *Nani* had given me, and a miniature stone Shiv lingam, like the ones I had first learned about in the *galis* of Benares. *Creation and destruction combined.*

The sheets were cold when I got into bed. A copy of *Full Moon* sat on the floor beside the night table. Brett and Jasmine hadn't come back for the second attempt. Instead, two women from Canada would assist Giles and teach me. I was sad not to see Jasmine and Brett. I had never forgotten Jasmine's patience as she taught me about lenses in the back of the camera truck in Benares. The two Canadian women hadn't arrived yet, but I had already received an e-mail from the first assistant cameraperson asking me if I could find a plastic trolley for the camera gear. The e-mail was quick and impersonal. I don't think she even signed it.

I looked at the miniature Shiv lingam, curved and full, despite its size. I had what I wanted—a job camera assisting and a degree. But something felt vacant, and lacked a spark I remembered.

THE LOBBY WAS BUSY as I walked to the production office the next morning. I passed the fountain and the lounge where the waiters had stood at attention, and through a small corridor, which connected the new wing to the old one. A group of European men and women stood talking near the fountain. I overheard strains of Spanish and French, and noticed one of them had a bag printed with the EU symbol, twelve gold stars in a complete circle. I wondered who they were.

I bumped into Dolly as I turned the corner from the corridor into the old wing. She was just the same, wearing a simple, yet tasteful, *salwaar kameez* and flowing *dupatta*. She gave me a big hug.

"You must come down and see wardrobe."

"Where is it?" I noticed she was holding a call sheet, the schedule for our first day of filming.

"In the basement of the new wing, near the Cheers pub."

I promised I would visit.

All of our original costumes were useless. Dolly and her team had to completely redo the entire wardrobe of the film, from the widows' white saris to the period brocade of Narayan's mother, Bhagwati. The originals had been placed carefully in metal trunks in a storage space in Delhi. But four years later, it was discovered that the storage space had leaked. All of her Benares research—silks, dyed cottons, and saris—had practically disintegrated, leaving only a greenish mush.

The old wing was built in the seventies, and all the floors overlooked an atrium with a raised area on the first floor, which was rented out for functions and conventions. There was a study-abroad convention on at the moment. Booths were set up advertising technical degrees in Malaysia, and how to get a BA from a Canadian university. Sri Lankan students milled about with backpacks slung over their shoulders, collecting papers and pamphlets and stuffing them into their bags.

Our offices were relatively quiet. Pearl, our Sri Lankan office manager, was busy confirming pickups from the airport, as the rest of the international crew would be arriving within the next couple of days. She had brown hair cut just below her ears and wore round gold earrings. During filming, it would be Pearl and the production team in the office who would hold fort while we shot at a handful of locations in and around Colombo. I looked at a big white travel board behind one of the desks. It showed the arrival dates of cast and crew, and our first day of shooting, written in blue marker. Dylan would be arriving tomorrow from Goa, where he just finished working on the *Bourne Supremacy* with Matt Damon. I had last seen him after we arrived back from Nepal.

Outside the production office window guests swam in the hotel's pristine blue swimming pool, shaped like the Red Cross symbol. I looked around the production office, at files and scripts and schedules. We had set all of this up before. What made us think that a plush hotel and four years' distance from India would protect us or allow the Hindu right to forget? We were still only a land bridge away.

"Pearl, what do you think will happen with the Sri Lankan elections?" I asked.

She looked up from her computer.

"I think Wickremasinghe will win." She seemed confident. "People are tired of the war."

Prime Minister Wickremasinghe's photograph was plastered all over Colombo as the UNP geared up to challenge President Kumaratunga in Sri Lanka's often volatile elections. The president had run Sri Lanka for seven years under the People's

Alliance. She had a glass eye, having lost it when a Tamil Tiger suicide bomber attempted to assassinate her in December 1999 at her last campaign rally before the general elections. The suicide bomber was a woman fighting for Eelam. We had been lucky in Benares.

I picked up the first day's call sheet and checked the camera department's mailbox for any changes to the script or memos, but there was nothing there. I walked back to the apartment. Students were still searching for the perfect education, their footsteps and queries making a low din in the atrium of the old wing, a benign background to the comings and goings of the Colombo Plaza. David approached me near the stairs leading down to the breakfast room. He had aged since Benares. The hair above his ears had gone from brown to grey, and his face was heavily lined. It was as if the injustice of Benares had left its physical mark.

"I have a proposal for you."

"What is it?" I thought he might want me to do some extra work in the office before the camera department arrived.

"How would you feel about doing the stills photography for the film?" The sound of the students' footsteps echoed through the atrium. He must have made a mistake.

"What do you mean, 'stills photography'?"

"I mean we don't have a photographer yet, and we thought you would do a good job," David said.

It was impossible. The responsibility. All the images to be used in press kits, film reviews, the poster—the visual representation of the film in photographs. I remembered the first time I knelt down with a camera at the fish market in Turkey—the naked light bulbs against the watery darkness of the Bosphorus, the blood-stained cardboard, and my father, encouraging me to move in closer with my uncle Dilip's old hand-me-down Canon F-1. Encouraging me not to be afraid.

But I hadn't picked up a camera since Benares, since Assi *Ghat*. Since Vikram. David was waiting.

"I need a day to think about it."

"Okay. Come by my office when you've decided." David walked past me to the elevators, and the din from the convention once again filled my ears.

What about Giles? But then wasn't this the opportunity I was looking for? The opportunity to avoid repeating what I had already done. I wanted to talk about it with Mom.

The elevator operator pushed the Up button as soon as he saw me walking toward him. There was already someone inside, a large man wearing a navy blue blazer and khakis. He looked as if he was in his early fifties, with greying brown hair and pale white skin that seemed rosied and raw just below the surface. The European Union symbol, the twelve-star circle, was pinned to his lapel.

"Excuse me, what's the EU doing here?" I had been curious since I overheard the group speaking Spanish and French in the lobby.

"We're the EU elections observation mission." He spoke with a thick Irish accent.

The man pushed the button for the fourth floor. I pushed eight.

"We're hoping it goes smoothly, without the violence of previous years."

He reminded me that Sri Lanka's general election was only a few days away. The EU observation mission would monitor the election to make sure it passed democratically. Calling oneself a democracy was quite different from being one. I remembered our censorship in Benares, despite the full permission of the central BJP government. In 2000 and 2001 Prime Minister Wickremasinghe and President Kumaratunga had accused each other's parties of intimidating voters. There had been murders and thousands of reported cases of election violence.

He looked tired. A thick file of papers bulged out from underneath his arm.

"Where are you from?" I asked, curious about his accent.

"Belfast." He pulled a small white business card out of his jacket pocket. His name was printed in the centre, in fine black lettering.

John Cushnahan
Chief Observer
EU Election Observation Mission

It was embossed with the same EU symbol.

I had a friend from Northern Ireland in university. We had spent two weeks together in Ulster. He was Catholic, from Derry. I remembered walking with him through Derry's Catholic and Protestant neighbourhoods early on a Sunday morning before the streets were awake with people, before the church bells rang. The neighbourhoods were identical, down to the cheap housing with thin windows and plastic children's toys scattered on the front lawns. Identical except for the strong visual demarcation of territory—sidewalk curbs painted in the alternating red, white, and blue of the Union Jack on one side of the road, and orange, white, and green, the Irish tricolour, on the other. High walls, topped with barbed wire, loomed over the city. They surrounded the Royal Ulster Constabulary, the British law-enforcement presence in Northern Ireland, now renamed the Police Service of Northern Ireland in an attempt to appear more secular. It was similar to the Sri Lankan army in Jaffna—faces hidden behind green walls and sandbags. Even the IRA cemetery, on a hill overlooking Belfast, reminded me of the LTTE graveyard—rows upon rows of gravestones; one, volunteers fallen for a united Irish Republic, the other, cadres fallen for Eelam. Did the earth smell the same for them? Sweet with national pride, bitter with unrealized freedom.

The elevator door opened on the fourth floor, and John Cushnahan said goodbye, still fingering the thick file under his arm. There was a table covered with a maroon cloth just outside the elevator doors. A stack of in-box trays were placed at one end with a small sign reminding EU delegates to pick up their daily memos.

The door to Mom's suite was slightly ajar. I knocked quietly.

"Come in."

Sarala and Lisa were sitting on the floor, going through lines in the script. Mom was on the couch, directing the rehearsal with Sarala's tutor beside her, translating the direction into Sinhala. I closed the door behind me and waited until they finished. The sky was overcast, throwing a pale grey light into the room, across Lisa's and Sarala's faces, and Mom's collection of one hundred DVDs lined up neatly against the wall. The plastic spine of *Hiroshima Mon Amour* caught the grey light. When they took a break I went and sat next to Mom.

"David just asked me to do the stills for the film. Did you know about this?" I whispered, as Sarala and Lisa drank water and laughed.

"Yes, David told me."

"Did you have anything to do with it?" I asked.

"No, in fact, it was Dilip's idea. He thinks you have a great eye. David and Mark wouldn't have offered you the job if they didn't believe you could do it. There's too much at risk."

Dilip. He had taken a break from photojournalism to do the production design for the film. Mom trusted his eye, and felt he could make the look of the film come alive beautifully. But I still didn't know what to do. The potential responsibility weighed on me as much as it threatened to set me free.

I sat in the lounge and scribbled on a thin paper napkin the pros and cons of third assistant cameraperson versus stills photographer. The sun poured in through the windows as the waiters served afternoon tea to guests and Sri Lankan businessmen. I looked at my napkin, stained blue as the pen ink seeped through the fibre. There was only one thing under the pros of camera assisting—working with Giles. Under photography, there was everything.

DILIP OPENED THE DOOR. He was surrounded by a mess of papers, blueprints of the widows' house, swatches of upholstery fabric, and photography reference books he had brought from India. Sumant Jayakrishnan, the art director, was sitting at the table with his laptop, organizing lists of period furniture to be rented from local homes and stores.

A table
A chest of drawers
A 1930s gramophone

All the small details that go into making a script come alive.

"Come in, *beta*." Dilip spoke affectionately, and then turned back to his work.

"Do you want a cup of tea?" Packets of Ceylon tea were stuffed into a porcelain container on the desk. He began sorting through papers and reference photographs. Copies of *Time* and *Newsweek* were scattered among them, both magazines that he had shot for as a photojournalist.

"David asked me if I want to do the stills for the film." Dilip looked up from his papers.

"I said yes."

It was hard for me to tell him. I had always admired his work, but never felt I could talk to him about it. Those years away from India had created a distance between us, a barrier. I left him that day when I left Mom in Cannes.

"Good," he said.

"Thank you for your recommendation." I hesitated, awkward with the ties that gratitude infers.

He was looking at diagrams. I noticed they listed the exact distance, in feet, between funeral pyres on the Benares cremation grounds.

"Here, you'll need this." He placed a black camera on the desk. "And this." He pulled out a small white instruction manual for the Olympus E-20 digital camera. I had never shot on digital before. It had a lithium battery pack attached to the bottom and a fixed lens. I began to realize that my job had drastically changed in the course of one afternoon. We spent the next hour going through the camera functions together, as Sumant assembled the prop list.

A hackney carriage

A four-poster bed

Round-frame reading glasses for Gandhi

"Where do I begin?" I asked Dilip as he wrapped the Olympus in a white hand towel. Condensation would develop in the lens as it moved between the air-conditioned hotel and Sri Lanka's humidity if it didn't have a buffer. Dilip handed me the Olympus and placed both his hands on the edge of the desk.

"If I were you, I'd begin with the river."

PEARL ARRANGED A production car to meet me outside the lobby at seven the next morning. I carefully packed the Olympus in a white towel, and placed it in my small black backpack, now a camera bag. The dawn sky was wide and pink over Galle Road and the Indian Ocean appeared vast as its rough waters hit Sri Lanka's shoreline.

I sat in the back seat as the driver sped down the empty road heading south. Pearl told me that it would take the crew an hour to get to the location, but only forty-five minutes if we beat rush hour. The city was silent, except for the sound of birds and the occasional Muslim call for prayer. The deep-throated, mystical call was a sound I didn't associate with Sri Lanka, and a reminder of the country's small, but powerful, Muslim minority.

A BBC production team was poised to shoot Salman Rushdie's *Midnight's Children* in Sri Lanka in 1997 when the Muslim minority requested that the film be stopped as fallout from the controversy surrounding the author's novel, *The Satanic Verses*. The Sri Lankan government's decision forced the pre-production team to return to London after they had already begun to prepare the movie.

We passed off-track betting agencies, casinos, and gem shops. A neon horse and jockey flickered on a sign above the agent's, the horse's legs moving in animated gallop as the electric charge ignited neon gas passing through different tubes. The gem shops advertised sapphires and rubies for sale, with big photos of the cut stones placed on signs above the store. It reminded me that the name Ceylon was said to be a corruption of the word *Sihalam*, Pali for 'Place of Jewels.'

The streets began to stir as we passed through the suburb of Mount Lavinia and the small towns south of Colombo. Buildings were replaced by dense green rice paddies and lush palms. Vendors placed freshly cut lotus flowers on folding tables outside the entrance to a Buddhist temple—offerings for sale. I thought of how people buy candles at a church, or incense at a Hindu temple. Worshiping God costs. The deep pink blooms were still closed, picked as they slept that very morning.

The driver pulled off the main road near a rural photography studio. Pictures of Sinhalese couples in traditional wedding dress were plastered on plastic signboards and hung from the balcony railing. I wondered what happened to Sinhalese women when their husbands died. Did Buddhism prescribe a life of asceticism for them? The road curved past rural houses and thick banana groves. As the driver slowed on a turn, I noticed two old women walking along the edge of the road. They both wore white blouses and colourful sarongs. One of the women wore large gold earrings. They walked fast, balancing a shopping bag in each hand. Whether they were widowed or not, they were definitely active participants in society.

The car slowed to a stop at the end of a straight dirt road. I could see the glassy reflections of water less than a hundred metres away. Grabbing my camera bag I walked toward it. As I neared the water I saw the bare wooden back of a large structure, and heard the sound of hammering. It was the back of an enormous set. Sri Lankan construction workers and carpenters moved back and forth between a small white bungalow and the river, through a door cut into the massive wooden façade. I walked through, and was transported into another world.

A wide river stretched to an opposite bank covered with lush green foliage. The early morning sun reflected lightly off the water and illuminated a long bamboo fishing dam cutting across the river on a diagonal. But it wasn't the river that made me stop, frozen in wonder. It was what I was standing on.

Surrounding me, on the banks of a rural Sri Lankan river, was a Hindu temple town, constructed out of plywood, wire mesh, and concrete shaped like stone—the *ghats*. I was standing on six hundred metres of *ghats*. We had created our own mini-Benares an hour outside of Colombo, with a Sri Lankan river as our Ganges.

I started taking photos of the construction as workers spread fresh concrete on the steps, shaped them like stone, and aged them with spray paint. The façade blocked any view of the white bungalow and surrounding Sri Lankan countryside. It was just the *ghats* and the river. Carpenters worked on a large dome for a Hindu temple, sweating as they cut through the plywood. Even trees from the natural landscape were incorporated into the set.

I walked behind the set to the bungalow. A man was working at a large drafting table on the verandah, studying blueprints. He introduced himself as Errol Kelly, the master set builder who had created everything. Errol was the art director for *Indiana Jones and the Temple of Doom*'s Sri Lankan unit, under the direction of Steven Spielberg.

I introduced myself as Deepa's daughter, and looked over his shoulder at the plans, detailed sketches, and dimensions, chalked out in black ink and fine blue pencil. A temple, a boat station, the main washing *ghat*—all the places we had left behind in Benares. Through the door in the façade I could see a ferry crossing the river. It was built out of a piece of wood stretched over two red pontoons. An old woman and a man with his bicycle stood patiently as the ferryman rowed them across with a wooden paddle. There was a peaceful rhythm to this river, like the simple comings and goings of the ferry as it moved slowly from shore to shore. It was so unlike the chaos of the Ganges in Benares with its religion, and worn steps imbibed with spiritual meaning. I looked through the lens of the Olympus, and believed we had a chance.

The last of the international crew arrived later that evening, with only ten days left before we began filming. I lay in bed, unable to sleep. Avani had arrived, and the room now had the warmth of two bodies. Her clothes hung neatly next to mine in the closet, and our toothbrushes shared the same narrow ledge next to the sink. I looked at my alarm clock. It was eleven forty-five.

I woke up at seven. The sky was the same pale grey, streaked with pink, which seemed to herald all Sri Lankan mornings. Avani was still asleep, bundled in her grey blanket with her faced turned toward the window. We had decided to take the train to a beach an hour south of Colombo in our last few days off before filming.

The train had open windows and ran along tracks that paralleled the sea. The spray from the breakers left a fine layer of salt on our faces and hair.

Vasant, Avani, and I talked and laughed. We stood in the open doorway between carriages, as an old Sinhalese woman moved through selling shrimp patties out of a wicker basket balanced at the hip. A Sri Lankan university student practised his Hindi with us. He thought Vasant and I were an Indian couple. I felt I belonged.

We sat on the beach the whole day, and drank and ate and played volleyball until the sun set over the thatch huts and palms of Hikkaduwa, and our legs were covered in sand. The sky began to darken, so we walked along the beach until we found a guesthouse with cabins for rent. The owner gave me a thin metal key and pointed to cabin #1. The guesthouse dog, a German shepherd, had dug herself into a shallow hole near the door. She panted and tried to dig deeper to keep herself cool.

Listening to the sound of waves, I remembered the university student's mistake. *A couple. An Indian couple.* If I had that, maybe the threads of my life would knit together the way they had on the Vaibhav landing so many years earlier. I went to sleep dreaming of an idyllic world, down to the fine grains of sand that gathered between the sheets.

But when I woke up, the pale morning light was seeping in under the door. It fell across my face and reminded me that perhaps belonging might always elude me. Maybe that wasn't such a bad thing. I remembered a line that Shakuntala says in the script, "*sab maya hai.*" It's all an illusion.

I went out onto the beach. The sun hadn't risen, but the sky was already light. The cabins were dark, and the only sound was of the waves as I walked on the sand, smooth and untouched so early in the morning. The German shepherd was awake. She ran on the beach and lay down next to me on her haunches, close enough that I could smell the salt in her fur.

The sky warmed from grey to pink and then to orange. I hugged my knees and dug my toes into the sand, which was still cold from the night. A woman with a surfboard walked across the beach. She was Japanese. Far away, small black shapes drifted down the beach and into the water—surfers catching dawn waves. A few minutes later a young couple followed the path the woman had taken. They were also Japanese. She wore a brown bikini, and her short hair was neatly tied in pigtails. His black hair was spiked, and his back was covered in a large tattoo of angel wings. They walked hand in hand, balancing their surfboards under their arms.

14

Voting day arrived on April 2, 2004. Pearl was in the production office after she returned from the polls. She felt confident that Wickremasinghe would win and that the peace process would continue. What she was uncertain about was the possibility of post-election violence, and what it might mean for the film. I looked out at the pool. Guests swam and sipped drinks under a still afternoon sun. It was a perfect day, at least within the cloisters of the Colombo Plaza. The curfew was scheduled to begin at six p.m. and last until six p.m. the following day. With nothing for the crew to do, the producers had arranged a pool party in the evening. The little finger of Pearl's left hand was stained a deep purple. She noticed me staring at her finger.

"They do it to everyone who's voted—dip their finger in ink so they won't double-vote."

Pearl lifted her hand so I could see.

The crew gathered by the pool a few hours later. The light had faded until the sky was an even indigo. The polls would be closed by now. The hotel had opened a new bar under a pagoda. I walked up to the counter and ordered a drink.

"Devyani, I want to introduce you to someone." David stood at the bar with an attractive Sri Lankan couple. "This is Suresh and Mandy. We're using their home as the set for Narayan's house."

They were well dressed, and in their early forties. Suresh's hair was greying at the edges, but his face was sculpted and youthful. Mandy was petite, with gentle eyes.

"You went to Oxford, didn't you?" Suresh asked.

"Yes."

"So did I. I read maths at Christ Church College."

"I lived right behind Christ Church Meadows," I said, remembering the winter cold that left a light frost on the edges of the tall meadow grasses. I searched their faces.

"What will happen with these elections? Will Wickremasinghe win?"

"Actually, the prime minister is Mandy's cousin." Suresh looked at his wife. "We don't know. President Kumaratunga comes from a powerful political dynasty."

Both of Kumaratunga's parents were former prime ministers of Sri Lanka. And I knew dynasty meant power in this part of the world. I had seen it in India. It was being used for the upcoming Indian elections, a little more than a month away. Sonia Gandhi's familial connections, as wife of former Prime Minister Rajiv Gandhi and daughter-in-law of former Prime Minister Indira Gandhi, was being pushed heavily by the Congress Party. Familial dynasties spoke of power, familiarity, and lineage, and held weight in both countries.

We drank in silence. They invited me to visit them at their home whenever I wished. Although they smiled and spoke politely about how excited they were about the film, their eyes were distracted and tense. I wondered what a Kumaratunga win would mean for the Indian elections. Would Sri Lanka's choice of the familiar hard line be reflected in India's choice? Maybe Hindutva was here to stay. Images of the stadium in Calcutta rose in my mind, along with the journalist's talk of India's "saffronization." I took another sip of Lion Lager and turned off my mind.

THE LOBBY WAS EMPTY the next morning. There were no businessmen in the lounge, or Sinhalese wedding parties crossing the foyer with the bride wrapped in a gold sarong. There was only the sound of water from the fountain, delicate and sooth-ing. I couldn't stand a day spent by the pool or in my room, waiting to hear the election results, waiting to see if they would affect the film. I pushed open the lobby door and walked out into the heat.

Galle Road, normally heavy with buses spewing fumes and yellow rickshaws, was now empty. There were no roadblocks and no police or army. I looked both ways, and walked cau-tiously into the middle of the street. I could see clearly in both directions—the Galle Face Hotel to the right, and the endless line of stores, casinos, and bookies lining the road south toward Mount Lavinia. The only sound was the sound of the breakers against the Sri Lankan coast.

A horn blared behind me. I spun around to see a yellow autorickshaw parked at the side of the road. The driver motioned me toward him. I had no idea why he was out or what kind of fare he'd get on a day like today. But I was curious. Why not? He was wearing a loose button-down shirt and sarong. I had seen him before; he often took hotel fares.

"Where do you want to go?" he asked.

"Nowhere. There's a curfew."

He looked up and down the empty road. "No problem. All okay."

I considered for a moment. I didn't have to go *far*.

"Okay. Take me to the Galle Face Hotel." I jumped into the back of the rickshaw, breaking the curfew.

The rickshaw sputtered down the deserted Galle Road. The hotel was less than five minutes away, and we soon pulled up in front of its grand wooden doors. I paid the driver half the fare and asked him to wait. He turned off the engine and lay back as if it was just another Saturday afternoon.

I walked past the reception desk, past a polished plaque list-ing all of their famous guests, and out onto the verandah. The verandah was decorated with black-and-white tiles, low-hanging lamps, and little wooden tables overlooking the sea. The lamps swayed gently in the sea breeze. A hotel waiter started to come toward me. I began to feel tense about my momentary freedom, and went back to the rickshaw.

I spent the evening alone in my room. The small silver statue of Shiva rested on my bedside table. It was tarnished from my travels. If the elections didn't go smoothly, I'd return to India and visit my grandmother. She had given the statue to me only a month earlier. I had never grown up religious, but I felt like some ritual or prayer would help. I closed my eyes. Born into both Judaism and Hinduism, different religions were just different ways of understanding God. My appreciation of all religions was made even greater by the presence of a South Indian Catholic *Amah*, or nanny, in my childhood.

Theresa Anthony, my *Amah*, was from the southwestern state of Karnataka. She had dark brown skin and blue tribal tattoos on the backs of her hands and the tops of her feet. The ink had been applied with a sewing needle and had seeped so deeply into her skin that the patterns were hardly visible. Her parents were probably converts from Hinduism, untouchables who wanted to escape the confines of caste and found that Christianity offered a way out. When I was four weeks old, she was hired to move to Canada and take care of me when my parents were away working.

I opened my eyes and looked at the statue, realizing I had said a similar prayer in Benares when Mom went to New Delhi for re-permission. Now, we were about to go to sleep in Sri Lanka, *Amah* had retired to New Delhi, and my dad was just waking up in Toronto. When my father had tried to explain time zones and jet lag to *Amah* before she immigrated to Canada, she had laughed and said, "*Saab*," respectfully addressing her employer, "everyone knows it's the same time everywhere!"

PRESIDENT KUMARATUNGA won the general elections. We found out in the morning, to the surprise of Pearl, Suresh, Mandy, and many others in Colombo. Her party, the People's Alliance, had allied with a pro-Sinhalese Marxist party called the Janatha Vimukthi Peramuna, or JVP. Together they formed the United People's Freedom Alliance, and won forty-six percent of the vote, while Ranil Wickremasinghe's United National Party won only thirty-eight percent. The Alliance, taking the cultural hard line, won the majority. It seemed the city was the anomaly, favouring Ranil Wickremasinghe, but most of rural Sri Lanka had voted for the Alliance.

It had turned out to be one of the most peaceful elections in recent Sri Lankan history. The curfew hadn't even been officially called. That explained the rickshaw driver, but the empty roads showed that people were still not taking chances. With the elections behind us, we began to shoot the film.

15

We started shooting on Easter Sunday, the day of resurrection. My alarm went off at nine in the morning. The shower was running, and steam was rising from below the bathroom door. Avani was up and ready to take the actors to makeup and wardrobe. I fumbled to turn off the alarm, caught in the blankets of my single bed. The sky was grey and flat outside the window. I felt nervous, the same nervousness I felt on my first day of school. My palms began to sweat. I wiped them on the cotton pillowcase before reaching for the camera and packing it into my bag. Mom told me that she always threw up on the first day of shooting. I could see her room in the new wing from the apartment window. Was that what she was doing now, alone in her bathroom, before facing an eighty-person crew?

The crew gathered in the lobby. It was silent except for the sound of the fountain. Mom sat on its marble ledge, where I had seen the Sinhalese girls playing the night we arrived back from Jaffna. She was talking with Giles, her script in a black binder open across her lap. Dylan crouched next to them, listening as they planned how they would shoot the first scene.

We were going to start by shooting the beginning of the film, where Chuyia is brought by bullock cart across a tropical vista to the house of widows. It's unusual to shoot a film in sequence. The schedule is often constructed so that all of the scenes that take place at one location are shot in the same block of time, but it just happened that our schedule would begin at the beginning. I opened the script to the first page.

CREDITS OVER: *FADE IN:*

1. EXT. TROPICAL VISTA—DAY

A green lush landscape, peppered with coconut trees and banana groves as far as the eye can see.

CLOSE UP of creaking wooden wheels as they enter the frame, fill it and then wipe it clean.

We are behind a bullock cart as it plods along, its passengers hidden by their own long shadows.

ON two tiny, bare feet, encircled with silver anklets, dangling by the side of the bullock cart. The small bells on the anklets ring sweetly as the feet swing back and forth to the easy rhythm of the cart.

We reveal seven-year-old CHUYIA.

Giles wore a black turtleneck and black jeans, despite the heat. Mom and Dylan both wore loose cotton shirts. The lights from the fountain played against their backs. This was the same group who had been the last to leave the set the day we were shut down in Benares. We left with two minutes of footage and memories that would last a lifetime. Vasant brought them coffee from the lounge. The waiters were wiping off the tables and placing a cart displaying their tea selection near the entrance. I went and sat next to Mom on the fountain.

"Were you sick?" I asked quietly.

"No, it's strange. It's the first time I haven't been sick before a film." She looked down at her script. Handwritten notes were scribbled in the margins. "I think it's because I really know what I want to do with this one."

Vasant called to her from the lobby entrance. Their transport had arrived. She picked up her script and got into the van.

WHITE VANS CONTINUED to pull up to the entrance, and the crew piled in under the direction of our transportation coordinator. I placed my camera bag near one of the marble pillars outside the lobby and waited. Dolly and her wardrobe team had a van of their own, as did the sound department, two men from Canada. I looked at my call sheet. I had been placed in a van with the camera crew.

The transport coordinator motioned me to van number 3. The two female camera assistants I would have been working under stood drinking coffee out of disposable paper cups from a deli attached to the hotel. Deli-France advertised croissants and fresh baguettes under a white sign painted with the French tricolour. The sign, an anomaly amid the betting agencies and gem shops of Galle Road, always grabbed my eye.

I piled into the van with the two women and two Canadian men—Bob, the gaffer, who would ensure Giles's lighting design would be set up by the electrics team, and Johnny, the dolly-grip. The group was new to me. They had been brought in to fulfill the requirements of the Canadian government financiers. The production had to spend a certain amount of the budget on Canadian talent. It made for a strange mix. We now had a crew made up of people who had been in Benares, including an Indian art and wardrobe department, a Canadian contingent who knew each other from working on the same American productions that were shot in Canada, and the Sri Lankans—who had no attachment to either.

As the van drove toward the tropical vista, I listened as they talked about malaria medicine between sips of coffee, and the possibility that their families would come to visit over the next two months. I felt the bulk of my camera bag on my lap and thought of what a different world Dylan, Giles, David, Dolly, Mom, and I had inhabited in Benares. For them, it was their first day of work. For us, it was a victory that took four years to achieve.

We travelled in convoy, this time without armed accompaniment, down winding backroads until we reached the location, Kalanimulla. The van pulled into a clearing surrounded by lush palms and shallow pools of water, dense with lily pads. What most of the crew didn't know was that Mom had asked me if I wanted to come with her and Giles the previous day to do an unscheduled day of shooting with a reduced crew that included Dylan, Johnny, David, and Dilip. We took one van, a box of lenses, and the film camera to the tropical vista. A guerrilla unit.

Ingmar Bergman talked about guerrilla filmmaking in his account of shooting *The Virgin Spring*, which was released in 1959. He described working with a small crew in the northern Swedish province of Dalarna. Everyone, from the actors to the makeup men, helped with the equipment. When someone noticed a crane flying overhead, they dropped their work and went to get a better look. Bergman said that this is what it meant to make a movie with little money and teamwork—when you could leave everything to appreciate a beautiful, passing moment in nature.

I lifted the hard-cover lens box out of the van and placed it on the grass. Giles carried the camera body to the edge of one of the pools. He knelt in front of the sea of lily pads as Johnny crouched behind him, supporting the weight of the camera from behind. The bank was soft and damp. I sat cross-legged on the slope and watched as the camera rolled, capturing the fading pink light as it reflected in the water and bounced onto the smooth underside of the lily pads.

There was no sound being recorded, and no actors. We were there only to shoot beautiful details, images of nature that could be used as inserts within the film, like icing spread between the layers of a cake. Mom sat silently next to David, and the quiet seemed a communal appreciation of something we never would have been able to do in the pandemonium of Benares.

As Giles balanced the camera, leaning back on the muddy bank, I remembered that he had started out as a BBC cameraman, shooting documentaries in the Amazon. My mom had started out doing documentaries with my father in the seventies after she immigrated to Canada. She recorded sound while my father directed. They had been temporarily separated while shooting in apartheid South Africa while going through customs and immigration at Johannesburg Airport. She had been singled out for greater scrutiny. He was, after all, a white man travelling with his brown wife.

Storm clouds moved across the sky, obscuring the reflections in the water and the fine outlines of the lily pads. We were losing the natural light. Giles called it a day. The experience was easy, simple even, and was about to be replaced by the reality of full production.

THE CAMERA VAN pulled into the clearing among a dozen other white transports. The equipment trucks, makeup trailer, and wardrobe were already parked among the lush palm groves and rice paddies. The production nurse, a small Sri Lankan Christian sister with a gold cross pinned to the lapel of her nurse's uniform, had set up a medical station under a white tent. It was midday and the air was quickly becoming hot and sticky near the pools of water. I felt the Olympus to see if it was still cool from the hotel air conditioning, scared of condensation in the lens. The towel was cold. I left it in the bag to acclimatize.

The bullock cart that would take Chuyia across the tropical vista to the Hindu temple town, her husband's cremation, and widowhood, was parked on a dirt track between two pools of water. The driver was already dressed in period Indian clothing, barefoot in a white *dhoti* and vest. I walked over to the large wooden cartwheels. They were painted blue, and came up to my chest. The bullocks were tethered through their nostrils, and stamped impatiently on the dusty ground. It was where we would do our first shot, and where we would hold the *pooja*.

Sarala was sitting on the back of the cart with her small legs dangling over the side. Dolly had dressed her in a striped indigo sari and red blouse, typical of 1930s Bengal. Giles was already sitting in the bullock cart beside her, balancing the camera on his lap. Assistant directors, with walkie-talkies clipped to their belts, ensured that the vista was clear of any curious Sri Lankan farmers who might wander into the frame. I unwrapped the Olympus from its towel and put it over my shoulder.

Dylan called everyone to gather around the bullock cart over his walkie-talkie. Seema and Lisa emerged from the crowd. Seema's head was freshly shaven. She smiled as the crew commented on her widow's haircut. Mom stood next to one of the large blue cartwheels, and Giles held the camera as Dylan helped her up into the cart. She squeezed in beside Sarala and the Sri Lankan actress playing Chuyia's mother-in-law. I pushed my way through the crowd until I was standing next to the same blue cartwheel.

Dolly held a small brass tray in her hands. Her white *dupatta* fell off her shoulder, nearly catching on the small lit candle placed in the middle of the tray. A few grains of rice and some red *tikka* paste were carefully spread around the candle. The crew fell silent as she reached up toward Giles and moved the tray in small clockwise circles around the camera. The flame flickered from the motion. Light blessing light. A wardrobe assistant began handing out red *rakhi* strings to tie on each other's wrists. The vegetable colouring was not washed away by water or wear, but still deep and vibrant. There was no Hindu priest this time, and no elaborate ceremony like the one in Benares. We were practising a different type of religion, one rooted in camaraderie.

As the assistant directors went to their positions around the vista, Dylan cleared us away from the cart. Sarala sat quietly, chewing on a piece of sugarcane given to her by the art department. Mom gave her direction, and Kay translated it into Sinhala. I looked through the Olympus viewfinder as Dylan called for quiet on the set, and focused the lens on Mom. She wore her Lennon sunglasses and a Tilly hat slung casually around her neck. She grabbed tightly to the side of the cart.

"And…Action!"

The driver whipped the bullocks and the cart lurched forward. I fell back into the waiting crew, and wondered how Mom felt as the cart moved slowly down the dirt track. How it felt for something to be reborn. Does it remember the integrity of what it was, or move freely into a new state, as gracefully as a leaf fallen from a tree? I leaned my hand on one of the actors' canvas chairs, as a strange wave of dizziness passed over me. Within an hour I had sunstroke.

As the cart moved back and forth, repeating take after take, I sat on the grass fighting waves of nausea. The Olympus rested at my feet. Drinking a small bottle of water only temporarily relieved the burning which radiated throughout my body. Our line producer noticed me sitting off to the side. She helped me walk to the nurse's makeshift medical station, a white wooden box filled with aspirin, packages of electrolyte powder, and bandages. The sister smiled and poured electrolyte crystals into a bottle of mineral water. They dissolved in a puff of light green powder, giving off a faint citrus smell.

In the distance I could see the cart, and insisted on going back to work. The nurse checked my temperature. It was 101. She suggested I lie down in the wardrobe tent, and held me under one arm as we walked down a narrow dirt path. Two couches and a changing screen were set up next to one of the shallow pools. I felt like a failure, bowing out on my first day.

The sister left me on the couch. I rested my head on its hard wooden arm, with the Olympus balanced on my stomach. The sun had begun to descend, casting a soft orange glow across the vista. I faded in and out of sleep and dipped into feverish semi-consciousness, like dipping into a swimming pool with your ears below water, accompanied only by the muffled sound of people's voices and feet touching the bottom of the shallow end.

The line producer woke me up. The sun had already set behind the dense wall of foliage that surrounded the clearing. She told me we were moving to a nearby location, breaking for lunch, and then shooting the next scene. Our one meal of the workday was always called lunch; it didn't matter if it was noon or the middle of the night.

We were about to shoot one of the most important scenes in the script: Chuyia's head-shaving, the ritual that would complete her transformation to widowhood. Without hair a woman was without vanity, shorn of a basic symbol of being female. It was the only scene we had fully completed in Benares, holed up in the back garden of Clarks while RSS protesters burned Mom's effigy on the other side of the garden wall. I had highlighted it with a pink highlighter in my script, taking Dilip's suggestion to mark key images I wanted to capture with the Olympus. I pulled myself off the couch and walked slowly to the transport vans.

The clearing was dark by the time the unit shifted. The location was only a field away, but the five-minute distance took more than an hour with packing up the equipment, moving, and setting up again. The night was heavy with humidity, and enveloped in a blackness that seemed to seep out of the surrounding jungle. The art department had set up a fake *ghat* in the clearing. It was a wooden platform and a few steps covered with concrete shaped like stone, a little more sophisticated than the apple boxes we had used in Benares. The platform was surrounded by gas fires, which gave off deep orange flames with the flick of a switch, mimicking funeral pyres.

I stared at our artificial flames and fake cremation grounds, and remembered Manikarnika *Ghat* in Benares, where the air had been thick with the smell of woodsmoke and camphor. The only smell now was the smell of Sri Lankan food—lunch, served out of stainless-steel trays in an open tent filled with rows of wooden tables and benches.

Vasant helped me pile yellow *dal*, rice, and curry onto my plate. The steam from the lunch trays rose and hit my forehead, making me sweat even more. We sat down at one of the long wooden tables, but I couldn't eat. I rested my fork against the yellow *dal*. The hum of the portable generator filled my head, drowning out all thoughts and doubts. I began to shiver. A cold sweat was forming under my arms and in the small of my back. It ran down my spine and competed with the humidity. I asked Vasant to help me find a place to lie down.

The equipment trucks and transport vans were parked so close together it felt like we were in the midst of a travelling circus. I could see Champika, the new third assistant camera-person, loading magazines with fresh film in the camera truck. He moved fast, preparing a number of them for the night ahead. The Canadian second assistant called to him from the bottom of the narrow metal ramp that led to the truck. He stopped what he was doing and ran down to help her lift the heavy black lens boxes onto the camera gear trolley. I remembered Jasmine's gentle face, teaching me about lenses in the back of the camera truck in Benares.

I would have been doing that, married to the job, in sickness or in health. Departments had an established hierarchy that they needed in order to function like a well-oiled machine. Instead, I found myself in my own department, my own boss. I had the freedom to lie down with fever, but I also had a growing fear that I belonged to no department, and maybe to no one.

Vasant guided me to one of the white transport vans. The driver's seat had been pushed back, and the driver was asleep with one arm shading his eyes from the glow of the set. I held on to the side mirror as Vasant pulled open the sliding door. The sound woke the driver, who helped me into the van. Lunch was over. Vasant slid the door shut and returned to the set.

I curled up in the back seat in darkness. The seat fabric smelled musty and still held the faint scent of coffee and croissants. It started to rain, slow, heavy drops, not enough to stop the filming, but enough to streak the windows. Rivulets of water caught the light from the surrounding trucks until all I could see were white veins of liquid, small rivers, pulsing as they flowed. I could feel the sweat on my back seeping through my shirt and into the seat. But the more I tried to sleep, the more I felt I was missing something. I began to feel guilty. The guilt seeped out of me like sweat. I covered the Olympus with a plastic bag and pulled open the sliding door.

The air outside smelled sweet, of rain and earth and wet leaves—that clean smell when there's no dust left in the air, and the world feels naked and new. The ground was slippery underfoot, muddied and torn up by the truck tracks. I walked with the Olympus under the shelter of my arm, even though the rain was light now. A few hundred metres away the set was lit up by two large lights and Chinese lanterns, round white balls that softened the light. The flames from the gas fires threw flickering shadows across the back wall of the set. Sarala sat on the middle step, wearing a small white sari, as a Sri Lankan barber—dressed like an Indian—shaved her head.

The crew sat under the shelter of a white tent placed a few metres away from her. Mom leaned forward on a black canvas chair, staring intently at a video monitor, which fed everything the camera shot to the small screen in front of her. The only sound in the blackness was the gentle rain and the metallic *snips* of scissors cutting hair. The camera was rolling. I waited.

"Cut!" Mom leaned back in her chair.

I went and crouched beside her.

"Go home." She felt my forehead with the back of her hand.

"I can't." I held on to her chair, and felt my body becoming weaker as the electrics moved the lights for the next camera angle.

"Why not?"

"I have to get this shot." I thought of the pink highlighter.

"You must stop beating yourself up." She looked into my eyes, and I loosened my grip on the chair.

She was right, it was my habit—hide behind perfect grades, then perfect university essays, and now perfect photography. If I fed the weight I felt inside with perfection, then maybe it would be appeased.

I waited to hear her reassure me, to tell me that it was okay to leave, to miss the shot, to fuck up, to make the choice I had made. To not be perfect.

"Here, take my key and go back to the hotel and get into bed." She handed me a grey electronic hotel key. The pale plastic shone in the artificial light.

I asked Dilip if he would take the Olympus for the night, in case he had time to take some shots, and went to look for a way to get home. The driver of the transport I had rested in agreed to take me. I lay down in the back seat as he started the engine. But when I tried to close my eyes, they burned with sweat. There was a knock at the window as we began to pull away. One of the assistant directors slid open the door and handed me a call sheet for the next two days. I folded it and tried to sleep.

The rain increased as we drove along the rural roads that led back to Colombo. I could barely see the rice paddies and jungle that surrounded us. By the time we reached the main road into the city, the rain was coming down in sheets. The driver leaned forward over the steering wheel, and tried to see through the cascade of water that flowed down the windshield. I lay in the back seat with my face close to the window as the lights from Galle Road, with its continuous line of casinos and neon bookies, blurred through the rain-streaked glass. I thought of the crew. Had they packed up? Or maybe the storm hadn't hit them. I leaned my head against the sweaty seat. It had taken four years to get here, and I hadn't even heard Mom call it a wrap at the end of our first day.

The van pulled past Deli-France, the tricolour sign aglow over the entrance, and up to the lobby of the Colombo Plaza. The doorman, dressed in a maroon uniform with flat brass buttons, opened the sliding door. "Evening, ma'am." He smiled politely. I held the grey electronic key between sweaty fingers, and walked into the air-conditioned lobby. As soon as the cool air touched my skin, I began to shiver. The lounge singer with her curly hair and shiny shirt was crooning a Bryan Adams song to a small audience of drunken ex-pats. I walked as fast as I could toward the elevators.

Mom's suite was cold when I opened the door. I went into the bedroom and turned on the bedside light. There were two small chocolates wrapped in gold foil and a small purple orchid placed in the middle of the pillow. The king-size bed was turned down. The sheets shone, white like ice. I stepped into the shower and let the hot water burn away my sweat. I imagined the crew packing up. The first of forty-five days down.

The sheets were painful against my skin. Before turning off the lamp, I unfolded the call sheet that had been handed to me. It listed the next day's schedule, and the location—the widows' house.

16

The heavy curtains were drawn, and the air conditioner had been turned down when I woke the next morning. The room felt like a cave, a neutral space blocked from any view of the outside world. As my eyes adjusted to the darkness, I could see the faint outline of Mom's body in the bed beside me, buried under the thick duvet. I felt angry that I had needed her reassurance, and turned and faced the wall, resting my cheek against the cool pillowcase. I remembered how good it had felt when Vasant and I were mistaken for an Indian couple, and became even angrier. Was I a woman whose self-worth was connected to another? Like the widows? I thought of a line Madhumati says to Chuyia. I had highlighted it in the script: "Our *Shastras* [holy books] say a wife is her husband's half-body when he is alive, and when our husbands die we become their half-corpses."

Half.

Why was I only *half* without someone else?

The alarm went off on the bedside table. Mom stirred under the covers and reached to turn it off in the dark. I wanted to talk to her, about my life, about photography. About love. But I knew she would be frustrated, tired of the same old routine. When would I stop having to ask her if I was okay. When would she stop having to tell me. My voice stuck in my throat, that little piece of glass still lodged between muscle and skin. The clock read seven. She got up and drew the curtains.

"How was the rest of the shoot?" I asked, casually.

"Fine. It didn't rain for very long." She glanced at me on the way to the shower. "How are you feeling?"

"Weak, but I can go." I had to go.

The crew had already gathered in the lobby. Giles and David sat on the edge of the fountain, sipping coffee out of flimsy Deli-France disposable cups. I went outside and waited with the camera team. The air was still cool, pale and placid like the bed-sheets. Giles, Vasant, Dylan, and Mom got into the first van, and I found my seat among the Canadians. They talked about drinking beers by the pool the previous night, and the big American television productions they had worked on in Toronto. I always felt like a Canadian in India. But as we drove along Galle Road to the *ashram*, I couldn't pinpoint exactly what was Canadian about me.

The majestic Galle Face Hotel sat like a queen ready to receive her court. She was one of the oldest hotels in Colombo, a colonial building with cream-coloured pillars and a curved grand staircase. Vivien Leigh had stayed there in 1953 while shooting *Elephant Walk*. The story was that she had a mental breakdown during the shoot, and wandered around the hotel in her nightgown, suffering from hallucinations. The production replaced her with Elizabeth Taylor.

The hotel's court was Galle Face Green, a one-kilometre stretch of lawn in front of the hotel, bordering the ocean. In World War II Japanese planes raided Sri Lanka on an Easter Sunday. One of the bombs fell on Galle Face Green. A concrete promenade was laid down between the ocean and the grass, lined with lampposts corroding from the salt spray. At night, Sri Lankan families would stroll by the sea, buying coconut water or Coke from vendors lining the promenade. Now there was almost no one, only the sea, wide and grey and alive, and a group of Sri Lankan army soldiers doing their morning exercises. They ran back and forth in formation, wearing white T-shirts, green combats, and army caps pulled low over their foreheads. I thought of the upcoming Indian elections. They were on May 12, less than a month away. The Sri Lankan army's exercises reminded me of the way Mom described the RSS, swinging their sticks in efficient militaristic patterns, that cold winter morning in New Delhi. What would happen to the film if the BJP won again?

The van continued past Galle Face Green and curved away from the sea just before a yellow roadblock, manned by a handful of soldiers.

"What is that?" I asked the driver.

"That's the president's house."

I caught a glimpse of what looked like an old clock tower a few hundred metres from the roadblock. I thought of Temple Trees, the prime minister's residence down the road. Had he vacated it immediately? When I first saw its smooth white walls and golden crest, I'd taken the name literally, mistaking it for a place of worship. We passed the Colombo docks, where huge industrial cranes pivoted and turned, and transferred cargo behind walls and chain-link fences. Local fishermen, dressed in worn sarongs and flip-flops, sold their wares off the sidewalk in front of the walls. The fish were laid on newspaper in shallow woven baskets. They were damp and beginning to rot in the heat of the sun. The smell of fish filled the van.

The van pulled up in front of an alley opposite a Tamil Hindu temple. Ornate carvings of gods and goddesses lined the tall pyramidal structure. They were painted in bright pinks and blues, like the temples of south India. Our equipment trucks were parked in an empty lot beside the alley, white and practical next to the colour of religion. The camera assistant opened the sliding door and we piled out onto the street.

Slinging the camera bag over my shoulder, I walked down the short alley to our location. We had taken over the house of a Tamil temple trust, where the priest of the local Hindu temple would once have lived. The house would be our main location, the widows' *ashram*, and the centre of Shakuntala, Kalyani, and Chuyia's austere lives. It was now home to a handful of Tamil families, who were relegated to two small rooms in the front of the house for the duration of the shoot.

The alley itself was home to a number of displaced families, Tamil refugees from the north. Both sides were lined with narrow houses made of brick and corrugated iron. Open sewers ran below the doorsteps. The sewers collected water from the women bathing and washing clothes in front of their houses. I walked past a Tamil woman dipping a plastic container into a bucket of water and then pouring it over her head and already-drenched *kaftan*. A child ran naked between the houses, wearing only a thick black smudge on his forehead, to ward off the evil eye. The bathing woman looked at me as I walked by, soapsuds still in the corners of her eyes. She must have wondered who we were—all these people in baseball caps and shorts, taking over her alley. As a woman, I was advised, like all female crew members, to wear long-sleeve shirts and pants to avoid offending the alley's residents and observers at the local Hindu temple.

The location was one hundred years old. I walked down a musty corridor with six-metre ceilings and emerged into a central courtyard surrounded by several small dark rooms. It reminded me of an Indo-Lankan version of the traditional Chinese house in Zhang Yimou's *Raise the Red Lantern*. The courtyard was grey and desolate, and the walls had been aged by the art department until they had a palpable griminess. Dilip had used research photographs from Benares to set up every detail in the house. As I walked through the open courtyard I could feel the same sense of desolation I felt in the Sunview in Benares, in the world below the German tourists eating marmalade and the oily guesthouse manager chewing his *paan*.

The electrics had already set up the lights for the first shot of the day, Chuyia's arrival into the *ashram* and her initial run-in with Shakuntala. A constant flow of human traffic moved in and out of the courtyard, carefully avoiding the piles of black power cable on the floor. Avani came in leading Seema and Sarala. They went into a makeshift green room off the entrance corridor, both wearing their white widow's saris. As their world came alive, ours would fade behind the camera— a silent exchange of realities. While the crew moved the gear into the centre of the courtyard, I could see the displaced residents continuing their lives as we worked. Women cooked *hoppers* and curry as their children slept behind curtains made from torn bedsheets.

I unwrapped the Olympus and went into the small room off the courtyard where we would be shooting our first scene. It was Shakuntala's room. There was almost no space inside. Seema knelt on a reed mat on the floor, bending over a stone tablet used for grinding spices. Sarala crouched just behind the door. Lights were set up in the door and window, preventing me from getting a clear view. They gave off a low, stifling heat. Giles knelt next to the camera, set low on the floor, while Mom stood behind him watching a small monitor attached to the camera body.

There was only one space left to stand.

I squeezed into the corner of the room behind the camera, as makeup put the final touchups on Seema. It was a good position, and I hoped to get some nice shots, but I felt out of place and in the way. The light fell softly into the room, creating deep shadows on the walls and highlighting Seema's stark white sari.

Someone tapped me on the shoulder.

"Sorry, you're going to have to move." It was the boom operator. He held a long metal pole with the microphone attached to its far end.

I was in the only position from which the sound department could record the scene. I took the Olympus and went through a connecting door into the next room.

The room was dark and filled with camera gear. I could make out the shapes of people sitting on apple boxes—electrics and members of the Sri Lankan crew. They sat silently, waiting. Most of our time was spent waiting to set up for the next scene, hours of patience for a moment of drama—life intensified. Dylan stood in the doorway between the rooms. I squeezed in beside him, with no clear view for shots, but with a view of Giles and Mom, silhouetted against the light.

I had acted under Mom's direction once, while I was still living with my dad. I was thirteen and given the opportunity to be in a pilot for a teen television series. We did rehearsals together in a production office in the west end of Toronto, among old warehouses and streetcars that travelled unhurriedly along their metal tracks.

I was excited to go through makeup and wardrobe and turn up in front of the lights with my mom behind the camera. But we ended up fighting before the scene, to the side of the sound stage, in the darkness away from the lights. She told me that I had never loved her. The weight slowly descended. *I had made my choice.* One of her friends took me aside and told me what a horrible daughter I was. Mom cried before the shot. In those days I was too young to understand what it must have been like for her to live and work alone, separated from her family, her daughter, in a cold, adopted homeland.

She was quiet now, and intensely focused. Beautiful in a way I had never seen before. Passionate. She held her chin in her hand and looked at Seema.

"Action!"

I stood in the darkened doorway as the soft sounds of Hindi dialogue came from Seema and watched, not Seema, but Mom as she stared at the little colour monitor attached to the camera, focused and silent. Seema motioned for Sarala to come and sit with her back to her, so she could rub medicinal tumeric on her newly shaven head to cool the nicks and cuts. Sarala slumped her shoulders as Seema applied the thick yellow paste to her bare scalp. Chuyia's rite of passage was complete.

"Cut."

The silent space of their world broke, and the electrics were up and moving behind me, preparing for the next shot. Vasant brought Mom coffee. I watched as she knelt next to Sarala, this little Sri Lankan girl, and spoke to her carefully, lovingly, as Kay translated her praises into Sinhala. Sarala nodded and they laughed. I couldn't remember when I had seen her like that, laughing and kneeling on the ground. I had hardly ever seen her be physical. The one memory that remained, a piece of the fragmented glass of our relationship that shone instead of cut, was of her swimming in the neighbour's pool in Toronto, laughing and smiling like a child.

Dylan called lunch. I hadn't gotten the shot. The Olympus hung loosely around my neck. I was angry with myself, and wanted to escape the widows' house, grim and hot and grey.

I walked to lunch alone. The bathers' alley was empty in the intense afternoon heat, except for thin stray cats, stunted from lack of food, who wound their way between the open sewers and plastic buckets left out for washing. The air was oppressive and humid, lined with the rancid scent of burning coconut oil. I walked out of the alley and onto the main road. Colombo traffic was thick. Three-wheelers, like the rickshaws I had taken in Bombay, spewed out brown emissions. I avoided the oncoming rickshaws and cars, and walked past our base camp parking lot to the church where our lunch tent was set up. The road curved down past small shops and houses. Blood ran down the edge of the asphalt outside a Halal butcher's. A group of men, wearing sarongs, shirts, and Muslim skullcaps, sat beside the skinned carcass of a goat. They watched as I walked by, a lighter-skinned woman alone in a T-shirt and pants.

The lunch tent was set up on the grounds of a small church, only a five-minute walk from the widows' house. Another church sat on the opposite side of the road, freshly whitewashed, with banana fronds tied to the entrance pillars with coconut-fibre rope, leftovers from Palm Sunday. I walked up the dirt driveway to our tent, set up in a clearing behind the nave. Some of the Sri Lankan crew had already arrived and were lined up at one of two buffet tables set up opposite each other under the tent. One had spicier food for the Sri Lankans.

I took a white china plate and visited both tables, making a mix of yellow *dal*, rice, thin, hard *paapads*, and macaroni salad. I found a place at one of the long lunch tables overlooking the church grounds. It was built on a hill above the port authority, and I could see the cranes in the distance, cold and industrial against the palm trees and red flowers of the church garden. The *dal* was spicy and heavy with coconut oil, spicier than Indian food. I picked at the macaroni salad. The Olympus sat unused in the bag at my feet.

The crew filled the tent. Vasant sat with Avani and the other production assistants at a table a few feet away. It reminded me of high school, where I spent most of my lunches sitting in a hallway in the basement, eating alone out of a Tupperware container packed with Indian food made by my *Amah*. My dad didn't know how to cook, and I didn't live with my mom. "Lonely little lunchbox girl" was what a friend called me. I felt that same sense of isolation now, a distance that wouldn't allow me to enjoy myself. Why did it still haunt me? I left my plate and walked back to the widows' house.

The house was silent and peaceful without the crew. It seemed to have returned to its original state, where one could imagine that it once was the residence of a priest. Voices drifted out of the green room. I went in. Seema, Lisa, and Mom were eating lunch off a coffee table surrounded by old couches and chairs. Half-eaten Deli-France baguettes lay scattered on the table in clear plastic containers.

"Mmmm... Have some." Lisa lifted up her sandwich.

"No, thanks. I've eaten."

"Come, sit." Seema patted the space on the couch beside her.

I sat down as they continued to natter away about Bollywood gossip in a mix of Hindi and English. The room had a greenish tinge from a halogen strip high up on the ceiling. It was the only source of light. The families' furniture hadn't been removed, just pushed into the corners of the room, like dust after a cleaning. I looked into a large glass cabinet beside me. It was filled with porcelain dolls and photos from school ceremonies.

"Hey! What's wrong?" Lisa shook my arm and pushed a cup of cold coffee into my face. "Have some."

She had smiling eyes, green eyes. I knew she was half Indian, half Canadian, but I hadn't really talked to her before. Her relationship with Mom was relatively new, and I had missed the shooting of *Bollywood/Hollywood*. When Chuyia meets Kalyani for the first time, the only word that escapes her lips is "*pari*," "angel."

I thanked her and took the coffee.

"Come on, ladies! Time for makeup." Avani came in and gathered Seema and Lisa. Lunch was over. The green room was silent. Mom leaned her head against the back of the chair and closed her eyes.

"It's tiring, isn't it?" I asked.

"Exhausting."

"Yes, I know." The crew slowly began to trickle in, and the house was no longer a place of refuge. Mom kept her eyes closed, despite the movement around her.

"Vikram's coming down for a few days to help with the choreography of the songs."

A plastic Santa Claus was suspended from a nail above one of the glass cabinets, its hat lined with sparkles and grey dust.

I thought of Vikram, of how much I had felt for what seemed like so long. It was incredible that one event in one's life could manage so much of the future. I held the memories in, tight, hard, away from the surface, and picked up the Olympus and went to set.

LISA PHONED THE apartment after we wrapped that evening.

"Do you feel up for a walk?" she asked.

I wanted the air.

We met outside the lobby and walked down the street, which was peppered with people and cars.

"I hear there's a Buddhist temple on the small lake behind the hotel."

"I'd like to see that," I said.

We strolled along a road that curved behind the hotel and around the lake. Lisa wore a baseball cap and a T-shirt. She must have been a few years older than me. She'd gone to Bombay to model when she was sixteen. It was a life that seemed so different from my own.

"Are you really half Indian, half Canadian?" I asked. I hadn't met anybody else in my life who was the same mix as me.

"Yes. My father's Bengali and my mom's Polish."

"Really? My mom's Punjabi and my dad's a Ukrainian Jew. We both have this Eastern European thing." I don't know why, but it excited me, and somehow made me feel I belonged.

The lake was black, and the sidewalk encircling it was littered with garbage. We picked our way along in silence.

"Do you ever think that you'll always be alone in life?" I asked.

"All the time. It's good to be alone, shnookums."

I laughed, but secretly I loved the affection. She was like an older sister. Something I never had.

We walked by a set of steps that led to the outside of a small amphitheatre. Lisa ran up.

"Come on!"

I followed her. It was an old amphitheatre on the side of the lake, littered with junk—exercise equipment, scattered school desks, and a red London double-decker bus, sitting off to one side, gutted and rusting.

"Why in the world?" But Lisa was already looking through the glass door of the bus and poking at the windows. When had I lost that? I was only twenty-four, but I envied her playful curiosity.

"I have no idea." She rubbed the dusty passenger windows and then continued past the Sri Lankan Housewives Association building and toward the Buddhist temple.

The temple was built at the end of a jetty out in the lake. We removed our shoes at the entrance and walked along a wooden causeway to a small stone square, which seemed suspended in the water. Night had fallen, and we were surrounded by darkness, except for the light from naked bulbs strung between three trees planted in the centre of the temple. Large stone Buddhas were placed around the square, with small, well-maintained offerings at their feet: oranges and sweet cakes and incense. We walked around the periphery in silence, in newfound companionship, as the lake lapped at the causeway.

17

The crew waited outside the lobby to be shuttled to the set. The clouds over the sea were the colour of slate, threatening rain. It would be wonderful if it rained, and washed away the grime of working in the widows' house. There were so many people enclosed in such a small space that by the end of the day, the camera assistant's shirt was soaked with enough sweat that I could see the rainbow tattoo clearly etched on her back. The sound department had stopped calling it "Madhumati's house" and begun calling it "dirtydirty's."

I thought of Pearl's finger, dipped in deep aubergine ink. If Colombo had been so wrong about the outcome of the elections, its priorities so different from rural Sri Lanka, how reliable was the information I heard about the upcoming Indian elections from middle-class family and friends in Delhi? My grandparents hoped the Congress would win, and maybe return India to a more secular state. But Gandhi had always said that India was in her villages.

The majority of Indians were still rural Hindus. The BJP's India Shining campaign and Hindutva probably appealed greatly, as Kumaratunga and the JVP did to the rural Sinhalese population. My ears were tuned only to the urban in both countries, and then only poorly so.

A white car pulled up to the entrance. Seema walked out of the lobby in her normal clothes—a pair of khakis and a pink cotton shirt. She headed for the car. She was such a strong woman. I secretly wished for her grace and composure.

"Devyani." She stopped near the car door. "Do you want a ride to set?"

I was surprised. But the camera crew hadn't arrived yet, and the transports sat idling in front of the lobby as the sky grew dark with rain.

"Yes, thank you." Happy to be released from the monotony of our daily routine, I grabbed my camera bag and got into the back seat.

The car was cool, and smelled faintly of perfume, clean rather than flowery. We pulled out of the driveway and onto Galle Road. The green was dotted with early morning joggers. They ran past the closed kiosks and four large cannons that sat facing the sea at the end of the promenade, rusting reminders of colonial rule. The streets in the centre of town were quiet and peaceful, oblivious to the recent shifts in political power.

"You know, when you were in Benares, I was following what was happening from Assam," Seema said.

She was from the troubled northeastern Indian state, but I thought she lived and worked in Bombay.

"What were you doing in Assam?" I asked.

"I was acting in a mobile theatre for seven months."

Her character, Shakuntala, was a stoic woman struggling with what her faith had prescribed for her. When I looked at Seema's short widow's haircut and dark eyes, I could see her doing the same. Both actor and character seemed to have an infinite reserve of silence, an internal space that no one could touch. I admired that.

"What an amazing experience."

"Yes, we travelled all around Assam, performing in small towns and villages." Seema touched the edge of one of her long earrings. "But I was worried for all of you in Benares, and for what was happening to India," she said.

The car passed the Colombo docks. The smell of fish filtered into the back seat, reminding me of the sea. The fishermen were setting up their baskets beside the port authority wall, their backs burned black by long days out in the sun, and their sarongs stained with fish oils. The schedule of filmmaking had taken over so insidiously that I hadn't noticed how out of sync we were with the local rhythms of life. The days had become an endless cycle of call time, lunch, and wrap, a cycle that would continue in a consistent rhythm until we were released on June 12, our final day of shooting.

"Are you enjoying the photography?"

"Yes." She was the first to ask.

I was reminded of the work I was doing. I had always dreamed of being a photographer or a writer, but I never thought I would get the chance. For a moment, my doubts and fears faded, and I felt like I knew where I stood. We pulled in front of the bathers' alley, and the rush of activity swept us in different directions—Seema to wardrobe and me to the set for another day of shooting.

DYLAN AND KAY WERE busy placing the widows at different positions around the courtyard. We had cast a group of ten women who could pass as background widows and make the home more believable. Dylan squatted on the ground, and tried to show an extra how to hold her body. She didn't move, confused by his mixture of English and Kay's Sinhala interjections. Dolly had wrapped her in a white sari, and her grey hair was shaved to a buzz cut, but she was a Christian Sri Lankan, not a Hindu widow.

I looked at the women's faces, at their dark skin and wrinkles. They were bored as they sat on the cold concrete rim of the courtyard, waiting for Dylan's direction. Most of them were over sixty, and all were poor Sri Lankans who had been found by our local casting director. Their thin, dark bodies wrapped in white cotton made them look like Indian widows, but in reality they were Muslim, Christian, and Buddhist women desperate enough to shave their hair for money.

It began to rain. The sky broke and the courtyard filled with water. The widows moved to find shelter, upsetting the positions Dylan and Kay had spent so much time setting up. Dylan looked at the sky, and then at his watch. Frustrated, he announced that we would have to wait.

I went into the small temple trust kitchen to make myself a cup of tea. It had been converted into a food station for the crew. A middle-aged Sri Lankan man had been hired to make coffee and tea throughout the day. Premadasa served sandwiches and digestive biscuits in the afternoons off a red plastic tray lined with paper napkins. He had a drooping moustache and greasy black hair.

"Tea?" He looked at me with wide, worried eyes. A tray of disposable plastic cups sat on the table in front of him, waiting to be filled and served to the crew. The kettle began to boil, vibrating on the gas stove.

"Yes, please." I waited beside the fridge, out of the way of the electrics and wardrobe girls rushing in to pick up handfuls of biscuits for breakfast.

Premadasa reached for a plastic strainer full of used tea leaves and crushed, soggy ginger. He lifted the heavy kettle and poured boiling water through the flattened black leaves, letting them soak for a moment before adding condensed milk and sugar. An old Sri Lankan Airlines poster hung above the stove, curling at the edges from the steam. A photo of a pretty flight attendant, with her palms together in the gesture of greeting, was printed in the centre. *Ayubewon*, Sinhala for "welcome," was written below her.

Premadasa passed me a hot plastic cup, and placed the strainer on the table. A swarm of flies immediately gathered on its sticky rim. I walked back to the edge of the courtyard and watched the rain. Mom, Lisa, and Seema were sitting on a low wooden platform on the other side of the courtyard. It was a traditional bed frame. She sat smoking a Rothman's and talking with her actresses.

The rain began to lighten until it eventually ceased altogether, leaving the courtyard partially flooded. I watched as the production carpenter broke a hole in the corner of the concrete, allowing the water to drain out between the cracks. A schoolgirl in a pressed, white uniform and braids stood in the corridor watching us work. She was from one of the families in the front rooms. She watched shyly, holding the edge of a braid in her hand. When we arrived in the morning, the family was still in the small kitchen. They were chopping vegetables and making *hoppers* in a stainless-steel *thachiya* or flat pan. The smell of burning coconut oil continued to permeate the set.

I felt a hand on my shoulder.

"Hello, *chutku*."

I turned and looked into Vikram's face. The steam from the tea rose slowly above the edge of the disposable plastic cup, as drops of rain continued to fall from the eaves in the courtyard. I had first started to fall in love with him in the courtyard of the widows' house in Benares. It seemed a strange twist of fate that we would meet in a replica of that house four years later and a country away. I had taken a Polaroid of him that day in Benares. Unsuspecting, he came out wide-eyed in the white of the flash. "Deer caught in headlights," I scribbled in black marker on the bottom edge of the photo, long buried in some drawer now.

"Hello, Vikram." I held the Olympus close to my body, as if it could give me the warmth of a lover. But it was cold against my side.

He looked older. His hair was longer, his body heavier.

"I'm doing the stills for the film." He looked at the camera dangling from my shoulder. "And I hear you're helping choreograph the song situations."

I thought of the six songs A.R. Rahman had composed in 1999, and how we had heard them together for the first time on the yellow couch in Benares.

"Vikram!" Dylan came over and put his arm around Vikram's shoulders. The water had drained from the courtyard, and the art department was laying towels on the concrete to soak up the dampness, and using hair dryers to speed up the process. Their whirring hum filled my ears. Vasant came over and slapped Vikram affectionately on the back as the crew began to set up for the shot. I moved away, and sat on the wooden platform next to Mom and Lisa.

"What are you doing?" I asked.

Mom was crossing out dialogue lines in the script.

"I'm simplifying, cutting out unnecessary dialogue."

I watched as her black pen cut through the text. Lisa sat beside her with her Discman headphones on. She listened to the soundtrack of the film religiously, a source of inspiration for her character. Across the courtyard, Vikram laughed and joked with Vasant and Dylan. Maybe I was blind, continuing to imagine what was not there.

"I want to tell this story visually." My attention strayed back to Mom. She seemed to be speaking to herself. I could see her evolving as a director, through her desire to simplify, to take the time to do detailed shots of nature, which added ambience to the story. She had never done those things in earlier films. I looked at her eyes, focused and clear, her hair pulled back in a tight ponytail, and her worn, working-woman's running shoes.

"I'm proud of you, Mom ... for doing all of this." I thought of the years it had taken—the politics, the organization.

"Really?" She looked at me in disbelief, and I realized how little I actually told her I appreciated her.

"Excuse me, Deepa. We're ready to go." Dylan crouched near the edge of the platform.

Mom put the script down and began a final rehearsal with the actors.

I lifted the Olympus and went to look for the best position to shoot from. They filmed quickly, making up for lost time due to rain, and went straight into blocking the next scene.

LISA AND SARALA SQUEEZED into a small wooden rooftop room, a *barsati*, built on top of the widows' house. The space was so small that the production carpenters had constructed a set of wide portable steps that could be placed in the courtyard, allowing the crew and their equipment access to the room. It was Kalyani's room, which was separated from the rest of the house because she may pollute the others with her long hair and association with prostitution. Giles set up the camera to shoot the scene where Chuyia meets Kalyani for the first time.

There was no space inside. I tried to sit on the steps, but had to leave enough room for Dylan. I needed to deliver 500 colour photographs for the final distribution package, but there was no clear shot.

"Dylan..." I tried to get his attention, but he was focused on Mom and Giles. We were about to shoot.

"Can I do stills after the shot, before they change the lighting setup?" He considered for a moment.

"Yeah, sure. Just make sure to remind me."

I climbed back down the stairs and sat next to the monitor. Dylan shouted for quiet on the set. The courtyard fell silent, and I could hear Mom say "Action" from the rooftop room. I studied the composition of the frame on the monitor. Lisa and Sarala talked in silence on the small flickering screen. I looked to see where Giles's light was falling, calculating where I would have to position myself when they finished the shot, and how little time I'd have to get it.

"Cut!" I jumped up and headed for the stairs.

"They're going again." An A.D. put his hand on my shoulder, stopping me.

I waited patiently until they completed three takes and finished the scene.

"Checking the gate," Dylan called the end of the shot. "And we're moving on to..."

"Stills!" I shouted, and rushed up the stairs to the rooftop room. Dylan stopped the crew from starting the next setup, and spoke into his walkie-talkie.

"Taking a moment for stills."

I knelt on the rough wooden floor and asked Lisa and Sarala to hold their positions. Their faces filled the Olympus viewfinder, highlighted and warm in Giles's lighting. I composed, clicked, and thanked them.

"Stills are done," I said.

"Stills are finished...and we're on to..." Dylan relayed his instructions over the walkie-talkie, and I went back down to the courtyard feeling satisfied.

Vikram was sitting next to the large blue statue of Krishna, which presided over the courtyard from the widows' shrine. He casually smoked a cigarette, and leafed through a copy of the script. I remembered the first widow I met, Sundarbai, in her narrow, damp room in Benares, and how she reached for her small statue of Krishna, absorbed in devotional love. The first thing Kalyani asks the pimp Gulabi, after she meets Narayan, is whether Krishna can take on human form. I was sick of women seeking salvation in the image of a perfect man.

I went and sat next to Manorama. She was resting on a plastic chair placed close to a portable fan, chain-smoking. Avani had to help her walk to and from makeup and wardrobe. She was seventy-seven and in ailing health. Manorama's white sari billowed over her immense body, and a fine line of sweat gathered in the folds of her skin. She was the perfect Madhumati, the true empress dowager of the widows' house. Mom called her the Gloria Swanson of Indian cinema. With her husky voice and English tinted with the faintest British accent, she was truly a former Bollywood queen.

"*Aajao, beti.* Come here, child." She patted the seat beside her, inviting me to sit down.

"How long have you been acting, Manorama*ji*?"

"Oh ... I doon't knoow ... Since I was twelve." She stretched her vowels, each syllable imbued with *draama*. "That was in 1940, you know."

Manorama took a long drag from her cigarette. This was the first movie she had done in years, and it sucked the energy right out of her, like water going down a drain. Despite it, she valiantly showed up every day.

"Manorama is my celluloid name. My real name is Erin Isaac Daniel. I'm half-Irish, you know."

I was surprised. I would never have known looking at her light brown skin and brown eyes. She reminded me that a small Anglo-Indian community still existed in India, a human vestige of the Raj. Anglo-Indian actresses were often cast as vamps in Bollywood, fulfilling the common Eastern view of the loose Western woman. They were a marginalized group in Indian society, and actresses like the curvaceous 1960s Anglo-Indian Helen found work by wearing skirts, smoking cigarettes, and doing cabaret numbers in film. Manorama had played the same kind of vamp in her younger days.

"I told your mother I want this to be my last film." She took another long drag from her cigarette, letting the ash fall to the ground. The fan blew her thinning grey hair, the smoke from her Gold Flakes drifting out into the courtyard.

Mom finished the scene and returned to her refuge on the wooden platform. Her forehead was furrowed.

"What happened?" I asked.

"John's dates!"

John Abraham, who was playing Narayan, was supposed to come for a week of rehearsals. His agent had called from Bombay and reduced it to four days. He had just called again to tell her that John would be arriving the night before his first scene. Mom lit a Rothman's.

"I don't even know if he's learned his lines. He won't even have any time with Lisa, and they're supposed to be in love." She held her head in her hands and asked Vasant to get her an aspirin.

It was the Bollywood system at work. John was involved in three other films at the same time as *Full Moon*. Most actors and actresses worked on multiple films simultaneously, changing roles as many times as they changed costumes. On average a Bollywood film took two years to complete because of juggling actors' dates. Rehearsals and tight shooting schedules were a Western phenomenon. I could understand her fear about John, a handsome Bollywood star who had just come off a heist film about motorcycles, about to play a poetry-spouting Gandhian idealist. He was also bringing his manager to Colombo.

Dylan called lunch.

"I need to lie down." Mom felt her forehead with the back of her hand. "I feel like I'm getting sick."

She left to find a quiet place to rest.

The crew moved quickly, covering the camera and dismantling the metal dolly tracks. Soon the courtyard was blissfully empty. I studied the indigo writing which had been carefully hand-painted in Hindi along the walls of the house. *Hare Krishna Hare Krishna*, the chant of Vaishnavites, followers of Krishna. It was a small but powerful detail that the art department had lifted from photographs of an *ashram* in the north Indian city of Vrindavan. The paint had been aged and faded, and the words looked as if they had always been on the walls.

I packed the Olympus and walked to base camp. The bathers' alley was slick with water from the constant exercise of washing. I wondered how they could afford to use so much of it. Maybe it was one of the freebies included in their resettlement as refugees from the north. It seemed to be their only luxury, to stay clean in poverty.

The base camp was almost empty. Most of the crew were gathered at lunch at the church. Only a few people were relaxing in the parking lot. A group of Sri Lankan drivers ate under a tent, and Johnny, the dolly-grip, sat in the back of the grip truck with his Sinhalese crew, talking in sign language and broken Sinhala.

There was a natural divide between the Sri Lankan and international crew. They sat at different tables at lunch, and lined up at the more spicy of the two catering buffets, while the rest of the crew gravitated to the cold macaroni. Someone had painted a sign on a piece of wood outside the lunch tent. It had an arrow pointing toward the two buffet tables, "Catering: Foreign and Local."

I asked the drivers if they had seen my mom. One of them pointed to Sarala's small trailer, parked in the middle of the dusty lot. I knocked gently at the door.

"Come in."

The trailer was heavily air-conditioned. Mom lay on a narrow bed built into the wall, and the venetian blinds were tightly shut. The sudden change in temperature made my skin prickle, and reminded me to wrap the Olympus in its towel.

"Mom, what's wrong?" Her arm was resting over her eyes.

"I'm just exhausted."

I sat on the edge of the bed. Piles of candy and Sprite were scattered on a table in the corner of the trailer, next to a small TV and DVD player. Sarala's collection of Bollywood movies were placed lovingly beside them. She was the only actor with a trailer, but then she was just a child and often had to take rest breaks between scenes. Avani would come and ask her after a scene, "Sarala, trailer?" Sarala would nod her head, put on little pink flip-flops and a robe over her widow's sari, and be taken to base camp for a break.

I had also opted for my own space, and moved out of the apartment into a room in the new wing of the hotel. It was at the end of a long hallway, at the very back of the building, secluded and safe, away from the now claustrophobic apartment full of unwashed dishes and tired film-set gossip.

David pushed open the trailer door.

"How's she feeling?" He looked at me.

"Not well." He went and felt her forehead.

"Deepa, there's something I have to talk to you about." She didn't open her eyes.

"You know the music we've been hearing in the evenings..."

Sometimes Sri Lankan pop would filter into the courtyard from somewhere near the set. The sound department picked up on it, forcing us to stop shooting until it died down.

"Well, it's coming from the local cinema. The owner heard there was a Canadian film crew shooting here and he wants to be paid to turn off the music."

Extortion from politicians was one thing, but extortion from cinema owners seemed just a little below the belt.

"Oh God..." Mom turned over and faced the trailer wall.

THE SOUNDS OF SINHALA pop filled the courtyard as a soprano sung a particularly lamentable passage that could only have been about love. The delay from rain in the morning and the music from the cinema meant that we worked well into the night. I imagined the refugee families sleeping peacefully, freshly bathed and lulled by the purring of thin cats. Vasant brought Premadasa's tea to Giles and Mom, who were crouched on the floor in the stifling heat of Madhumati's room. They were trying to get the final shot of her stoned on *ganja*. She lay

sprawled out on her metal cot as the art department kept restuff-
ing a small clay pipe with tobacco from her Gold Flakes.

Dylan called wrap an hour later, and the crew left the house
half-asleep, in search of quick transport back to the hotel. Seema
had left with the car in the afternoon, so I found space in a van
with Mom, Vasant, and Giles. They slept during the short drive
back to the hotel. The streets were dark and silent. A metal gate
was pulled shut in front of the entrance to the Tamil temple
across the road, and the Halal butcher's was boarded up for the
night. Only the whitewashed church was lit up, with its blue
neon cross radiating against the black Colombo sky.

The crew dispersed to their rooms as soon as we arrived. I
waited by the elevator, listening to the sound of the fountain.

"What room are you in?" Vikram was standing next to me.

"I'm on the second floor, and you?"

"The fourth." The elevator door opened, and we both
stepped in.

There have been others, I wanted to say, reminding him of his
own words, spoken in Anurag's apartment that night in Bombay
four years ago. He was twenty-seven now, and had written two
screenplays. One was about the troubled relationship between
a father and his son. It looked like it was about to be funded. I
tried to remember how far I had come.

"I'm engaged . . . We're going to get married after I make my
first film."

Vikram looked at me as if he were waiting for a reaction.
There was something calculated and cool in his expression,
something I hadn't seen before in his eyes.

The elevator door opened on the second floor.

"Goodnight." I smiled politely, and swiftly turned into the
corridor.

The Olympus felt heavy in its black bag, like it wanted to pull
me down into the carpet. I was confused. Why would he deliver
his news with such strange coolness? Maybe time had just bred

dispassion, or maybe he didn't like seeing that he was no longer the centre of my attention, that maybe I had moved on.

I opened the door to my room. Camera equipment and dirty clothes lay scattered on the floor, next to unread back issues of the *Daily News*, a Sri Lankan English-language newspaper. Kumaratunga's face covered the front page. *A room of my own.* But it held none of the excitement of the Vaibhav, or the painful growth of Oxford. It was impersonal and realistic, practical and lonely. Adult.

I went to up to Mom's suite on the eighth floor.

"Mom..." I knocked at the double doors, and listened to see if she was awake.

She opened the door in her *kaftan*, her hair brushed down for the night and her eyes sleepy with fatigue.

"What's wrong?" I had woken her.

"Nothing...I just need to talk." I felt the old desperation growing inside me, the familiar weight, almost reassuring in its heaviness.

She turned on the living room light, went and sat on the couch and lit a cigarette. I closed the door behind me, at a loss for what to say. Why wouldn't she just tell me what to do?

"Vikram's getting married," I blurted.

"Oh, no. Not the doubt again."

"Why don't you listen?"

"I am listening!" she snapped back.

"Why are you getting angry? I came to you for help."

"I'm not angry. Why are you attacking me?"

"You always bring it back to you," I said.

"I'm tired of listening!" She put her hand over her face. "Why don't you just call your father. You chose him."

A strange silence descended over the room. It left a ringing in my ears, as in the aftermath of an explosion. Why could we never get over this wall? I remembered Greece. The crying, and the taste of blood from my split lip. How I had to go to the hotel pool and swim alone after the fight, just to breathe again. There was no *ouzo* involved this time—just the piece of glass still lodged in my throat, neatly inserted between muscle and skin. I looked at her sitting on the couch, rigid with anger. My own anger was numbed, but it was tinged with a clarity I hadn't felt before. I didn't run away to cry, or to call my dad. I saw the same piece of glass lodged in her, older, harder—the matching piece of pain I had never seen before.

"Mom, I chose Dad because it felt safer. I was eleven. I'm twenty-four now."

She looked at me, tears beginning to stream down her face. But I felt no tears, no anger, only fatigue from our constant cycle.

"Mom...we must break free of this. There's too much good here." I sat down beside her. "Look at how far we've come."

She nodded in agreement, and wiped her tears with the edge of the *kaftan*. The salt began to dry, leaving faint white stains on her skin.

18

The river was still in the early morning, the colour of ink. It reflected the pale outline of clouds in the predawn sky. The small passenger ferry I had seen a month earlier was tied to a piece of bamboo jutting out of the water. It drifted lightly with the current, pushing up against its yellow mooring. We were almost halfway through the shoot. Our unit had moved in the night, and the white equipment trucks lined the dirt road behind the set of the *ghats*. They were completed now—painted, aged, and dressed. Cows had been brought in by an animal wrangler, and a hundred Sri Lankan extras, dressed as devout Hindus, had been placed throughout the six-hundred-metre set. It was a living temple town.

The little white bungalow, where I had first seen the master set builder studying the blueprints for the *ghats*, had been converted into the actors' green room. A sign on the door read "Actors Only." I ignored it, and put my camera bag inside. The house smelled of urine or vomit, covered lightly with cleaning fluid. The art department had lit incense sticks near the crew toilets in the widows' house, sticking them into cracks in the walls to ward off the smell. Maybe they would do the same here.

I liked the quiet of the river, free from the sound of Tamil temple bells and the cinema owner turning down his music for money. I placed my camera on a tripod and knelt down near the edge of the water to shoot the dawn. Dilip suggested they would be useful images for the film poster, a pastoral background against which photos of the actors could be superimposed. He had shot the posters for both *Fire* and *Earth*, and the Canadian distributor wanted him to do *Water* as well. It would be an organized photo shoot with lights, makeup, wardrobe, and assistants. I wanted to do it myself, even though I was painfully aware of my own inexperience.

The opposite side of the river was dark, and I stared hard to see the outlines of the trees. An A.D. placed a female extra in the water and tried to explain to her to make washing motions when the director called "Action." A man was placed waist-deep beside her, and shown the *surya namaskar*, the sun salutation practised in Hinduism. He lifted his arms, palms upturned, from his waist up toward the Eastern sky, emulating the Indian A.D. kneeling on the nearby steps. Drops of water fell from his cupped hands, and disappeared in the river.

I flipped through my copy of the script until I found scene 53. We were beginning with a shot where Chuyia runs away from the house of widows, searching for a way to get home to her mother. Shakuntala finds her on the *ghats*, playing alone with a toy boat made of banana bark, a leaf for a sail. I read the description, marked through with my pink highlighter:

> EXT. GHATS—DAY
> SHAKUNTALA
> Chuyia! Chuyia!
> There's a tug at her sari, she turns. Chuyia stands in front of her. Shakuntala, first relieved and then angry, gives Chuyia a good shaking.
> SHAKUNTALA
> Where were you? I've been looking for you! Where were you?
> CHUYIA
> You're always angry.
> Deflated, Shakuntala sits down on the ghats. After a beat, she pats the place next to her.
> Reluctantly, Chuyia sits beside her, keeping her distance.

I shut the script. *You're always angry.* Chuyia's words ran through my mind, as did the image of Shakuntala, who realizes her own bitterness for the first time. It reminded me of Mom and me.

JOHN HAD FINALLY arrived from Bombay. Our Narayan hadn't only learned his lines, but he had practised wearing his *dhoti* between motorcycle stunts for his latest movie. Our fears about a star doing an independent film without the trappings of Bollywood—coffee-boys, assistants, personal stylists, and drivers—were quelled when he politely offered his black canvas chair to one of our makeup assistants. He was half Syrian Christian and half Irani with forefathers from Persia, but grew up in Bombay, and had a master's degree in business.

While he waited for the scene between Shakuntala and Chuyia to finish, John joked with Lisa and text messaged back and forth to Bombay on his small silver cellphone. Their chemistry was lovely, even though they were about to act with each other for the first time. Narayan offered Kalyani the opportunity to escape her destitute life. Their relationship embodied the innocence of first love. But, then, they were just characters penned at our kitchen table early one morning.

The *ghats* were insufferable by midday. They baked in the sun. I sought shelter under a leafy tree covered with yellow flowers, which grew out of the riverbank and had been incorporated into the set. The concrete had been spread on wire mesh up to the edge of the bark, leaving the tree with just enough room to breathe.

John had brought news from India. A few articles had appeared in the national dailies announcing *Water*'s rebirth as *Full Moon* in Sri Lanka. David worried about a possible impact in Sri Lanka by the RSS or its affiliates, and shifted the schedule to shoot some of the more important scenes first. One Bombay magazine "exposed" John's planned nude scene with Lisa. *Water* was, after all, purported to be pornography. The Indian election campaigns were coming to a close, and the BJP was making one last strong push.

Their campaign was based on two slogans: India Shining and Feel Good. Both expounded on India's supposed economic boom. Prime Minister Atal Behari Vajpayee and Deputy Prime Minister L.K. Advani were confident that the India Shining campaign, coupled with Hindutva, would touch a national chord—India was well on her way to becoming a *developed*, no longer developing, nation.

They had an added advantage. Despite having the weight of the Gandhi dynasty behind her, Sonia Gandhi, head of the Congress Party—the RSS's and BJP's main opposition—was actually foreign-born, an Italian whom Rajiv Gandhi had met in his student days at Cambridge. The RSS and BJP were ready to crucify her based on her "foreignness."

After Kumaratunga's re-election in Sri Lanka, it seemed that voters liked to choose the safe familiarity of a hardline candidate. I thought about a possible BJP win. Four more years to consolidate India's Hindu identity. There would be no way that *Water* could ever be safely shown in India. The RSS would only grow in power under the protection of the central government, and who knew what lengths they would go to censor and oppose anyone who challenged the vision of India Shining? I thought of the Hindu right's shutdown of cinemas screening *Fire* in 1998—the posters torn, the windows smashed, and the sets burned on Assi *Ghat* in 2000, still smouldering as they were thrown into the Ganges.

Vikram came and sat next to me under the shade of the tree. He arrived on set late. His schedule was determined by whether or not we were shooting a song situation.

"Hey, what do you think of this?" He held a copy of the script and sketches in his hand. "When Kalyani goes to meet Narayan in the song 'Piya Ho,' I want her to stop by a small temple and line her eyes with *kohl* from the edge of a clay oil lamp."

I tried to remember what it had felt like to line my eyes with *kohl* the night before we started shooting in Benares. But I couldn't. It had already faded in my mind, like a piece of paper left too long in the sun.

"That sounds good," I offered.

He had grown up with the tradition of the Bollywood song. It was a classic device used in Indian cinema, often associated with a heroine singing and running around a tree in the Swiss Alps. But the form was much older, and much more important than the comical images one saw looking in from the outside. Bollywood songs were like the libretto in an opera—they pushed the story forward.

A lyricist in Bollywood is paid an average of $4,000 U.S. per song, and each film has an average of eight songs. Even before the film is shot, the music is composed and the director meets with the lyricist to explain the song situation. The lyricist then takes the director's vision and the composer's score and writes the accompanying words. During filming, actresses and actors lip-sync the words to the songs, which are actually sung by professional playback singers. The same singers tend to sing for the same heroes or heroines, providing them with a musical identity. The choreographer is brought in to create the dance movements and to help the director *picturize*, or visually design, the shots, while the actors mime the lyrics.

Like symbiotic organisms locked in a mutual embrace, the Indian film industry fuels the music industry, and the music industry fuels the box office. Even before a film is released in India, the soundtrack is released, and it alone can influence the film's success or failure.

The actors didn't lip-sync to the songs in *Water*. It was a creative choice of Mom's, and one that reflected the influence of both East and West on her work. Bollywood had influenced her enough to insert six song situations in the film, but a love of Japanese director Yasujiro Ozu's restraint and Ingmar Bergman's meditations on psychology had made her leave room for silence. She chose to let the characters experience their songs, not sing them.

"The wardrobe assistant's pretty hot, isn't she?" Vikram asked.

The question came out of nowhere, inserted into the middle of our conversation. Vikram gave me the same look he had in the elevator, as if waiting for my reaction, waiting to see if he still held something over me. I wanted to leave and go back to my stills, but something deep inside said *there once was love here*, and waited to see if any traces of it were left. I looked into his eyes and at the curve of his nose. A dry wind blew across the *ghats*, lifting the tiny yellow flowers that had fallen from the tree. They were tied to the branches with wire by the art department.

"Look!" Dolly cried out and pointed to the river.

The crew stopped preparing for the next scene, and stared at the water. A monitor lizard, almost two-metres long with thick, dark green scales, swam lazily along the length of the *ghats*, less than ten feet away from us. Johnny and Bob left their equipment and followed the monitor's course along the edge of the set until they reached the end of the *ghats*, where the set fell away into the banks of the river. The monitor's round black eyes were just visible above the waterline. It showed no fear, and used its long tail to navigate and then dive underwater toward the marsh-lands behind the set.

I thought of Bergman's experience on *The Virgin Spring*, how the crew dropped everything they were doing to watch the crane fly above the tops of the trees. I felt lucky we could do the same.

WHEN WE BROKE FOR LUNCH, the Sri Lankan extras were taken to a separate tent down the dirt road. The crew tent was set up behind the bungalow in a soggy field, wet from the nearby marshlands. I walked past the sign "Catering: Foreign and Local," and went to rest in the green room, ignoring the sickly sweet smell. I was tired of yellow *dal*, cold macaroni salad, and the smell of coconut oil, which was getting worse in the heat as summer approached.

The green room was dark and peaceful. The curtains were drawn, filtering a soft white light across two single beds with an air-conditioning unit placed between them. I shut the door to keep in the cool. Someone stirred on the far bed.

"Sorry. I—"

"Hey, sweetie." Lisa stretched and sat up.

My eyes adjusted to the darkness until I could see the side of her face, a green eye, and her hair, cut ragged and short from a scene shot earlier in the week. Madhumati had cut Kalyani's hair as punishment for her love with Narayan, as punishment for thinking she could ever free herself from a widow's life.

"I'm just preparing myself for the big scene tonight." Her Discman sat on the bed beside her. "Come." She patted the crumpled white sheets.

"Oooh...I get to commit suicide tonight." She made a cutting motion across her neck. I remembered when I first read the script, five years earlier, and had come to Kalyani's suicide. I cried and felt a hollowness in the pit of my stomach. Kalyani, afraid to tell Narayan that she's a prostitute, and desperate not to return to the widows' house, chooses death as her only way out.

The scene originally took place on the houseboat of one of her wealthy clients. Kalyani slips into the river, unnoticed by the drunken party. The houseboat had been built for $10,000, and sat unused, baking in the sun at the end of the *ghats*. Mom had cut the scene completely, and decided that Kalyani's death should be a solitary one. She would walk down the steps and into the river, late at night when the *ghats* were empty. I thought of a painting I had seen at the Tate Gallery in London by Pre-Raphaelite John Everett Millais. It was an image of Ophelia, drowning alone in *Hamlet*, tangled in reeds and flowers. It reminded me of Shakespeare's verse:

> When down her weedy trophies and herself
> Fell in the weeping brook. Her clothes spread wide
> And, mermaid-like, awhile they bore her up;
> Which time she chanted snatches of old tunes,
> As one incapable of her own distress,
> Or like a creature native and indued
> Unto that element; but long it could not be
> Till that her garments, heavy with their drink,
> Pull'd the poor wretch from her melodious lay
> To muddy death.

SUICIDE BY DROWNING seemed a natural escape for Hindu widows, most of whom spent their lives in holy cities on the edge of the Ganges. Assamese writer Indira Goswami had written about it in her novel *Neelkanthi Braja (Shadow of Dark God)*, published in English in 1986. Her widow heroine, Saudamini, drowns in a river, as does a widow in the opening of Rabindranath Tagore's *Chokher Bali*, written in 1902. I had met Indira Goswami earlier in the year in her small home on the Delhi University campus. I was granted an interview late at night, as part of research on widows for the film.

She served me sweet tea and biscuits and spoke with a thick Assamese accent. There was a photograph of her receiving an award from V.S. Naipaul, covered carefully in plastic and hung on her living room wall. She gave me a signed copy of her book before I left, even though we had just met.

The crew prepared for the scene as the sun began to set. The sky over the river faded from blue to a deep indigo. As soon as the sun had dipped completely, bats began to appear. They were large, almost the size of seagulls, and swooped over the river with their black bodies silhouetted against the darkening sky.

Two boats, made of wooden platforms connected to large pontoons, were brought out onto the river. We were going to shoot the scene from the water. Giles, Dylan, and Mom were positioned on one with the camera. The sound recordist and script supervisor were balanced precariously on the other. I watched from the *ghats*. There was not enough room on either boat.

Lisa came to the set with a pink towel around her shoulders. Dolly followed her with an extra white sari. She would have to change after every take of walking into the river. The sky had become black, and the only light was the cool grey of Giles's lighting and a small fire in a temple in the background.

The crew fell silent as Lisa handed the towel to Dolly, and stood alone at the edge of the steps. *A solitary figure in white.* The water lapped gently against the *ghats*, and the camera boat maintained its position, anchored with bamboo poles. Mom quietly called "Action," and Kalyani placed her only belongings by her side—a coarse cotton cloth and holy beads—and stepped tentatively into the water. She lifted her hands to her face, washing her skin, and walked into the river, leaving only a ripple.

I found Lisa crying alone in the green room after the scene.

19

Giles leaned back against the courtyard steps. They were covered with grime and dust. A brass band was playing "When the Saints Go Marching In" somewhere in the distance. The coarse, tinny sound came from the direction of an elementary school behind the widows' house. Lunchtime band practice. Giles rested his elbows on the concrete and relaxed after a demanding shot—something I rarely saw him do. Vasant, glued to his mobile phone, was wildly text messaging back and forth to a friend in Delhi and relaying the incoming news to Mom. She sat on a plastic chair next to the kitchen, as Premadasa strained steaming tea into disposable cups behind her.

"It looks like the BJP's won Gujarat," Vasant called out to the surrounding crew. It was mostly the Indians who clustered around him like Premadasa's flies to sugar.

In a few hours India's choice would be known. It was May 13, 2004, the day after the general elections, and four weeks before the end of our shoot. Chief Minister Narendra Modi's re-election in the western state of Gujarat didn't bode well for a Congress Party win. He was a staunch BJP chief minister, and a devoted member of the RSS. Modi had sat in office while Hindu fanatics butchered more than 1,000 Gujarati Muslims in 2002 in retaliation for an attack on a train carrying Hindu pilgrims. His police force had stood by and watched as Muslim women were raped and mutilated, while their husbands were killed. Many participated. Another four years of Hindutva terrified me. The brass blasted through "The Saints." I listened as it echoed through the otherwise silent courtyard.

"So Colin Monie's interested in editing the film. He edited *The Magdalene Sisters*." Giles mumbled so fast I barely understood him.

But I knew of *The Magdalene Sisters*. I had seen it in my last year at Oxford. It was a powerful film about the Irish convent laundries, sweatshops run by Catholic nuns, where "sinful" girls were sent to work for their penance. Girls who had committed "sins" like having a child out of wedlock, or being raped. The last laundry had closed in the mid-nineties.

It seemed amazing to me that two religions with such different histories, mythologies, and religious texts—Catholicism and Hinduism—could demand such similar forms of penance from their women. The widows had to absolve for the sin of their husbands' death as much as the laundry girls had to absolve for their sins. Both lived in a state of denial. The widows denied themselves certain foods and colours, and the laundry girls were denied freedom and forgiveness. I clearly remembered a scene in *The Magdalene Sisters*. One of the girls comes to an open door in the wall surrounding the laundry, and has a chance to escape its confines. She stands, looking out over the open fields. No nuns are watching. The wind blows gently through the meadow grasses less than three metres away from her, and she goes and closes the door. At some point, we all internalize our own prisons.

"Colin and I worked together on *Young Adam* with Ewan McGregor," Giles continued chatting. It was funny, but I realized I'd never had a full conversation with him as an adult.

"What's *Young Adam* about?" I knew it had just been released in Europe.

"It's about a man who has no moral conscience."

I listened as Giles went into a full monologue about morality and existentialism. He spoke about reading Camus and Sartre when he was younger, and how much he loved them. I looked at him, dressed in his black shirt and jeans, and I could see a once-young and intense man exploring those questions, and perhaps finding some answers in the way he saw light, and thus, the world.

"But it was all shit, really, wasn't it?" he added. And he laughed, a wry laugh, and smiled.

The electrics were almost finished placing the lights. I could hear the low hum of the power as it filtered from the generator into the black cables criss-crossing the courtyard. Manorama was having a lengthy conversation with Winnie near the wooden platform—the Anglo-Indian actress and the Chinese-Canadian script supervisor. I thought of Dylan, Giles, Seema, and Sarala. It was amazing—we truly were an international motley crew.

"My God! Congress just won Maharashtra!" Vasant shouted across the courtyard as he read the incoming text.

"Let me see!" Dolly ran toward him, almost tripping over the cables.

I looked over my shoulder at Mom. She sat silently, sipping her tea. There were many more states to go.

Giles continued talking about *Young Adam*. The producers and studio wanted an ending where Ewan McGregor's character, Joe, finds some form of moral retribution. Giles and Ewan fought them, and ended up secretly shooting an ending where the audience is left feeling the nothingness Joe feels.

Giles looked at me.

"But it's hard to sell nothingness."

And then he was up, and preparing for the next shot.

SEEMA WAITED IN the courtyard, holding the end of her white sari up to her face. Avani stood behind a pillar, ready to give her a signal to walk into Madhumati's room. The camera was set up facing Manorama, who lay sprawled on her bed, stoned on *ganja* made from her crushed Gold Flake cigarettes. It was a key scene. Shakuntala was about to find out that eight-year-old Chuyia had been taken to one of Kalyani's clients by Gulabi, replacing Kalyani after her death. It was one of the darkest scenes in the script, hinting at child prostitution, a problem Sri Lanka had also been dealing with for years. The original version had Shakuntala slapping Madhumati full across the face. It was now deceptively simple, the action crossed out one afternoon on the wooden platform while Mom rested between takes. Shakuntala now had to react in quiet horror.

Seema stood silently, her eyes focused on the concrete floor and her broad bare feet. She swayed slightly, still holding the end of her sari. Avani gave her the signal, and she walked purposefully into the room and out of view. But take after take, she collected herself in the courtyard, preparing for her reaction as if in a trance. I watched, transfixed by her incredible focus. She swallowed a mosquito before a take, and ran, gagging, to the bathroom at the back of the house. It created the right feeling for the scene, but then Seema wasn't a method actor.

As she prepared for each take, the Canadian sound recordist and gaffer were already talking about their next projects back in Canada. sars had badly hit the Canadian film industry the previous summer. American productions, the bread and butter of Hollywood North, were afraid to bring work into the country. The sound recordist was planning to work back-to-back projects through June to make up for lost time.

Full Moon was ending, and it felt impossibly fast. Soon we would all go our separate ways, and there would be this finished entity, this film. Mom always talked about how a film stays with the director the longest. Long after the crew moved on to new work, she would be in the darkness of the editing suite, and then the sound-mixing studio.

Mom returned to the wooden platform after the take and lit a Rothman's. Vasant came and stood in front of her with his cellphone gripped tightly in his hand.

"*Haan beta*, what is it?" she asked.

"Deepa *masi*..." Vasant's voice seemed to stop in his throat. "Congress won... It's a miracle! The BJP are out!"

The courtyard fell silent. It lasted for less than a second, but in that space of time four years of memories flooded through my mind. I could have sworn I heard the ash falling from the tip of Mom's cigarette.

"It's an amazing, unprecedented triumph for the Congress!" Vasant began jumping up and down. The Congress and its allies would form a coalition government.

The sound of shouts and celebration filled my ears, drowning out all activity in the courtyard. A wave of possibility washed over us. It was a miracle. The BJP had been so sure of themselves.

It's hard to sell nothingness. Giles's words rang in my ears. India Shining was a sophisticated ad campaign wrapped in a shiny package, but it had held nothing for the majority of the population—a poor population where the IT boom, biotech, and back-office processing meant little to daily life. Sixty-five percent of the population in India didn't even have bank accounts. The BJP lost on a campaign that catered to the urban-elite, and when they relied on Hindutva to appeal to a wider voter base, they rediscovered that India is, and always has been, a country beautiful in its religious and cultural diversity.

"Who won Uttar Pradesh?" Dolly asked.

The crew fell silent as Vasant text messaged his friend. I remembered the green carpet of the district magistrate's residence in Benares, and how he confirmed the shutdown of the film, the Uttar Pradesh tourism poster hanging on the wall behind him.

"The Samajwadi Party!" Vasant read the incoming text.

Samajwadi was the Hindi word for socialist. The democratic socialist party purported to be anti-communal violence, and anti-Hindutva. Its platform even favoured a confederation of India, Pakistan, and Bangladesh. It was truly a miracle. The BJP had lost Uttar Pradesh.

"Let's go back to Benares!" Mom shouted across the court-yard, so loud that one of the Tamil refugees poked her head out from behind a curtain.

I felt elated, so much so that I couldn't breathe. The film would return to India, free of the politics that had haunted it for so long. We could go back and shoot establishing shots of the real *ghats*—their majesty, their scope. We could return to where the idea for the film had been born eleven years earlier, on the set of *Young Indiana Jones*. Without the BJP in power, the RSS had lost its political front. They still existed, but their ability to move through avenues of governance would be severely weakened.

But Mom fell silent as soon as she had said it. Premadasa's tea steamed in her hand. Her eyes were clear and ecstatic, but I could see, somewhere below the surface of the iris, beneath the fine veins that ran along the whites of her eyes, that she didn't really want to take it back to Benares. Not even now. We were free of the hassles of shooting in India, and Sri Lanka had allowed the story and characters to take precedence over loca-tions and logistics. It had given us the freedom to make a more pure film. The Congress Party win would hopefully ensure that no one else would have to experience what we did while film-ing in India in 1999.

The light from Giles's Chinese lanterns threw a warm glow across the courtyard. It highlighted the edges of the Sinhalese widows' saris, but left the pillars in shadow. The evening was like a box lined with velvet, soft and sheltered. The camera whirred silently, the frame filled with Sarala's face. The crew waited patiently for the scene to end, sitting and standing in the shad-ows out of view. A venerable Sri Lankan theatre actress leaned over to Mom after the take.

"So, the film is called *Full Moon*."

Mom put both hands on the woman's arm, and answered quietly.

"No, it's called *Water.*"

The invisible shirt of sadness had begun to melt.

FIVE DAYS LATER Sonia Gandhi declined the position of India's prime minister. It was the most strategic move she could have made. Instead, she named Manmohan Singh, an Oxford-educated economist and former finance minister, India's first Sikh P.M. As in a game of chess, she silenced the BJP in one unexpected and brilliant move. Queen takes King. The BJP could no longer debase the Congress government on the grounds of having put forth a "foreign" prime minister. BJP members of Parliament who had threatened hunger strikes if Sonia Gandhi won, and its female members who had sworn to shave their heads, were left speechless. Manmohan Singh was bulletproof.

More than twelve days later, former BJP deputy prime minister L.K. Advani spoke out for the first time since his party lost. He stood in front of a hand-painted banner, dyed saffron, and addressed the failure of the India Shining campaign.

"In retrospect, it seems that the fruits of development did not equitably reach all sections of our society," he said.

Gyanvati sifted grains of rice, as weak rays of sunlight filtered into the *ashram* below the Sunview guesthouse. I imagined how each grain felt between her swollen fingers. A poster from the BJP's India Shining campaign drifted into my mind. It was a photo of a young married woman playing cricket with her son, dressed in a saffron sari. *Myth-making.* There was a lot left to be done before women like Gyanvati, before the widows I had met in the dark, dusty *ashrams* of India, could live such privileged lives.

The plush red carpet of the Colombo Plaza sank beneath my bare feet as I walked along the corridor. The eighth-floor hallway was empty and cool. The door to Mom's suite was open, and David and Dolly sat on the green couches, whispering.

"How is she?" I asked, shutting the door quietly behind me. David had called at eleven p.m. His voice sounded tired on the other end of the line, as if he had just finished running a silent marathon in his head.

"Her fever's still at 104."

Mom had fallen violently ill, and had to be taken off the set, sweating and shivering. David and Dolly were taking shifts to look after her. She lay in bed in the adjoining room.

There was no time or money to stop shooting until she recovered. Dylan and Giles were doing their best to lead the crew and complete scenes that involved anything but the performance of the lead actors. And tomorrow was our biggest day. We were scheduled to shoot the finale of the film. The scene took place in a colonial train station the production had rented in central Colombo. They had also rented a period engine, eight carriages, and hired 800 extras.

"It's strange. Everybody's doing their job, but the morale is low." Dolly pulled the edge of her *dupatta* through her hands. "It's like a ship without a captain."

David glanced at her, his eyes heavy with sleep.

"No," he said. "It's something more spiritual than that."

He asked me if I'd take the night shift, checking her temperature every four hours until morning. I agreed, and they said goodnight, closing the door quietly behind them.

Her bedroom was dark, and smelled stale. The curtains were drawn, and I could hear the faint sound of irregular breathing. I used it to guide me to the edge of the bed, groping for the metal wine cooler that David had filled with ice water and hand towels. My fingers touched dampness. The ice had melted, and the towels felt warm. I lifted it carefully, and went into the bathroom.

The illness had come so close to the end. It was as if her body could not wait to release the memories of violence stored since

1999, letting go as soon as it was given a moment's peace. They say the body remembers. I poured the water into the basin, and squeezed out the towels before refilling the cooler. I looked into the mirror. My hair was dishevelled and long, and I could see two fine lines that I had never seen before, one under each eye. But I felt strong. Maybe it was a strength that came with age, maybe not. I don't really know. I carried the bucket into the bedroom and switched on the bedside light.

"*Chutz...*" Mom rolled over.

"Time for cold compress, Mom." I took her temperature. It was running at 103. Squeezing a cold, damp towel, I carefully placed it on her forehead. She moaned as it touched her face.

"Bergen...fj...fjor...Norway..." She began mumbling, lapsing in and out of consciousness. I placed a fresh towel on her forehead as she continued to mumble about the fjords. Days later she would tell me that thinking of Norway was the only thing that kept her body cool. It was a mother–daughter trip we'd taken together in the spring of my final year of university.

I switched off the lamp and went to make my bed in the living room. The reflection of the room played out on the windows, skewed and elongated, like a distorted film. I pulled four green cushions off the couch and arranged them on the floor next to her bedroom door. It was midnight. I set the alarm on my cellphone for four in the morning, and turned off the lights. The darkness was soothing. Lying on the narrow, hard pillows felt like lying on the train berth I had occupied en route to Benares four years earlier. But this time I drifted to sleep with my mother in the room next door, and without the benefit of wheels rocking gently against the rails.

The alarm rang at four a.m. I felt like turning over and going back to sleep, but the sky was already beginning to lighten over Sri Lanka's coastline. I fumbled for the thermometer, and went into her room. The distance from the door to the bed felt immense in the darkness.

"Mom?" I reached for the lamp. It cast a dim light across her face, slightly swollen and pale. She opened her eyes, but they were weak, and the lids hung low and tired.

"Temperature. Last time for the night."

She propped herself up against the white pillows and patted the space beside her.

I waited patiently, sitting on the edge of the bed, both of us silent, the silver-white thermometer sticking out of her mouth.

Four minutes.

I pulled the thermometer gently out of her mouth, and studied the mercury carefully. It sat stubbornly at 103. A hard silver line.

"I always loved you." Her voice was weak.

I continued looking at the hard silver line.

"And I know why you made your choice . . . I understand."

I felt the final piece of glass shift and move in my throat, and fall to pieces.

I looked at her, perhaps clearly for the first time. Her black hair was spread across the pillow, lined with a few strands of grey.

"I know, Mom. I know."

I had also begun to forgive myself.

And the weight I had felt holding me down on the train berth—the weight of guilt—seemed to release completely, washed away by forgiveness.

20

The rain poured over the windows of the van—torrential rain, the beginning of the monsoons. They would start in Sri Lanka and move up the coast of India, reaching Bombay and Delhi in late June and early July. The Colombo streets were flooded. Sidewalks glistened and long damp streaks stained the sides of buildings, runoff from the eaves. A rickshaw cut in front of us through the water, sending an arc of spray toward a woman waiting for the bus, her face hidden under a black canvas umbrella. I held the blanket around Mom. She shivered with fever, but had refused to stay in bed.

"I have to go," she said.

We drove through the downpour toward the train station, the location for the last scene of the film, where Shakuntala hands over Chuyia to Narayan, freeing her from life as a child-widow and helping her attain *moksha*, self-liberation.

The van pulled into a long driveway next to the station. The monsoons created a lushness. The foliage shone. We sat in the van as the windows began to fog up. I called David on my cell-phone. He was waiting in the station.

"We're here."

"I'll send someone to get you." His voice crackled over the line.

An A.D. with a black umbrella ran through the rain to the passenger door.

"Are you ready?" I put my hand on Mom's shoulder.

"Yes," she said.

I leaned across her and opened the sliding door.

Water ran down the slope of the road, carrying gravel and dead banana leaves in its stream. We huddled under the umbrella and walked toward the station. I held Mom's arm in one hand and the Olympus, wrapped in its towel and covered with a plastic bag, in the other. Pieces of cardboard were laid down on the driveway to cover the mud. They sank into the water under the weight of our feet. We shuffled across, and under the corrugated-iron roof of the station.

The platform was filled with people, a sea of bodies, like my first morning in Benares. Women in saris and men in white *dhotis* and *kurtas* were dressed as followers of Gandhi, patiently waiting for the shooting to begin. Hundreds of people sat in front of a raised white dais, where an actor hired to play Mahatma Gandhi was sitting in front of an antique microphone, dressed in a white loincloth. He was preparing to deliver Gandhi's famous words: "For a long time I thought God was truth. Now I know truth is God."

Words that inspire Shakuntala to place Chuyia on the train.

Behind Gandhi, billowing steam and slick with rain, was the Bengal Express, a beautiful 1930s black engine with five carriages that the art department had put together from old trains in the Colombo railyards. It was filled with extras and laden with period luggage. As the train began moving, Shakuntala would run alongside, begging Gandhi's followers to take Chuyia. She would eventually see Narayan and hand Chuyia to him.

I wove through the crowd, holding Mom's hand. The A.D.s ran along the platform, trying to control the extras. They had been outfitted with megaphones, and were shouting instructions in Sinhala to the waiting crowd.

I led Mom to her director's chair and small video monitor. They were placed at the back edge of the platform, away from the train and behind the crowd. Dolly and David were waiting for her. The blanket was wrapped tightly around Mom, like the swaddling cloth of a baby. How vulnerable she seemed, and yet she was about to take control of more than 800 people. I left her at the back edge of the platform and went to find the best place to photograph the scene.

The crowd reacted to the A.D.'s instructions of "Closer! Closer!" like living coral, contracting around Gandhi's dais. My view was obstructed by a tight knot of saris and men's backs. There was no way I could see the scene from ground level. Halfway down the platform was a row of metal lockers. They were positioned evenly in the centre of the platform. The last one was placed up against a small ticket office. Its roof was flat, with at least three metres of headroom up into the rafters of the station.

I put the Olympus over my shoulder and pushed through the crowd as the A.D.s called for quiet on the set. But when I stood in front of the locker, it was at least two metres tall. I searched the rusting metal surface for a foothold, but it was surprisingly smooth. An extra dressed as a porter pointed to a wooden table at the end of the row. He helped me pull it over and held it as I climbed on top. The metal began to buckle under my weight, but from there it was one easy step to the roof of the ticket office. My head was now level with a heavy steel rafter. I grabbed it with both hands and pulled myself onto the flat office roof.

The platform spread below me, a living mass of bodies and colours. I looked down on the Bengal Express with a perfectly clear view. The rain had stopped and water dripped slowly from the edges of the corrugated iron roof. I knelt to position myself for the shot, bracing one arm against the rafter. The office roof was covered in a thick layer of dust. Obviously no one made regular trips to the rafters. My eye caught something shiny near my knee. I traced my hand over the brown surface. It was a coin, *Sri Lanka 1978*. The year before I was born. I picked it up, leaving a perfect circle in the dust.

Gandhi's favourite hymn began playing over the loudspeakers. The song reverberated through the station, signalling the beginning of the scene.

"*Vaishnav jan to tada kahayeh,*

Peer paraiyeh jana re."

"A truly realized person is one who recognizes the pain of others."

The crowd began to move into their final positions. I looked down over the edge of the office roof, and spotted Vikram's face among the throng. He was wearing a walkie-talkie and helping the A.D.s direct the extras, his hand on a man's shoulder. Vikram pointed down the platform and guided the man toward it. He walked swiftly below me, and disappeared into the crowd.

The train whistle blew and the Bengal Express lurched forward. My view was partially blocked by the rafter, and I didn't know where Chuyia's handover would take place. The crowd surged wildly, shouting, "*Gandhiji Zindabad! Gandhiji Zindabad!*" "Long live Gandhi! Long live Gandhi!" I lifted the Olympus to my eye as Shakuntala ran along the platform with Chuyia in her arms. They disappeared in and out of the throng, two small figures in white, swallowed in a sea of colour. I tried to follow their movements through the lens until I noticed them only a few feet away. As they passed below me, Shakuntala lifted Chuyia toward Narayan's outstretched arms, toward freedom from a life half-lived. I clicked, and heard the shutter snap the moment.

Moksha.

21

The swimmer took long strokes, stretching a pale arm far in front of her and pulling back the chlorinated water like it was the only substance worth touching. The hill dropped away steeply beyond the swimming pool, and the harbour was visible in the distance. I looked over my shoulder at our bungalow, and at the frangipani trees, fragrant and full, which framed it. Mom was sitting on a large wicker armchair on the verandah, a book open across her knees.

I was glad we were together for our last few days in Sri Lanka. The film had wrapped successfully, and most of the crew had already left the country. Lisa would be en route to London, and John and Seema would be back in Bombay, having returned to a Congress-led India. Mom suggested we go to Galle, a small town four hours south of Colombo on the southwest coast of the island. A mother–daughter vacation before parting.

In a few days she would fly back to Toronto, and within a week be in the editing suite, digitally splicing all the footage we had just shot until it emerged, a streamlined twelve dollars at the local cinema—a finished film. And as she closed her eyes and reclined her seat somewhere over the Atlantic, I'd be landing in London for a reunion with college friends. On all those evenings while growing up, sitting comfortably in darkened theatres, I never knew how much work it took to create what was flashing in front of me. Not until now.

The swimmer pulled herself out of the pool, and wrapped a towel around her waist. The hotel was a converted eighteenth-century Dutch admiral's house with only four rooms. Galle, with its small harbour, was originally a Portuguese colonial town until it was taken over by Holland. It was built around a fort, which I could see in the distance, a construction of heavy black stone that sat on an isthmus extending into Galle harbour. Its thick walls rose thirty metres above the Indian Ocean, churly and rough below.

I put down F. Scott Fitzgerald's *Tender Is the Night*, and walked back toward the bungalow, feeling the crabgrass crunch between my bare toes. Mom's small round reading glasses had begun to slip down her nose. She smiled as I walked up onto the verandah, and put her book down on the soft blue pillow beside her. I gently touched her hair with my hand. It was through her, through our relationship as mother and daughter, that I had been able to experience all that I had in the past four years. She held my hand, and gradually let go as I passed into our room.

The room was cool and comfortable. It was decorated in a colonial style with a few subtle hints of modern design. There was a large mahogany bed covered in mosquito netting, a cathedral ceiling crossed with wooden beams, and then a large oil canvas leaning against the wall, of a man, abstract, almost angel-like, curled up into a little ball. It was placed in such an unassuming way that one expected to see a Portuguese galleon emerging from the canvas in conquest of Ceylon, not a half-naked man in broad strokes of colour.

There was a knock at the door. I crossed the room and answered it. The swimmer stood on the verandah, fully clothed now, and wearing a broad-brimmed straw hat and sunglasses. She introduced herself as an Australian visiting her sister who worked on the island.

"Would you like to go for a walk with me? I was going to take the owner's dog into town."

The leash was already in her hand. I looked at Mom, but she had fallen asleep in the wicker chair.

We wound our way down the narrow street that led from the hotel into town. The dog strained at the leash, forcing the swimmer to extend a slender arm. We walked in silence, shaded by the full leaves on the trees, until Galle opened up below us, lazily, in the afternoon heat.

When she spoke, she told me she was a poet who worked part-time in a bookstore in Melbourne. She lived with her boyfriend, a highly successful chef, and she liked to swim. Her voice was soft and sweet, and hung between us like a fine cloud of perfume.

As we crossed a street, in the comfort of that shared moment of silence, she told me that she had suffered from mental illness, and was still on medication. It had come out so naturally that I wasn't shocked, but I was surprised to see a beautiful young woman, living an apparently perfect life with love, work, and family, struggling with such darkness. She continued to talk of loneliness and of the highs and lows as I listened.

We came to a roadside market. Vendors sold plastic hairclips and ripe mangoes off the side of the road, as a group of boys played a casual game of cricket on a worn-down green below the ramparts of the fort. She stopped to look. We said our goodbyes, and I walked in the direction of the fort.

I entered the fort through the old gateway, a large stone arch curved high above. I thought the black stones seemed almost burnt, but I was later told it was the type of stone, compounded by its age. I passed beneath the arch, almost missing the subtle reminder of time carved into the stone, 1682.

The road continued into the fort, and slowly rose until it was level with the ramparts. The interior was covered with tall grass, which shifted uneasily in the hot breeze as if searching for shelter from the sun. I followed a narrow dirt track up until I was on the wide-open expanse of one of the fort's many citadels. The cricket ground spread far below, as did Galle harbour, reflecting the sun like a piece of crumpled foil. Dozens of couples were huddled under black umbrellas on the citadel, shaded from the sun, and safely hidden from public view as they kissed. They perched in the old cannon recesses and on the narrow, crumbling staircase which led to the lower levels of the fort.

A whitewashed administrative building sat silent and dormant at the entrance to the citadel, as if sleeping in the heat. I crouched in the shade of the building with my arms stretched out in front of me. I could hear the rhythmic pounding of the waves, and the sound of the breeze through the tall grass.

As the sun slowly began to fall in the west, I realized we all carry our own weight, thinly disguised below the surface, and always possible to overcome. But the distances we have to carry it continued to amaze me—like an idea for a movie born eleven years earlier in India until its final realization in Sri Lanka. Like a pain formed in childhood, only to be faced in adulthood. Weight accumulated, weight released. They were all such incredible journeys. I looked out at the Indian Ocean, fading light refracting on its darkening surface.

Afterword

Parallels are often drawn between making a film and having a baby. Perhaps it's the arduous nature of the process and the absence of predictability of both their final outcomes that prompts this bizarre comparison.

This analogy doesn't let up even when the film is complete. Many a time after handing it over to the distributor, I've had friends inquire, not without some amusement, "suffering from postpartum blues, Deepa?" Walking around like a zombie, almost catatonic, seems to be the norm after finishing a film. The landscape of uncertainty slowly disintegrates into abject paranoia as the magnitude of what has been accomplished sinks in. The "baby" is now on its own, and to protect it zealously and keep it within the confines of the editing room is no longer possible. It's out there in the world, struggling to find its place, vulnerable to rejection, criticism, and maybe, with a bit of luck, an embrace or two. And many a night is spent reiterating to oneself that whatever lies in store for it, you love it and will continue to do so ever after.

What a long journey it has been for this film. I care deeply for *Water* and yet feel a sense of detachment from it. To preserve a sense of proportion about its tumultuous creation has been imperative for me. My relationship to it will be transitory, my relationship to Devyani, ever evolving.

The mother–daughter journey continues long after the film *Water* is completed. The weight has dissipated and no longer smothers. But sometimes I feel its shadow as it briefly touches Devyani and myself. Then, all we can do is acknowledge it and yet not give it any import. After all these years of hurt, guilt, and absence, here we are, Devyani and myself, living under the same roof in Toronto, or as she says, "camping out together." We laugh, fight, watch bad movies, exchange favourite books, and argue about garbage details. I drive her mad with my obsessive cleaning, and she has me bewildered by the disarray in her closet. For me, it is like making up for our lost time together. Whenever I saw her hunched over her computer writing this book with such fierce concentration, I turned away. I didn't want her to see me looking all soppy with the good fortune of having her with me and the delight with which I viewed her accomplishments.

Sadly, we can't rewrite our lives as we do film scripts. But with awareness and a bit of luck, we can sometimes nudge them in a different direction. The rebirth of *Water* coincided happily with the rebirth of my relationship with Devyani.

As I read her book, I alternately smile and feel perturbed. Perturbed by her pain—because as parents we let her down. Smile because her honesty and courage made this redemption possible.

Deepa Mehta
Toronto, January 2006

Epilogue

On September 8, 2005, *Water* was chosen as the opening-night gala at the Toronto International Film Festival. It was also the film's world premiere. Before it began, Mom and I waited in the dimly lit wings of Roy Thomson Hall, incredulous that the film was about to be seen by a public audience. With us were the crew and main cast: Lisa Ray, Seema Biswas, John Abraham, and little Sarala, who had traveled to North America for the first time from Galle. We were so excited that all I remember from the moment before we went onstage to introduce *Water* was the smile on my mother's face and the glow from the white clothes we were all wearing. White—a small tribute to the widows whose lives we had tried to portray faithfully.

Since that evening *Water* has been sold for distribution in over 30 countries. It will soon be seen in theatres across the United States, distributed by Fox Searchlight. It played in our local movie theatres in Toronto for a record twelve weeks, and garnered incredible reviews in the international press. *Variety* said, "Deftly balancing epic sociopolitical scope with intimate human emotions, all polished to a high technical gloss, Deepa Mehta's 'Water' is a profoundly moving drama." Salman Rushdie called the film "magnificent" and said that "to its great credit, it tells its story from inside its characters, rounding out the human drama of their lives, and unforgettably touching the heart." Sadly, as I write this, the film still does not have Indian distribution.

I find this heartbreaking.

The reasons behind it are complex. Some say the Indian

distributors are afraid that the Hindu right will try to prevent the film from being seen, as they did with *Fire*, and that therefore it might lose money.

I find it disturbing that the film is having trouble being released in the country it portrays, especially when that country is a democracy of over 1 billion people. Yet, there is interest and awareness. After a private screening in New Delhi, *The Mumbai Mirror* said that "*Water*, without a doubt, is the Canada-based director's best film." *Tehelka*, a weekly with the tagline "The People's Paper," reported that "*Water* is a very moving film. Due for release worldwide it's a shame the film could not be shot in India. And a bigger shame it still cannot be shown here." In the many book readings I've been invited to give across Canada, one of the first questions that comes up is "Will the film be shown in India?" We hope that day will come soon.

But I am happy that our story—the five-year odyssey of making the film, personal transformation, right-wing politics, freedom of speech, and Hindu widowhood—will be able to be *read* in India. Penguin India will publish *Shooting Water* in spring 2006. I look forward to seeing it on the shelves of the Khan market bookstores near my grandparents' home in New Delhi. Maybe one day it will even be available in the little bookstore I stumbled upon near Assi Ghat, Benares, in 1999, before I met the widows.

Since the release of the film and this book, Mom and I have had the joy of being on the road together from time to time. We've supported each other through interviews, events, and jet lag. We've also had the honour of sharing our works with a number of wonderful organizations working towards social change and the empowerment of women. These include World Literacy of Canada, the YWCA's Week Without Violence, and Women of Influence, a group promoting the success of women in business.

At one screening in a small town outside Toronto, a middle-aged Indian man stood up during the Q & A. He didn't have a question. Instead, he said that the conditions of Hindu widowhood portrayed in the film "do not exist today," nor did they in the 1930s, when the film is set. "Maybe two hundred years ago," he said.

I did not get angry. Instead, I remembered the women I met below the Sunview. Gyanvati sifting grains of rice as the light streamed in through the broken shutters. I remembered the power of national myths, and I suggested that he look into it himself by reading *Perpetual Mourning*, a socio-ethnographic study of Hindu widows today by Harvard scholar Martha Alter Chen.

He didn't have to believe me. But by *seeing* the film, he had the option of engaging in a greater dialogue. That's what mattered.

Devyani Saltzman
January 2006

Acknowledgements

I extend my deepest gratitude to my editor, Janie Yoon, and publisher, Anna Porter, Michael Levine, my friends and family in Canada and India, including David Hamilton, Patricia Aquino, Lyndsay Green, Hubert Davis, Maria Thomas, Mehernaz Lentin, Anne Mackenzie and Dilip Mehta, for their valuable comments on the unfinished manuscript.

Many thanks to my friends in Oxford, including Gautam Patel, who confirmed which direction the Thames flows through Oxford; my friends in Mexico for their support and company; my friends in Sri Lanka; Elizabeth Gruszka for saving all those articles from Benares; and George Lucas, Rick McCallum, and Lucasfilm Ltd. for putting out that wonderful ad in *Daily Variety*, and standing by *Water*.

I'm also grateful to Michelle Lefolii and Velma Ruschin, my high school English teachers, for enriching my life with books, as well as to Pico Iyer, for our continued correspondence.

I am indebted to the following writers for their words and wisdom: Patrick Kavanagh for the opening quotation from *Raglan Road*; John Boorman for the concept of "money into light" from *Money into Light: The Emerald Forest, A Diary* (Faber and Faber, 1985); Pavan K. Varma for his insights on Indian society, and especially his concept that "all nations indulge in a bit of myth-making to bind their people together" from *Being Indian* (Penguin/Viking India, 2004); Jyotirmaya Sharma for his thoughts on political Hindutva from *Hindutva: Exploring the Idea of Hindu Nationalism* (Penguin/Viking India, 2003). The beautiful description of the Sinhala alphabet is from Michael

Ondaatje's *Running in the Family* (Vintage, 1993). I am grateful to Salman Rushdie for the phrase "imaginary homeland" from *Imaginary Homelands: Essays and Criticism, 1981–1991* (Granta, 1992), and I am grateful for the translation of the *dhyana mantra* of the widow goddess in David Kinsley's *Tantric Visions of the Divine Feminine: The Ten Mahavidyas* (Motilal Banarsidass Publishers, Delhi, 1997). I also want to thank Martha Alter Chen for her extremely informative study on Hindu widows, *Perpetual Mourning: Widowhood in Rural India* (Oxford, 2000), and Indira Goswami for our lovely tea that night in Delhi and the beautiful signed copy of *Shadow of Dark God and the Sin* (Gaurav Publishing House, 1986).

Index

A

Abraham, John, 181, 236, 244
Adam's Bridge, 165, 166
Advani, L.K., 245, 257
Ahluwallia, Dolly, 31–32, 186
Amritsar, 136
Anil, 135
Annapurna Mountain, 111, 113
Anthony, Theresa, 202
Apu Trilogy, 140, 141
A Room of One's Own, 50
Asoka, 165
Attenborough, Sir Richard, 137
Aurobindo, Sri, 90
Autumn Sonata, 45
Avani, 185
Azmi, Shabana, 26, 59, 179–180

B

Bandit Queen, 180
Basu, Jyoti, 134
Beach, The, 63, 64
Bee Season, 182
Benares (Kashi), 23–24
Bengal Express, 262, 263, 264
Bergman, Ingmar, 45, 207, 247
Bhagwati, 34, 186
Bharat (India), 69
Bharati, Uma, 129
Bharatiya Janata Party. *See* BJP

Bhatt, Mahesh, 89
Binoche, Juliette, 125, 182
Biswas, Seema, 180
BJP
    and coalition government, 39
    government, 91
    and permissions, 55
    purification campaign, 99
    and RSS, 69, 245
    wins Gujarat, 251
BJP government, 91
"Blood on the Tracks," 124
Blue, 122, 125
Bollywood/Hollywood, 154, 159,
    180, 224
Bollywood
    song tradition, 246
    system, 236
Bombay, 117–134
Bombay, 28
Bombay Dreams, 28
Boorman, John, 21
"bordering," 112–113
Bourne Supremacy, 187
Boyle, Danny, 63
Brigitte, 32
British East India Company, 135
Burton, Mark, 165, 168

C

Calcutta history, 138–139
Cannes Film Festival, 18
Champika, 212
Chari, Seshadri, 90, 92, 93, 94
Chatterjee, Soumitra, 140–141
child marriage, 20
Chisungu, 158–159
Chokher Bali, 249
Chuyia, 20
Cinema Paradiso, 45, 122
Congress Party, 39, 200
    and elections, 251, 253
    as opposition, 39
    and Sonia Gandhi, 200
    winning elections, 255
cremation grounds, 39–40
cultural nationalism. *See*
    Hindutva
Cushnahan, John, 190, 191

D

Dalai Lama, 33, 34
Damon, Matt, 187
Daniel, Erin Isaac, 235
Dante, 91
Das, Nandita, 26, 179–180
Devi, Phoolan, 180
DiCaprio, Leonardo, 63
Dilip, 30
Doordarshan, 105
Dutt, Guru, 71
Dyer, Edward, 136
Dylan, Bob, 124

E

Earth
    and Das, 48

    posters, 242
    and producer, 25
    soundtrack, 28
    story, 20
Echo Lake Productions, 168
Eelam ("precious land"), 169
elections
    campaigning in India, 167,
        245
    election day in India, 251, 253,
        255–256
    imminent, in India, 217–218,
        227
    results, Sri Lanka, 201–203
    Sri Lanka, 187, 189
    voting day, 199
Elements Trilogy, 20
Elephant Walk, 217
EU elections observation mis-
    sion, 189–190

F

Fanny and Alexander, 45
Feel Good campaign, 245
Film Location Services Sri Lanka,
    165
Fire
    actors in, 26
    casting, 48
    and exploitation, 76
    posters, 242
    and producer, 25
    shutdown, 1998, 245
    soundtrack, 28
    and Sri Sudarshan, 91
    story, 19
Full Moon (Water), 168
    as disguise, 168

film crew, 237, 248
first shot, 209–210
Indian rights for distribution, 180
shooting begins, 204

G

Galle, 265–268
Gandhi, Indira, 137, 200
Gandhi, Mahatma, 34, 39, 69, 227, 262–264
Gandhi, Rajiv, 200, 245
Gandhi, Sonia, 167, 200, 245, 257
Gere, Richard, 182
Ghandi, 137
Gokani, Urvi, 78
Gorapani, 111–114
Goswami, Indira, 249
Granth Sahib, 136
Great Railway Bazaar, The, 89
"growing the girls," 158–159
guerrilla filmmaking, 207
Gulabi, 56
Gupta, Ram Prakash, 104
Gyanvati, 44

H

Hamilton, David, 25
Hamlet, 249
Hendry, Joy, 158
hijras, 56–62
Himalayas, 113
Hindu gods
    Brahma, 27
    Dhumavati, 45
    Ganesha, 27
    Kali, 137

Krishna, 38, 234, 236
Laxmi, 27
Ram, 69
Shiva, 58, 185
Sita (Janaki), 92
Vishnu, 38
Hindutva
    and elections, 251, 255
    and protests, 91
    goals, 69
    and India elections, 245
    Jhandewala, 88
    as political-cultural belief system, 90
    and rural India, 227
Hindutva: Exploring the Idea of Hindu Nationalism, 90
Hiroshima Mon Amour, 191

I

Indiana Jones and the Temple of Doom, 196
Indian humanist cinema, 138
Indianness, 98
India Shining campaign, 167, 227, 245, 255, 257
Inferno, 91
International Cinema Club, 160
Iqbal, 34
Ishika, 121

J

Jaitley, Arun, 93
"Jana Gana Mana," 146
Janatha Vimukthi Peramuna (JVP), 203, 227
Jayakrishnan, Sumant, 192
Jhandewala, 88, 90, 92

Jism, 181
Junior Statesman, 123
JVP, 203, 227

K

Kalyani, 20
Kalyani's suicide, 248–250
karma, explained, 49
Kashi moksha and Sundarbai, 37
Kashi moksha, 31, 37.
  See also moksha
Kashyap, Anurag, 49
Kathmandu, 114–115
Kay, 184
Kelly, Errol, 196
Khalistan (independent Sikh
  homeland), 137
Kieslowski, 122, 125
Kumar, Alok, 103, 104
Kumaratunga, Chandrika
  introduced, 169
  and People's Alliance,
    187–188
  and political dynasty, 200
  in previous elections, 189
  re-election, 245
  and rural population, 227
  wins, 203

L

La Dolce Vita, 122
Lagaan, 28
Leigh, Vivien, 217
Liberation Tigers of Tamil Eelam
  (LLTE), 168, 177
lip-synching, 246–247
Lucas, George, 30, 83, 117
Lutyens, Sir Edwin, 92

M

Madhumati, 235
Madhya Pradesh, 106
Magdalene Sisters, The, 252
Malick, Terrance, 64
Malle, Louis, 55
Mamta, 123
Mandy, 199–200
Mankoff, Doug, 168
Manorama, 234–235
Manusmriti, 20
Maria, 153–155, 157, 159, 160
Matthews, Brett, 63
McCurry, Steve, 182
McGregor, Ewan, 252
Mehta, Deepa
  award, freedom of speech,
    137, 138, 139
  background, 17
  in Benares, 27–28
  in Calcutta, 134–142
  childhood, 117–118
  in *Daily Variety,* 117
  death threat, 84
  divorce, 18
  and effigy, 80–81
  and freedom of speech award,
    134
  in hospital, 133–134
  illness, 258–260, 262–263
  leaving Uttar Pradesh,
    106–107
Midnight's Children, 194
Millais, John Everett, 249
Ministry of Information and
  Broadcasting, 86, 91, 93
  first permission, 55
  grants re-permission, 94

meeting with Mehta, 93
and re-permission, 86
and script, 91
Modi, Narendra, 251
moksha (self-liberation), 21,
    86, 261, 264. *See also Kashi
    moksha*
Monie, Colin, 252
Mount Everest, 115

n
Naipaul, V.S., 249
Narayan, 181
Neelkanthi Braja, 249
Nehru, Jawaharlal, 39
Nepal, 109–116
Nirmal, 135
Northern Ireland, 190
Nuttgens, Giles, 30–31

O
Ondaatje, Michael, 179
Operation Bluestar, 137
Ophelia, 249
Organizer, 90, 92
Other People's Worlds, 158
Oxford, 151–161
Ozu, Yasujiro, 247

p
Pandey, Pinku, 35–39
Pather Panchali, 99, 141, 143
Pearl, 187
People's Alliance (PA), 169,
    187–188, 203
Phantom India, 55
"Piya Ho," 246
Pokhara, 110, 114
Polo, Marco, 194

pooja, 70, 74–77, 208, 209
Prabhakaran, Velupillai, 177
Premadasa, 230–231
Pyaasa, 71

q
"Quit India" movement, 139

R
Rahman, A.R., 28, 181, 232
Raise the Red Lantern, 219
Rajdhani Express, 17
Rashtriya Swayamsevak Sangh.
    See RSS
Ray, Lisa, 154, 180
Ray, Satyajit, 99, 138, 140, 141,
    145
Republic of Love, 159
RSS
    in Benares, 68–70
    and elections, 251
    Jhandewala, 88, 90–91
    and protesters, 86
    supports *Water*, 92
Rupa, 135
Rushdie, Salman, 194

S
"saffronization," 145, 200
Sagarmatha (Everest), 115
Saltzman, Paul
    background, 17
    divorce, 18
    family, 52–53
Samajwadi Party, 255–256
Sarala, 183
SARS, 254
Satanic Verses, 194

Satya, 50
Sen, Aparna, 138
"Serendipity" (Sri Lanka), 194
Seth, Aradhana, 80–81
Shadow of Dark God, 249
Shakespeare, 249
Shakuntala, 20, 228
Shantiniketan, 142–147, 151
Sharma, Jyotirmaya, 90
Shastri Bhavan, 93
Shields, Carol, 159
Shivaji, 69
Shiv lingam, 58, 185, 186
Shiv Sena, 69, 100, 113
"Simple Twist of Fate," 124
Singh, Manmohan, 257
Singh, Raghubir, 182
Sinhala language, 183
Sinhala Only Act, 165
Sinhalese (Buddhist), 165
Sinhalese Buddhist Lanka, 165
Song of the Little Road, 99, 143
Spielberg, Steven, 196
Sri Lanka, 165–268
    colonial history, 174
    politics, 169–171
Stardust, 139
Star Wars, 31
sthaga (thug), 137
stills photography, 188–189,
    192–193, 233–234, 263–264
Sudarshan, Sri, 90, 91, 92
Sundarbai, 36–39, 234
Sunview guesthouse, 41–45
Suresh, 199–200
surya namaskar (sun salutation),
    126, 243
swastika, origins, 29

T
Tagore, Rabindranath, 142, 145,
    249
Tagore Museum, 146
Tamil Nadu, 166
Tamils (Hindu), 165
Tamil Tiger cemetery, 175–176
Taylor, Elizabeth, 217
Teen Kanya, 138
Telefilm Canada, 167
Theroux, Paul, 89
Thin Red Line, The, 64
Tiger flag, 176–178
Twain, Mark, 52

U
United National Party (UNP),
    169, 187, 203
United Nations High
    Commission for Refugees
    (UNHCR), 170
United People's Freedom
    Alliance, 203
Uttar Pradesh
    described, 17
    and elections, 255
    government, 29
    and shutdown, 99–102

V
Vaishnavites, 236
Vajpayee, Atal Behari, 39, 167,
    245
Varma, Pavan K., 99, 105
Vasant, 184
Vikram, 22, 231
Virgin Spring, The, 207, 247
Virmani, Ajay, 68
Vishwa Hindu Parishad, 69

W

Water
  actors in, 26
  and Ajay, 82, 84–86
  as anti-Brahmin, 55
  in Benares, 17–107
  and Chuyia's haircut, 78–80
  emergency press conference,
    75–76
  in Indian press, 244
  introduced, 17
  and mob rumours, 96–100
  and politics, 147
  pooja, 74–77
  prashad, 74–77
  and producer, 25
  production offices, 29
  protesters (effigy), 80–81
  protesters (rolling pins),
    66–70
  and re-permission, 90–94
  revived, 151, 160–161

  sets burned, 82
  setting, 20
  shut down, 107
  soundtrack, 28
  in Sri Lanka, 161, 165–286
  wrapped, 265
  writing of, 21
Webber, Andrew Lloyd, 28
Wertheimer, Bob, 29
West Bengal, 106
Wickremasinghe, Ranil, 169,
    187, 189, 199, 200, 203
widowhood, explained, 20
Woolf, Virginia, 50
World of Apu, The, 140, 141

Y

Yeats, W.B., 142
Young Adam, 252–253
Young Indiana Jones, 30–31, 83,
    117, 256
Yuen-Carrucan, Jasmine, 63

About the Author

DEVYANI SALTZMAN was born in Toronto, Canada. She received a degree in Human Sciences at Oxford University, specializing in Sociology and Anthropology. She was the recipient of the Young Professionals International Internship Grant to work on a feature-length documentary in India. She works as a photo-journalist and freelance writer, and travels extensively throughout the world.